New Casebooks

SEAMUS HEANEY

New Casebooks

New Casebooks Series
Series Standing Order 0–333–69345–0

You can receive future titles in this series as they are published by placing a standing order.
Please contact your bookseller or, in case of difficulty, write to us at the address below
with your name and address, the title of the series and the ISBN quoted above.

Customer Services Department, Macmillan Distribution Ltd
Houndmills, Basingstoke, Hampshire RG21 6XS, England

New Casebooks

SEAMUS HEANEY

EDITED BY MICHAEL ALLEN

First published 1997 by

MACMILLAN PRESS LTD
Houndmills, Basingstoke, Hampshire RG21 6XS
and London
Companies and representatives
throughout the world

ISBN 0–333–60885–2 hardcover
ISBN 0–333–60886–0 paperback

A catalogue record for this book is available
from the British Library.

This book is printed on paper suitable for
recycling and made from fully managed and
sustained forest sources.

10   9   8   7   6   5   4   3   2   1
06   05   04   03   02   01   00   99   98   97

Typeset by EXPO Holdings, Malaysia
Printed in Hong Kong

Published in the United States of America 1997 by
ST. MARTIN'S PRESS, INC.,
Scholarly and Reference Division
175 Fifth Avenue, New York, N.Y. 10010

ISBN 0–312–16502–1 (cloth)
ISBN 0–312–16503–X (paperback)

Contents

Acknowledgements

I am grateful to a considerable number of people for their help in the preparation of this New Casebook: in particular, Maureen Alden, Jim Arnott, Rand Brandes, Michael Durkan, Seamus Heaney, Ivan Herbison, Eamonn Hughes, Richard Kirkland, Christopher Ricks and Michael Smallman. Special thanks are due to Kate Arnott for expertly typing from a fairly illegible script. The Queen's University of Belfast Publications Fund gave welcome financial assistance.

I have, with the authors' agreement, shortened two essays republished here, those by Terry Eagleton and Patricia Coughlan, in order to exclude material not directly relevant to Heaney's poetry.

The editors and publishers wish to thank the following for permission to use copyright material:

Neil Corcoran for material from *Seamus Heaney* (1986), by permission of Faber and Faber Ltd; Patricia Coughlan for material from '"Bog Queens": The Representation of Women in the Poetry of John Montague and Seamus Heaney' in *Gender in Irish Writing*, ed. T. O'Brien Johnson and D. Cairns (1991), by permission of Open University Press; Seamus Deane for 'Seamus Heaney: The Timorous and the Bold' in *Celtic Revivals* (1985), by permission of Faber and Faber Ltd; Thomas Docherty for 'The Sign of the Cross: Review of *The Government of the Tongue*', *Irish Review*, 5, Autumn (1988), 112–16, by permission of the author; and 'Ana-; or Postmodernism, Landscape, Seamus Heaney' in *Postmodernism: A Reader*, ed. T. Docherty (1992), by permission of Harvester Wheatsheaf and Columbia University Press; Terry Eagleton for material from 'Recent Poetry: Review of *Field Work*', *Stand Magazine*,

21:3 (1980) 77–8, by permission of the author; Seamus Heaney for 'The Government of the Tongue' in *The Government of the Tongue* (1988). Copyright © 1989 by Seamus Heaney, by permission of Faber and Faber Ltd and Farrar Straus & Giroux, Inc.; Eamonn Hughes for material from 'Representation in Modern Irish Poetry' in *Aspects of Irish Studies,* ed. M. Hill and S. Barber (1990), Institute of Irish Studies, by permission of the author; Richard Kirkland for 'Paradigms of Possibility: Seamus Heaney', in *Writing and Culture in Northern Ireland Since 1968*, Studies in Twentieth Century Literature Series (1994) Longman, by permission of Addison-Wesley Longman Ltd; David Lloyd for '"Pap for the Dispossessed"; Seamus Heaney and the Poetics of Identity' in *Anomalous States: Irish Writing and the Post-Colonial Moment* (1993), by permission of The Lilliput Press; Edna Longley for material from '"Inner Emigré" or "Artful Voyeur"? Seamus Heaney's *North in Poetry in the Wars* (1986), by permission of Bloodaxe Books; Conor Cruise O'Brien for 'A Slow North-east Wind: Review of *North*', *The Listener*, 25 September 1975, by permission of the author; Christopher Ricks for 'Growing Up: Review of *Death of a Naturalist*', *New Statesman*, 27 May 1966, by permission of New Statesman; and 'The Mouth, the Meal and the Book: Review of *Field Work*', *London Review of Books*, 1:2, 8 November 1979, by permission of London Review of Books; Stan Smith for 'The Distance Between: Seamus Heaney' in *The Chosen Ground: Essays on the Contemporary Poetry of Northern Ireland*, ed. Neil Corcoran (1992), Seren Books, by permission of the author.

For copyright material included in the above essays:

Faber and Faber Ltd and Farrar Straus & Giroux, Inc. for extracts from Seamus Heaney's poetry; selections from *Field Work*. Copyright © 1976, 1979 by Seamus Heaney, *The Haw Lantern*. Copyright © 1987, by Seamus Heaney, *Poems 1965–1975*. Copyright © 1980 by Seamus Heaney, *Seeing Things*. Copyright © 1991 by Seamus Heaney, *Selected Poems 1966–1987*. Copyright © 1990 by Seamus Heaney, *Station Island*. Copyright © 1975 by Seamus Heaney; and Elizabeth Bishop, 'At the Fishhouses' from *The Complete Poems 1927–1979*. Copyright © 1979, 1983 by Alice Helen Methfessel; Penguin Books Ltd for Zbigniew Herbert, 'A Knocker' in *Selected Poems*, trans. Czeslaw Milosz and Pater Dale

Scott (1968) Penguin Books. Copyright © Czeslaw Milosz and Peter Dale Scott 1968.

Every effort has been made to trace the copyright holders but if any have been inadvertently overlooked the publishers will be pleased to make the necessary arrangement at the first opportunity.

General Editors' Preface

The purpose of this series of New Casebooks is to reveal some of the ways in which contemporary criticism has changed our understanding of commonly studied texts and writers and, indeed, of the nature of criticism itself. Central to the series is a concern with modern critical theory and its effect on current approaches to the study of literature. Each New Casebook editor has been asked to select a sequence of essays which will introduce the reader to the new critical approaches to the text or texts being discussed in the volume and also illuminate the rich interchange between critical theory and critical practice that characterises so much current writing about literature.

In this focus on modern critical thinking and practice New Casebooks aim not only to inform but also to stimulate, with volumes seeking to reflect both the controversy and the excitement of current criticism. Because much of this criticism is difficult and often employs an unfamiliar critical language, editors have been asked to give the reader as much help as they feel is appropriate, but without simplifying the essays or the issues they raise. Again, editors have been asked to supply a list of further reading which will enable readers to follow up issues raised by the essays in the volume.

The project of New Casebooks, then, is to bring together in an illuminating way those critics who best illustrate the ways in which contemporary criticism has established new methods of analysing texts and who have reinvigorated the important debate about how we 'read' literature. The hope is, of course, that New Casebooks will not only open up this debate to a wider audience, but will also encourage students to extend their own ideas, and think afresh about their responses to the texts they are studying.

John Peck and Martin Coyle
University of Wales, Cardiff

Introduction

MICHAEL ALLEN

Four narratives intertwine to provide a context for the materials collected here. The first tells of the amazingly rapid growth of a living writer's reputation over the last thirty years and is enlivened with Heaney's critical commentary on his own work and on poetry in general as he makes his bid to influence the climate of taste in which his poems will be read. The second involves the emergence within that same time-span of a challenging range of critical methodologies to compete with the Anglo-American 'New Criticism' which had governed the young Heaney's notions of poetic technique and schooled him as a critic in the early 1960s. In the third narrative, Britain and Ireland engage with their postcolonial legacy as the intercommunal conflicts endemic to the latter island break out, flourish and subside across the disputed territory where Heaney and other 'Northern'[1] poets have their roots. The fourth and core narrative, constantly modifying and modified by the other three, displays the development of Heaney's verse, from the rich sensuousness of *Death of a Naturalist* (1966), *Door into the Dark* (1969) and the early poems of *Wintering Out* (1972), through the myth-making that book shares with *North* (1975), towards a sinuous but plainer style in *Field Work* (1979) and *Station Island* (1984), often becoming parabolic in *The Haw Lantern* (1987) and *Seeing Things* (1991). (Visible in such poems as 'Fosterling' in the latter volume is an authorial capacity to reconstruct his own early literary identity which emerges fully in *The Spirit Level*, 1996.)

Later in this volume David Lloyd and Richard Kirkland (essays 11 and 15) give stimulating accounts of the way this body of work has been argued into a high place in the canon of Anglophone poetry; Lloyd also notes the large-scale cooption of Heaney to school and university syllabuses. Canon-making is a characteristic feature of what I called above Anglo-American 'New Criticism' (one way[2] of denoting the family resemblance or paradigmatic quality common to the work of such critics as T.S. Eliot, Cleanth Brooks and F.R. Leavis). Leavis, alongside Eliot, was probably the most influential representative of this approach in the United Kingdom during Heaney's apprenticeship. By 1966, when *Death of a Naturalist* was published, the approach had lost much of its urgent sense of poetry's spiritual mission (inherited from Matthew Arnold), but is still unmistakably identifiable in the review of that volume included as the first essay in this collection. There Christopher Ricks positions the young Heaney in the canon using a recognisable kind of inter-subjective persuasiveness. This poetry is better ('Is it not?'[3] as Leavis would say) than Peter Redgrove's[4] because its language actively reconstitutes the physical world rather than being enmeshed in that world's particularities. It does this by way of rhythm, rhyme, stanzaic form and linguistic complexity which 'enact' the meaning rather than directly stating it. Ricks's New Critical manoeuvres (comparison and analysis: the critic's essential tools according to Eliot[5]) are used to nudge Heaney into a 'tradition' stretching back at least to the English eighteenth century but defined without the fierce exclusiveness of Leavis's canon-making: the word 'stations' in the poem 'The Diviner', for instance, is commended because it has 'a simple and honourable place in traditional praises of nature (the stars in their stations)...'.[6]

In the contrasting essay (2) which follows, Conor Cruise O'Brien, an intellectual man of affairs rather than a literary academic, writes with a broad sweep, little methodological finesse and no interest in privileging the text as a discrete verbal structure. His critical mode, like that of the American critic Edmund Wilson, has its antecedents in the French school of Taine and Sainte-Beuve. For him Heaney's *North* is straightforwardly a presentation of the Ulster 'situation' in the 1970s from a Northern Catholic's point of view. In Part I of the book Heaney actually interposes a complicated mythic machinery between the topical material and the reader, while angling his language (as in the last lines of 'Punishment') towards a New Critical respondent on the lookout for the embodiments of conflict and tension. But O'Brien simply registers with trepidation 'the chasm' between Heaney's 'insider' view of 'the exact/ and tribal, intimate

revenge' ('Punishment', ll. 43–4) and his own hopes (as a cosmopolitan and liberal Irishman) for a satisfactory resolution of the
Northern situation.[7] In taking the poems of *North* as a vindication
of his own pessimistic view of historical events with little attention
to their formal qualities or canonical worth, O'Brien's stance is actually quite similar (because of its Continental antecedents) to one
which was by the 1970s significantly influencing English and
American academic literary thinking:

> criticism is not at all a table of results or a body of judgements: it is
> essentially an activity, i.e. a series of intellectual acts profoundly
> committed to the historical and subjective existence (they are the
> same thing) of the man[*sic*] who performs them.[8]

What is interesting about the third essay in this collection, Edna
Longley's '"Inner Emigré" or "Artful Voyeur"', is that it at once
fulfils and denies this well-known formulation by Roland Barthes.
The author is shaping her own intellectual contribution to the
debate initiated by O'Brien, but she is also assembling a 'body of
judgements' about Heaney's poetry up to and including *North* in a
characteristically New Critical way.

To take the latter point first: Longley places Heaney in a 'tradition' (in which he is preceded by Robert Frost and Patrick
Kavanagh) which 'travels a rich boundary between conscious and
unconscious' and 'fuses physical and metaphysical exploration'.
The success of the poetry in this tradition (and here she is like
Leavis[9]) is manifested in 'the movement of the poem' and its 'varied
physicality'. The best poems in Heaney's first three books she sees
as matching up to these criteria. But most of the poems of *North*
(Part I), unlike the 'epiphanic' 'Tollund Man' from *Wintering Out*,
seem to her to have a factitiously ritualistic quality (of which the
author shows himself aware in the last stanza of 'Strange Fruit');
while the more topical poems of *North* (Part II) tend to either accommodate and collaborate with the clichés they aim to expose or
to become melodramatic and over-literary. Only the first and last
poems of the book fully display the exploratory and rhythmical
qualities through which Heaney's authentic note is manifested.

Longley's essay shares a New Critical agenda with the Ricks
review from which we began but it has an extra dimension. She
aims to persuade a responsive reader that the imaginative failings
she sees in *North* result from its gestures of Catholic and

Nationalist commitment: 'has tribal preordination or ordination any petrifying effect on poetic life?' For Longley, partisanship in poetry falls too far short of its long-term solving and resolving power over social circumstances. This is because she retains – perhaps in Ireland it still has some relevance – Arnold's belief that good poetry provides a spiritual resource for a crisis-ridden society whose institutionalised religion is counter-productive. Her literary agenda and her cultural agenda clearly combine when she finds 'exploratory' qualities in the tentative rhythmic movement of 'The Other Side', a poem from *Wintering Out* which intimates the imaginative possibility of reconciliation between the two cultures and the two communities of Northern Ireland (and implicitly between a 'British' and an Irish allegiance).[10] Her reading here of the earlier Heaney points to the possibility of a less pessimistic political conclusion than O'Brien's.

Longley and the next essayist in this collection, Seamus Deane (essay 4), have both promulgated their cultural agendas beyond academic criticism, she through the Northern Irish Cultural Traditions Group, he through the Field Day Theatre Company.[11] (Both groups have, according to their adherents, contributed to the present [spring, 1996] prospect of peaceable negotiation between the two communities and the two governments.) Within the literary sphere the agendas of the two critics are very different, and Deane had already laid down a gauntlet for Longley to pick up[12] in urging on Heaney (and other Northern poets) what he calls 'politicisation' of their poetry as an antidote to New Critical attitudes (English in origin, and in his view too ready to see the 'well-made poem' as an end in itself and poetry as independent of the society which engenders it).

In the essay reprinted in this New Casebook Deane sees Heaney's poetry from *Wintering Out* on as displaying such 'politicisation'.[13] The implicit Nationalism of this is fleshed out early in *Celtic Revivals*, the book of which the essay is an integral part, when he revives (like Raymond Williams) an alternative definition of 'tradition' to the New Critical one: tradition for him is treachery against one's own dispossessed inheritance and insurgent allegiance.[14] Longley saw Heaney's authentic (exploratory and reconciliatory) voice as released within the 'tradition' of Frost and Kavanagh (both postcolonial writers who adopt and revitalise the English lyric). Deane sees Heaney rather as fighting to dislodge such alien influences in the course of the self-assertive struggle against father-figures postulated for 'strong' writers by Harold Bloom.[15]

Deane does concede some New Critical points to Longley: the 'Viking myths' of *North* 'do not correspond to Irish experience without some fairly forceful straining', in 'Strange Fruit' Heaney 'begins to doubt his own reverence, his apparent sanctification of the unspeakable'.[16] But he applauds in both *North* and *Field Work* what he sees as the alliance between Heaney's poetic practice and 'the experience of [an] oppressed culture ... the Catholic Irish one'.[17] In the latter book he particularly admires the way this point of view releases a visionary intensity within which a familiar world is set against the dimension of atrocity. Theodore Adorno[18] probably influenced his sense that the momentary resolution achieved by a Heaney poem is like the psychological equilibrium between id and ego: new disturbances caused by the unresolved antagonisms of postcolonial Ireland upset this balance and keep the developmental procession in motion. So if the poet leaves the North of Ireland to commit himself to a writer's career, it is the 'boldness' of his writing that Deane is able to set (within the dialectical framework of the whole essay) against the 'timorousness of being there' as an insurgent, 'gun, not pen in hand'.[19] If the latter possibility has been left behind, it is because the developing sequence of new art-works must inevitably engage with, if not vindicate (in terms drawn from René Girard's *Violence and the Sacred*); 'the ineffable, the unspeakable thing for which "violence" is our helplessly inadequate word'.[20]

It must be apparent that if Longley is privileging as critic some kind of transcendent power and force for poetry, Deane gives an almost equally transcendent value to Irish resistance to English tradition, influence and oppression. But there is obviously very little common ground between these two interpretations of Heaney (which are rooted in the confrontational potential of the Northern Irish situation). Another Irish critic, Eamonn Hughes (essay 5), tries to break the particular deadlock which centres on the significance and achievement of *North* by bringing into play some of the ideas of Saussure, Bakhtin (as mediated by Julia Kristeva) and Volosinov. He is drawing on a congruent cluster (which we might call Formalist/structuralist/poststructuralist) of the Continental influences which have recently widened the conceptual vocabulary of Anglo-American criticism: all of them are approaches which treat literature not only as made up of language (as do the critics we have already discussed) but also as though it is itself a language. Hughes adapts an influential distinction of Saussure's in seeing Part II of

North as 'parole', the personal voice of the poet, selecting and constituting itself out of the immense possibility of articulation presented by 'langue', the social order of language.

A logical consequence of the strict belief that each *parole* is a
working part of an impersonal system, *langue*, is the refusal to
accept that 'a free subject' (the author) can 'penetrate the substance
of things and give it meaning', can 'activate the rules of a language
from within and thus give rise to the designs which are properly its
own' (Foucault).[21] This is a model derived from Saussure's view (as
a linguist) of the way signifiers function in a linguistic community.[22]
Hughes is no purist in the way he appropriates it, but he finds its
metaphorical transfer of agency from the poet on the one hand or
'society' on the other to literary language itself very useful. What is
more, Kristeva's version of Bakhtin can be seen as poised 'between
traditional "high" structuralism with its yearning for "scientific"
objectivity' and 'a remarkable early form of "poststructuralism" or
the desire to show how the pristine structuralist categories always
break down under the pressure of the *other* side of language'.[23]
Hence Hughes suggests that the linguistic procedures of *North* open
up a 'carnivalesque' or 'dialogic' space where texts meet, contradict
and relativise each other. Heaney is to be seen in *North* as im-
mersed in the intertextual 'babble' of various idioms: of his own locality; of Wordsworth, or Yeats, or his own student contemporary
and friend, Seamus Deane; of Irish voices, English voices, even the
translated Spanish voice of Lorca. Within this 'dialogic' arena the
possibility of rejecting English voices (what Deane calls 'politicisation') is tested experimentally to the point of desolation represented
by the book's final poem, 'Exposure'. How is this desolation to be
interpreted? According to Hughes it demonstrably results from the
failure to comprehend and activate the variety of possible selves
available in earlier poems. Volosinov's thinking suggests that language (including Heaney's poetic language) is a site of social struggle and will opt to be as active as possible. So we can see rehearsed
in the later pages of *North*, says Hughes, the discovery that to
accept English language and culture 'may be to lose a measure of
independence'; but it provides opportunities to be active and to be a
representative voice. Hence, according to Hughes, Heaney's reas-
severation of English voices in his next book, *Field Work*.

Hughes, of course, had the advantage of retrospection in seeing
Heaney's developing 'parole' as almost involuntarily moving into
the space within the literary 'langue' which was waiting for it. His

sense in 1990 of Heaney's capacity to become a representative voice throws an interesting light back on two reviews of *Field Work* (1979) which appear as the sixth and seventh essays in this book. Christopher Ricks (in essay 6) had changed his critical idiom in the thirteen years since he reviewed *Death of a Naturalist*. He is less concerned to appeal intersubjectively to what Leavis, quoting Eliot, called 'the common pursuit of true judgement'.[24] Indeed, he engages in considerable critical 'play' which is very much his own in response to a Heaney text like 'Oysters'; and he may also be responding to the increasingly influential precedent provided for Anglo-American criticism by Roland Barthes:

> the text itself *plays* (like a door, like a machine with 'play') and the reader plays twice over, playing the Text as one plays a game, looking for a practice which re-produces it.[25]

Nevertheless, Ricks's playful pitting of his own urbane sense of English Augustan values against poetry with rather different qualities does find common ground where Heaney can be seen as displaying the self-undercutting 'irony' or 'ambiguity' dear to New Critics. And when Ricks detects the inter-textual presence of Wordsworth or exclaims 'pure Keats, this!' or illustrates Heaney's 'trust in other poets' by way of the poet's Shakespearian allusiveness[26] he is continuing the English New Critical mode of canon-making in a way which anticipates John Carey's euphoric account of *Seeing Things* in his *Sunday Times* review of that book.[27] One can see why someone like David Lloyd who shares something of Seamus Deane's political perspective might slyly attribute literary colonialism to Ricks's phrase 'the most trusted poet of our islands' by italicising the 'our'.[28]

Terry Eagleton (essay 7) is also suspicious of such canon-building and quotes a notorious example from Clive James.[29] He finds it difficult not to concede that Heaney is 'major', 'technically accomplished', 'probably one of the finest English language poets of the century'. But he insists that Heaney lacks 'much to say' or 'the impulse to totalise', that he makes no attempt to deal with 'global imperialist crisis'.[30] (There may be first murmurings here of the reductive view of Heaney's poetry that David Lloyd will be seen advancing later in this collection.) Eagleton's account of *Field Work* is, however, very positive and hinges on the same nexus of Formalist and structuralist ideas which sparked Hughes's essay. The first of these schools of criticism, as Eagleton was shortly to explain in his influential *Literary Theory: An Introduction* (1983), stood 'on its head' the New Critical notion of 'form as the expression of content' and the second clinched this inversion with its emphasis on 'the constructedness of human meaning'.[31] Hence Eagleton's pleasure that Heaney sees his own art as 'labour, craft and production', thereby conceding to language 'its own specific mode of materiality'. Eagleton sees Heaney's verse as having moved away from a 'densely textured' phase in which form was the expression of content (the imagery corresponding to physical reality in the way demonstrated by Ricks's review of *Death of a Naturalist*). The danger of the next phase had been that its 'rich technical virtuosity' would deprive Heaney of access to his unique repertoire of realistic materials. What poems like 'Glanmore Sonnets' III and 'Triptych' III now demonstrate by their subtly crafted 'modulations' between 'literary' and 'plainer notations' is how the best writing in *Field Work* grants to language 'its own material workings without detriment to its status as a realistic medium'.[32]

Like Hughes, Eagleton is partly talking about the language of literature and partly about literature as if it were a language (with that 'materiality' which Saussure was so fond of assigning to language).[33] But Eagleton is no more ready than Hughes was to dispense with the concept of reference (to a boyhood on a farm in County Derry, say) and see literature as an independent system on the strict Structuralist model. The reduction of Heaney to 'Heaney', to an 'author function' or 'labelling' line of print at top or bottom or front of the text[34] is something that neither Hughes, nor Eagleton (nor, in fact, any of the more radically 'theoretical' contributors to this volume) find themselves tempted to do. One reason for this must surely be Heaney's historical and textual proximity as an active contributor to the debates about his verse. As reviewer, occasional critic, public reader of his poetry, lecturer, Professor (at Harvard and Oxford), celebrated Irishman, as well as in his prose collections, *Preoccupations*, *The Government of the Tongue* and *The Redress of Poetry*, he constantly supplies ancillary materials to illuminate and justify his books of poems.

The essay by Neil Corcoran which comes eighth in this New Casebook illustrates how powerful the poet's collaborative presence can be, especially when it is reinforcing in the critic the kind of New Critical attitudes and techniques to which Heaney's own mind is attuned. This account of *Station Island* is the final chapter of

Corcoran's Faber Student Guide to Heaney: the Student Guides were, according to their editor,[35] to be a bastion against the way 'theory' was diverting attention from the 'text' (which so many sixth-formers and university students were assumed to be studying in a broadly New Critical way). The chapter was written shortly after *Station Island* appeared and not only relies crucially on a particular critical essay by the poet but acknowledges his practical assistance in clarifying a number of private references which give meaning to the book's title poem.[36] The collaborative role for the critic does not end there, however. Corcoran uses as his epigraph Heaney's aspiration (in a letter to Fintan O'Toole) to dispense with 'a Keatsian woolly line, textured stuff': 'I would like to be able to write a bare wire'.[37] The title, 'Writing a Bare Wire' in the context of the epigraph implies that by the time of *Station Island* Heaney has achieved this developmental aim. Furthermore, Heaney's own formulation is transparently close to Yeats's 'There's more enterprise/ In walking naked' ('A Coat'); its use implies a sympathetic view of Heaney's 'measuring of himself'[38] against Yeats in *Station Island* and reinforces Corcoran's canonisation of Heaney alongside Yeats and Eliot as 'the most significant poet now writing in English'.[39] He is, of course, quick to point out how different Heaney is from both Yeats and Eliot[40] and shows New Critical 'judiciousness' in approving the earlier and later lyrics of the book while demurring about its central sequence (too narrative and dramatic, he says, to display Heaney's truest poetic gifts[41]). But his readiness to minimise his critical distance from the living poet and to accept the collaborative role offered is clear when he hands over to Heaney the last words of his essay (and his book): 'the tune is not called for the poet, he calls the tune'.[42]

Heaney's essay, 'The Government of the Tongue', and Thomas Docherty's review of the book to which it gives its title (essays 9 and 10) show how Heaney's own critical presence sharpens the debate about his poetry. 'The Government of the Tongue' begins with a characteristic etymological device of the kind which Stan Smith writes well on below (essay 14).[43] Heaney breaks down his title into a binary opposition: the tongue (poetry) has authority/ the tongue (poetry) should subserve authority. This is, however, more what Smith calls 'a tic of rhetorical routine' than a real destabilising strategy of the kind we shall shortly see Docherty engaging in. The symbolist resonance of Eliot's *The Waste Land* may illustrate the first sort of tongue-government, the discursive tone of *Four*

Quartets the second, but Heaney's deeper purpose is to show us Dante, Zbigniew Herbert and Elizabeth Bishop combining the two modes (as, we are meant to conclude, does his own poetry). The synthetic conclusion that emerges from his thesis and antithesis is not unlike Edna Longley's: 'poetry is more a threshold than a path'.[44] Indeed, Heaney retains as critic a similar idea of the reconciling power of imagination to hers. He makes of the figures of Eliot writing in wartime London or Jesus writing in the dust emblems of an authority for poetry outside and beyond the political arena: a solving and resolving power, holding (he quotes Yeats) 'in a single thought reality and justice'.[45]

Docherty's review of *The Government of the Tongue* (essay 10 here) shows a readiness for self-assertive critical 'play' like that in the Ricks review of *Field Work*. For Docherty, though, this 'play' reflects the poststructuralist belief that signifiers, rather than being tied into a relationship with an appropriate signified within the sign as Saussure imagined, are slippery and unstable: that their meaning proliferates or is endlessly deferred. He allows his own meaning to do this throughout an essay which deliberately evades paraphrase; but his aim is to show thereby that the same tendencies are *unconsciously* present in Heaney's language. His argument as a whole provides a good example of the poststructuralist critical gambit of 'deconstruction'[46] and one which illuminates the Heaney essay collected here.

Elsewhere in *The Government of the Tongue*[47] (the book) Heaney chooses to give the word 'conscience' his own etymologically derived meaning: 'knowing the same thing together'. Docherty is aware how easily a meaning imposed upon a word can slide out of control towards something which is the opposite of the user's intention. He sees this happening when Heaney finds a *conscientiousness* in Robert Lowell which impels that American poet into knowing *differently* from others. Lowell became a conscientious objector according to Heaney when 'doctrine, ancestry and politics fused themselves in one commanding stroke'. To show that two can play etymological games Docherty mischievously italicises 'fused' and sees Heaney approving here of 'confusion' (fusing together) which is therefore almost a synonym of 'conscience' in Heaney's imposed sense. He shows Heaney approving of 'confusion' too (in its regular sense) when he takes pleasure in Auden's 'opacity' and his 'obscurity – even if it is wilful'. But in Heaney's frequent endorsement of Frost's famous view that poetry is 'a stay against confusion' there is, as Docherty says, a clear assumption that confusion is a bad thing.[48]

The contradictions in Heaney's language and discourse are taken by Docherty to undermine his essentialist and self-justifying conclusions. We are to see him driven back to his original dichotomy, with Auden and Frost now coming to exemplify (as *The Waste Land* and *Four Quartets* did) his two modes of 'tongue-government' which Docherty would call respectively 'alterity' and 'identity'. But the very instability of Heaney's own language seems to explode the claims of 'identity'. And since he has shown himself as acknowledging and displaying 'alterity', difference, incomprehensibility, 'the Other' as well as 'identity' (or 'knowing ... together'), he can be faulted, says Docherty, for subordinating the first of these options to the second, for 'imperialist thinking' and 'the desire not to hear the Other'.[49] A key example of such 'imperialist thinking' is the way Heaney sees the recent ideological predicament of Eastern European poets not as it is in itself ('difference') but as a mirror-image of the situation of a Northern Irish poet like him.[50] But it is interesting that the possibility of development for the living poet allows for Docherty a collaborative and communicative role in the literary process. While he insists that the association of poetry on Heaney's part with a reconciling and unifying understanding ('identity') is self-centring if not self centred, he can nevertheless prophesy that 'Heaney, as Ulysses' may yet crucify himself upon the mast in order to hear the sirens of 'alterity, the incomprehensible otherness'.[51] In the later essay by Docherty (13) in this volume he examines a poem from *North* where he thinks Heaney is already doing this.

The 'imperialist thinking' of which Docherty accuses Heaney is seen by David Lloyd (essay 11) as governing the whole Romantic and imperial tradition in which Heaney's writing stands and as already apparent in 'the initial formulations ... of Young Ireland's ideologists in the 1840s'.[52] The concept of a distinctive Irish literature in English aiming to uncover 'a common ground beneath political conflicts, whether between peasant and landlord, Catholic and Protestant or class and class' has always been counter-productive according to Lloyd. At every point a bourgeois hegemony has been deflecting the attention of the dispossessed from the fact of their own dispossession whether they are potential Irish insurgents or gulled and anaesthetised student-readers of Heaney within the Anglo-American education system. What Lloyd is arguing is that Heaney's poems are really functioning to reinforce the dominant hegemony of bourgeois consumer capitalism and to evade the insurgent implications of their postcolonial context. This is why they foreclose the issues that they claim to be opening up, so that what the poem is 'about' very quickly becomes a metaphor justifying the way its materials are used. Lloyd's illustrative analyses of the poems soon make it clear that what he is complaining about is very much what, early in this collection, we found Christopher Ricks and Edna Longley applauding. His version of cultural history and his way of reading dictate an ideological and methodological opposition to the premises of what throughout this introduction I have been calling New Criticism: premises which clearly correlate, to a considerable extent, with the avowed aesthetic of Heaney himself.

Heaney's writing may or may not be placed in an irredeemably vulnerable position by what Docherty calls 'the political dialectic, familiar to poststructuralist thought, of Identity and Difference',[53] as Lloyd interprets it. But there is no doubt that the 'Other' which threatens his totalising concept of 'the Sovereign diction'[54] most directly is difference seen in gender terms. 'Can poetry's claim to universality of utterance and to utopian insight,' asks Patricia Coughlan in essay 12, 'be upheld in the face of a reader's awareness of its gendered and therefore (perhaps unconsciously) partial perspective?'[55]

The linguistic analogy we have become familiar with shapes her answer to this question. In terms of 'parole', there is a definite 'vocabulary of roles allotted' to female figures in Heaney's verse; and he gives his own characteristic 'inflections' to the conventions governing such roles, thus conjugating a particular 'Heaney' version of a paradigm ('langue') endemic to Western literature and culture. According to Coughlan, Heaney either 'constructs an unequivocally dominant masculine figure, who explores, describes, brings to pleasure and compassionates a passive feminine one', or he proposes a woman who 'dooms, destroys, puzzles and encompasses the man, but also assists him to his self-discovery'. This vocabulary of female roles is unsatisfactorily limited in Coughlan's view in that the woman is invariably seen as 'Other' and not as an autonomous and equal 'subject or self'; whether Heaney is engaged in autobiographical or mythic construction (the bread-baking aunt of 'Mossbawn: Sunlight' or the Bog Queen of the eponymous poem), his practice, according to Coughlan, 'precludes the possibility of understanding history as the product of human actions', insists on seeing it 'as a fated, cyclical natural process'. And so deep is Heaney's involvement in these inadequate gender-constructions that his deterministic outlook colours his treatment of political and rural situations and processes in general.[56]

Coughlan's indictment here overlaps with Lloyd's but her values are liberal and humanitarian in their concern for individual choice, whereas he seems to look outside the liberal consensus for solutions. She is also more inwardly responsive to the textures and rhythms of Heaney's verse, showing in text and footnotes a certain amount of fellow-feeling for the New Critical aperçus of Edna Longley. Her quiet suggestion that Heaney is among those 'not always exactly choosing to take up the challenge to the notion of the unitary self offered by the "high" Modernists'[57] can be contrasted with Lloyd's unqualified attribution of the adjective 'minor' to the poet.[58] But Coughlan should still be coupled with Lloyd in the active ideological role she expects poetry and criticism to play, endeavouring as critic herself not just to describe reality but to change it: 'the social and cultural construction of gender is a continuously occurring process', she says, 'in which it is certainly not yet time to stop intervening'.[59]

Aesthetic value, subordinate to cultural value for Coughlan and Lloyd, returns to the fore for the next two contributors to this New Casebook; though their approach to Heaney is similarly distrustful of structures which override their historical context and propose a transcendent centre for themselves. Having detected these tendencies in Heaney's theory (in essay 10 here) Thomas Docherty proceeds in essay 13 to argue that some of his poetry breaks free of them through its 'postmodern' qualities. He meets the question of whether 'postmodernism' is a way of describing certain innovative art-forms or a historical condition that manifests itself in and through those art-forms by insisting that a postmodern poem (Heaney's 'The Grauballe Man') is an *event*. The ontological uncertainty, the destabilisation of all discursive origins and centres, influentially reflected upon by Jacques Derrida[60] has contributed in his view to a condition in which life is dominated by time rather than space; in which historical certainty has disappeared so that historical fact is abstracted into historical image, temporal event into electronic image, individual experience into pluralistic montage. 'The Grauballe Man', seen as an *event*, is both an engagement with and an embodiment of such a condition. The free and decentred 'play' of critical language which provides the chicken to the egg of Derrida's ontological view allows Docherty to follow Lyotard in interpreting the 'post' of postmodern as 'a process in "ana-", a process of analysis, of anamnesis, of analogy, of anamorphosis'.[61] By rooting his critical exposition of the poem in the active plurality and ambiguity of a Greek prefix ('up, in place or time, back, again, anew' – *OED*) Docherty gives himself great interpretive latitude. And to demonstrate that the poem functions as postmodern event rather than as a piece of misplaced or limited Modernism makes it possible to 'raise the stakes'[62] of the poem (though it is far from clear at first whether it is Heaney or Docherty who has given the poem the new status in question). However, as Docherty pursues these issues intertextually into the wider processes of *North*, tracing the influence on Heaney of *Hamlet* and Lowell's *For the Union Dead*, he can be seen as defending the poet against detractions voiced earlier in this collection by Eagleton and Lloyd; it is interesting, too, that his explication[63] of the way gender issues are explored in 'Grauballe Man' reflects back on to some of Coughlan's complaints.

It is possibly a measure of Heaney's presence in the critical debate about his poetry that a scholar as far from New Critical practice as Docherty should put a detailed analysis of a single poem at the centre of his critique. Stan Smith (essay 14) is equally concerned to justify the later Heaney; but he deploys his analyses of individual poems to illustrate what he sees as a steady transformative power in Heaney's language. He formulates more precisely an awareness earlier voiced by Eagleton that Heaney's mature practice undermines the traditional critical assumption that poetic language must be 'inflected either towards its signifieds or towards its signifiers'.[64] Smith argues that Heaney's late achievement of a 'classical austerity and bareness of diction' does not preclude a wide range of linguistically mimetic effects; he sees these as engineered by Heaney's syntax, which he explores along general lines established by Donald Davie's influential *Purity of Diction in English Verse* (1952). Heaney himself had seen the relationship of 'Place and Displacement'[65] as crucial to Northern Irish poetry: Smith follows the tendency in contemporary criticism which this introduction has been tracing by relocating this relationship between place and displacement in the achieved textuality of Heaney's written language. In particular he locates it in his *prepositional* manoeuvres.

His argument goes through several stages. He suggests that the parabolic mode of much of the later poetry (exemplified in 'Parable Island') promulgates the awareness that 'there are no authenticating origins: only a plethora of story-tellings which push the origin further back into an original emptiness scrawled over with too much meaning'.[66] (Not only Derrida's disbelief in 'origins' is invoked but also his idea of 'supplementarity' – his notion that articulation is always both replacing and adding to what is there.) Reading Heaney is thus engaging with something which is not historical or geographical but textual: 'It is in this area of dense secondary signification, where script dissembles an original emptiness, that Ireland "begins".'[67] What, then, of Heaney's explanation (in *Place and Displacement*) that the Northern Irish experience involved 'being in two places at once, needing to accommodate two opposed conditions of truthfulness simultaneously'?[68] Smith presents this as primarily a linguistic dilemma, its exploration one to be furthered through prepositional activity of the kind implied by the section-headings of his essay: 'A Place to Come From'; 'Sounding Out Through'; 'Thinking In and Back Into'; 'Drawing a Line Through'; 'Standing In and Standing For'; 'The Distance Between'.

At this point the arguments of Derrida's *On Grammatology*[69] (which has similar section-headings) become important. Derrida had set out to undermine Saussure's belief in the primacy of oral over written language. Under the heading 'The outside X the inside' he pressed his refutation of Saussure's position (using evidence like the common routine whereby one falls back on written equivalents when there is disagreement about what is being said). But this does not eliminate the older view that the oral is prior to the written, it merely supplants (or supplements) it, leaving the other articulable. The X in Derrida's section-heading represents 'erasure' which nevertheless does not remove the 'trace' of the opposite position: the new-found supremacy of 'writing' over 'living speech', of 'text' over 'experience', is only partial. From here Smith, perhaps more effectively than Eagleton earlier, can move to restore Heaney's mimetic potency. Heaney's achieved literary repertoire both encapsulates *and resembles* a linguistic repertoire. *Both* carry, in the way Derrida emblematises, the 'trace' of their experiential source: a moment like that when the young Heaney and his mother are linguistically 'allied and at bay' ('Clearances' 4) 'speaks from the central reticences of Heaney's verse ... the voices' echo or trace erased and yet co-opted in the lines of writing'.[70]

There is considerable difference between Smith's mode of critical advocacy and Neil Corcoran's but both display a commitment to the living poet. Richard Kirkland, in the final essay (15) of this Casebook, can be allied, perhaps, with the British school of Cultural Materialists[71] in wishing to rid not only poetry but all 'canonised' texts of any hint of privileged status vis-à-vis other texts. His concern is with ascertainable knowledge about cultural production[72] and he sees the 'writing' of this knowledge as excluding any special commitment (of the kind visible in most of the essays in this collection) to the writing of Heaney. He quotes Barthes: 'to go from reading to criticism is to change desires; it is no longer to desire the work itself but to desire one's own language'.[73] This balance of the utilitarian and the aesthetic excludes even the kind of political moralism displayed by David Lloyd (though Lloyd has clearly had considerable influence on Kirkland). Like so many earlier contributors Kirkland sees Heaney's self-presentation as dramatising the tension 'between a full individuation and the desire for assimilation'.[74] But this motif is seen as a product at once of the British/Irish politico-cultural situation as it emerges in Northern Ireland and of the literary critical establishment which monitors Anglophone poetic reputations. 'From the Frontier of Writing', he suggests, can be read as recognising this and so sidestepping the New Critical need for 'a reconciliation of issues – a perfection of form' (what Kirkland calls 'the Modernist reading')[75] which usually dominates Heaney's practice and his reception alike.

Kirkland's own larger emphasis (in the book from which this essay is taken)[76] is on the need for new initiatives to help in the reconstruction of Northern Irish society (which he sees as arrested in a pause or interval between two eras). With the possibility in mind that the poetic revival within the province may constitute such an initiative he constructs a paradigm[77] delineating the characteristic features of the 'Ulster Poet'. But he finds Heaney's literary project to be circumscribed and curtailed within this paradigm. There is a debilitating contradiction, in Kirkland's view, between the rooted and community-oriented elements in the paradigm which make the poet a representative of his society and the New Critical tenets which dictate the nature of the poetry he must write to receive institutional validation for his art. (An interesting contrast can be drawn between Kirkland's treatment of this subject and Eamonn Hughes's earlier). Kirkland analyses what he takes to be a representative 'late' work, 'Making Strange' (claiming that it asks *stern* 'questions of Heaney's relationship with his poetic'), to show that the crucial issues are 'evaded through its insistence on being judged [by New Critical criteria] as a well-made poem'. His conclusion seems to be that the mature Heaney raises questions about the contradictory forces involved in the production of Ulster poetry which if pursued might foster cultural regeneration; but is unable to escape the reductive parameters of the aesthetic which has brought him success. It seems appropriate to give Kirkland the last word here, not only because his is the most recent essay in the Casebook, but also because his brisk no-nonsense stance lends its own sense of an ending to what is obviously an on-going debate.

NOTES

1. See 'Further Reading', p. 268 below (Contexts: List A).

2. Other ways of labelling this approach would be: 'Practical Criticism' which is what Heaney himself calls it (*Preoccupations: Selected Prose 1968–1978* [London, 1980], pp. 13–14); 'Anglo-American Formalism' (which then has to be distinguished from Russian Formalism: I have simply called the latter Formalism); 'the Modernist Reading' (adopted by Richard Kirkland, p. 261 below from Anthony Easthope and Jane Tomkins). All such labels have their problems, including my own, which parrots the title of a book by John Crowe Ransom (Norfolk, CT, 1941) and is often used of a coherent group of *American* critics including Ransom, Allen Tate, Cleanth Brooks and W.K. Wimsatt.

3. '"This – doesn't it? – bears such a relation to that; this kind of thing – don't you find it so? – wears better than that", etc.' F.R. Leavis, 'Criticism and Philosophy', *The Common Pursuit* (London, 1965), p. 215.

4. Whose fourth book, *The Force* (London, 1966), appeared in the same year as Heaney's first.

5. T.S. Eliot, 'The Function of Criticism', *Selected Essays* (London, 1958), pp. 32–3.

6. See p. 22 below.

7. See p. 26 below. ('Punishment' is a *locus classicus* of Heaney criticism. [See below, pp. 25–6, 44–6, 70, 174–6, 195].)

8. Roland Barthes, 'What is Criticism?' *Critical Essays* (1964, English trans. Richard Howard, Evanston, IL, 1972), p. 257.

9. P. 35 below. Compare 'Imagery and Movement', *A Selection from Scrutiny* (Cambridge, 1968), vol. 1, pp. 231–47.

10. See p. 35 below.

11. For the origins of the first, see *Cultural Traditions in Northern Ireland* (ed. Maurna Crozier; Belfast, 1989); for those of the second, see *Ireland's Field Day* (afterword by Denis Donoghue; London, 1985).

12. See p. 59 below.

13. See p. 69 below.

14. See Seamus Deane, *Celtic Revivals* (London, 1985), pp. 18–27 and Raymond Williams, *Keywords* (London, 1976), pp. 268–9.

15. In Harold Bloom, *The Anxiety of Influence* (New York, 1973).

16. See p. 69 below.

17. See p. 66 below.

18. See *Negative Dialectics* (1966; English trans. E.B. Ashton, London, 1973); *Aesthetic Theory* (1970; English trans. C. Lenhardt, London, 1984). Deane acknowledges the influence of the first of these books, *Celtic Revivals*, p. 191.

19. See p. 73 below.

20. See p. 76 below and René Girard, *Violence and the Sacred* (1972, English trans. Patrick Gregory, Baltimore, MD, 1977).

21. Michel Foucault, 'What is an Author?' in Josue V. Harari (ed.), *Textual Strategies: Perspectives in Post-Structuralist Criticism* (Ithaca, NY, 1979), p. 158.

22. See *Course in General Linguistics* (1913, English trans. Roy Harris, London, 1983), p. 68: 'the individual has no power to alter a sign in any respect once it has become established in a linguistic community.'

23. Toril Moi, '"Introduction" to "Word, Dialogue and Novel"', *The Kristeva Reader* (ed. Moi, Oxford, 1986), p. 34.

24. F.R. Leavis, *The Common Pursuit* (London, 1965), p.v. (quoting T.S. Eliot, 'The Function of Criticism', *Selected Essays*, p. 25).

25. Roland Barthes, 'From Work to Text', *Image–Music–Text* (English trans. Stephen Heath, London 1977), p. 162. The New Critical version of 'play' which Ricks displays here can be seen also in critics like Frank Kermode and Richard Poirier (who theorises it in *The Performing Self: Compositions and Decompositions in the Languages of Contemporary Life* [London, 1971]).

26. See pp. 98, 100, 101 below.

27. See p. 254 below.

28. See p. 97 below.

29. See p. 102 below.

30. See p. 105 below.

31. *Literary Theory*, pp. 3, 107.

32. See p. 104 below.

33. See, for instance, *Course in General Linguistics*, Part Two, ch. IV, 3: 'Linguistic value: material aspect' (pp. 116–18).

34. See Foucault, 'What is an Author?' in Josue V. Harari (ed.), *Textual Strategies: Perspectives in Post-Structuralist Criticism*, pp. 141–60.

35. John Lucas, whose prefatory note to volumes in the series begins: 'In an age when critical theory promises or threatens to cross over into literature and become its own object of study, there is a powerful case for re-asserting the primacy of the literary text.'

36. See the quotation on p. 112 below from 'Envies and Identifications: Dante and the Modern Poet' (*Irish University Review*, 15: 1 [Spring 1985], 5–19), and the thanks expressed to Heaney in Corcoran's 'Preface' (*Seamus Heaney* [London, 1986], p. 9).

37. P. 107 below.

38. See p. 124 below.

39. Corcoran, *Seamus Heaney*, p. 9.

40. See p. 127 below.

41. See p. 119 below.

42. See p. 127 below.

43. Pp. 223–4 below.

44. P. 144 below. See Longley's words on p. 32 below: 'his poetry suffers when he forsakes the hovering suggestiveness of thresholds'. Longley, however, does seem to imply that some poetry (Yeats?) goes *beyond* thresholds.

45. See p. 144 below.

46. 'to deconstruct a text is to show how it undermines the philosophy it asserts or the hierarchical oppositions on which it relies, by identifying in the text the rhetorical operations that produce the supposed ground of argument, the key concept or premise.' Jonathan Culler, *On Deconstruction* (London, 1983), p. 86.

47. (London, 1988). Docherty gives references to this edition throughout.

48. It is in the nature of Docherty's strategy that I can only approximate to his meaning in this account of pp. 147–9 below. For the full statement of Frost's view, see 'The Figure a Poem Makes', *Complete Poems of Robert Frost* (New York, 1967), p. vi.

49. See p. 153 below.

50. See pp. 149–51 below.

51. See p. 152 below.

52. See p. 156 below.

53. See p. 148 below.

54. *The Government of the Tongue* (London, 1988), p. 137.

55. See p. 186 below.

56. See p. 188 below.

57. See p. 189 below.

58. See p. 180 below.

59. See p. 185 below.

60. Most famously in 'Structure, Sign and Play in the Discourse of the Human Sciences', *Writing and Difference*, ed. and trans. Alan Bass (Chicago, 1978), pp. 278–93.

61. See pp. 218–19 below.

62. See p. 206 below.

63. See pp. 215–16 below.

64. See pp. 240–1 below. The assumption seems to have been first voiced in this form by Barthes. See *Writing Degree Zero* (London, 1967), pp. 47–58.

65. See *Place and Displacement: Recent Poetry of Northern Ireland* (Grasmere, 1984).

66. See p. 235 below.

67. See p. 235 below.

68. See p. 234 below.

69. Trans. Gayatri C. Spivak (Baltimore, MD, 1977).

70. See pp. 244–5 below.

71. Catherine Belsey, 'Towards cultural history – in theory and practice'; Alan Sinfield and Jonathan Dollimore, 'Culture and textuality: debating cultural materialism', *Textual Practice*, 3 (1989), 159–72; 4 (1990), 91–100.

72. See pp. 256–7 below.

73. See p. 254 below.

74. See p. 254 below.

75. See p. 261 below.

76. *Literature and Culture in Northern Ireland since 1965: Moments of Danger* (London, 1996).

77. See p. 257 below.

1

Growing Up: Review of *Death of a Naturalist*

CHRISTOPHER RICKS

Literary gentlemen who remain unstirred by Seamus Heaney's poems will simply be announcing that they are unable to give up the habit of disillusionment with recent poetry. The power and precision of his best poems are a delight, and as a first collection *Death of a Naturalist* is outstanding. You continually catch yourself wanting to apply to the poems themselves their own best formulations. He remembers his father digging:

> He rooted out tall tops, buried the bright edge deep
> To scatter new potatoes that we picked
> Loving their cool hardness in our hands.

And 'their cool hardness in our hands' is just what we love in the words themselves – an unsentimental clarity which impinges with a sense of the physical and yet never becomes obsessed (in Peter Redgrove's way) with physical impingement. 'Digging' is even able to risk mentioning rhythm ('Stooping in rhythm through potato drills'), and then to manifest the very firmness of rhythm which it speaks of:

> The coarse boot nestled on the lug, the shaft
> Against the inside knee was levered firmly.

The extra syllable in 'firmly' braces itself – it sees the line through by skill and will. And the way that the skill of digging combines strength with delicacy is caught in the felicitous play of 'coarse' against the unforeseen but altogether apposite 'nestled'.

Again, 'Follower' is able to evoke the taut accuracy of the ploughman by itself evincing just such an accuracy: the poem tells how the memory of his expert father now stumbles behind him just as he himself once stumbled as a boy behind the plough. The wheel has come full circle, and the poet needs to manifest an expertness which is a counterpart of that skilled authority which he so poignantly remembers from childhood. Needs to, not merely in order to write the poem, but because self-respect and mutual respect insist that working with words is no less dignified, no more prissy, than working with earth.

'The Diviner' presents the intuitive skill of the water-diviner in a way which manages – without narcissism or sidelong glances – to imply that just such a skill is needed here and now by the poet too. One striking moment in the poem takes the kind of risk which the diviner has to, and then pulls it off: the twitch shows

> Spring water suddenly broadcasting
> Through a green aerial its secret stations.

Too clever, too *outré*? No, because 'stations' has a simple and honourable place in traditional praises of nature (the stars in their stations), and because 'broadcasting' did originally mean scattering seed: the modern sense is the metaphorical one, borrowed from country life, and so when Mr Heaney rotates the metaphor, he repays the debt or the compliment to country life. The wheel again comes full circle.

'Churning Day' is not only a finely evocative and unaffected description of how butter is churned from milk, but the poem itself follows the arc of those processes. It gradually becomes 'heavy and rich, coagulated sunlight', and then finally, itself a memory, remembers how the household remembered the recent churning:

> And in the house we moved with gravid ease,
> our brains turned crystals full of clean deal churns,
> the plash and gurgle of the sour-breathed milk,
> the pat and slap of small spades on wet lumps.

What is surprising is the dignity with which Mr Heaney invests such simplicities, such wet lumps. His subject is those things which are inherent or inherited. What he praises is to be praised in his own work.

The central subject is growing up. Wordsworth grew up 'fostered alike by beauty and by fear', and Mr Heaney writes with vivid strength about both. The beauty he finds in unexpected places – the farm machines glinting in the dark barn, the soft mulch at the bottom of the well. The fear he never exaggerates into that sensationalism, that sedentary violence, which currently passes for manly sensibility. Some of the poems present an adulthood achieved once and for all – say, a moment that conquered the fear of rats. Others show us an adulthood won in retrospect, not then. Frogspawn was quaint, but the multitude of frogs is suddenly terrifying. 'Death of a Naturalist'? Long live the naturalist, since Mr Heaney's powers enable him to transcend the limits of anecdote without kicking the anecdote away from beneath him.

The piercing nostalgia of 'Blackberry-Picking' does not cease to be literally itself in becoming furthermore a type of all that transitoriness for which we have all wanted to weep. The hoarded blackberries rot:

> Once off the bush
> The fruit fermented, the sweet flesh would turn sour.
> I always felt like crying. It wasn't fair
> That all the lovely canfuls smelt of rot.
> Each year I hoped they'd keep, knew they would not.

'It wasn't fair' calls across the years in the accents of childhood – only to be answered by the concluding and conclusive rhyme of 'rot' and 'not', so uncompromising after the half-rhymes of the previous lines.

The deploying of rhymes and half-rhymes, the subtle taking up of hints, the sardonic pitying puns – there can be no doubt about Mr Heaney's technical fertility, and it gains its reward in a directness, a freedom from all obscurity, which is yet resonant and uncondescending. The two poems on Ireland's great hunger are masterly. Only in some of the love-poems is there a note of mimicry (Robert Graves?).

From *The New Statesman*, 27 May 1966, p. 778.

NOTES

[This is the first of two essays in this collection by Christopher Ricks. It is included because it offers a characteristic analysis in the style of English New Criticism, albeit in the shape of a review, emphasising the form of the poetry and its relationship to other canonical poems. The reader is expected to be sufficiently familiar with the work of two English poets, Peter Redgrove (b. 1932) and Robert Graves (b. 1895), to be able to compare Heaney with the first and see the second as a possible influence on his love poetry. Ed.]

2

A Slow North-east Wind: Review of *North*

CONOR CRUISE O'BRIEN

> The pigskin's scourged until his knuckles bleed.
> The air is pounding like a stethoscope.
> ('Orange Drums, Tyrone, 1966')

I had the uncanny feeling, reading these poems, of listening to the thing itself, the actual substance of historical agony and dissolution, the tragedy of a people in a place: the Catholics of Northern Ireland. Yes, the Catholics: there is no equivalent Protestant voice. Poetry is as unfair as history, though in a different way. Seamus Heaney takes his distances – archaeology, Berkeley, love-hate of the English language, Spain, County Wicklow (not the least distant) – but his Derry is always with him, the ash, somehow, now standing out even more on the forehead.

A prehistoric body, dug out of a bog 'bruised like a forceps baby', leads to and merges with the image of a girl chained to a railing, shaved and tarred, with the poet as silent witness:

> My poor scapegoat,
>
> I almost love you
> but would have cast, I know,
> the stones of silence ...
>
> I who have stood dumb
> when your betraying sisters,
> cauled in tar,
> wept by the railings,

> who would connive
> in civilised outrage
> yet understand the exact
> and tribal, intimate revenge.
>   ('Punishment')

'Betraying' ... 'exact' ... 'revenge'. The poet here appears as part of his people's assumption that, since the girl has been punished by the IRA, she must indeed be guilty: a double assumption – that she did, in fact, inform on the IRA and that informing on the IRA is a crime. The IRA – nowhere directly referred to – are Furies with an 'understood' role and place in the tribe. It is the word 'exact' that hurts most: Seamus Heaney has so greatly earned the right to use this word that to see him use it as he does here opens up a sort of chasm. But then, of course, that is what he is about. The word 'exact' fits the situation as it is felt to be: and it is because it fits and because other situations, among the rival population, turn on similarly oiled pivots, that hope succumbs. I have read many pessimistic analyses of 'Northern Ireland', but none that has the bleak conclusiveness of these poems.

In a poem with the finely ironic title, 'Act of Union', Heaney has 'the man' addressing a woman pregnant by him, with the metaphor of England addressing Ireland:

> Conquest is a lie. I grow older
> Conceding your half-independent shore
> Within whose borders now my legacy
> Culminates inexorably.
>
> And I am still imperially
> Male, leaving you with the pain,
> The rending process in the colony,
> The battering ram, the boom burst from within.
> The act sprouted an obstinate fifth column
> Whose stance is growing unilateral.
> His heart beneath your heart is a wardrum
> Mustering force. His parasitical
> And ignorant little fists already
> Beat at your borders and I know they're cocked
> At me across the water. No treaty
> I foresee will salve completely your tracked
> And stretchmarked body, the big pain
> That leaves you raw, like opened ground, again.

The terms of the metaphor are surprising. After all, it is not just the 'obstinate fifth column' engendered by England – the Ulster Protestants – who wield parasitical and ignorant little fists; and most Ulster Protestants would be genuinely bewildered at the thought that it was they, rather than their enemies, who were beating at borders, or threatening England.

It is true that the act of impregnation can be thought of as producing the total situation in Northern Ireland, a fifth column relative to both England and Ireland: the poem is rich enough. (Elsewhere, Seamus Heaney writes of the *Catholics* as 'in a wooden horse', 'besieged within the siege'.) In a sense, the poet here is deliberately envisaging the matter mainly as 'the man' feels the woman (Ireland, the Catholics of Ireland, within the metaphor) feels it to be; and in relation to these feelings he is never likely to be wrong. In any case, there is a kind of balance at which Seamus Heaney is not aiming. He mocks at one of the protective Ulster clichés in 'Whatever You Say Say Nothing': '"One side's as bad as the other" never worse'. His upbringing and experience have given him some cogent reasons to feel that one side is worse than the other, and his poems have to reflect this.

Many people in Northern Ireland are in the habit of arguing that they 'have nothing against Catholics as such' (or 'Protestants as such', as the case may be). The trouble is that neither lot, in practice, can remain just 'such', they have to be the much more and much less that it means to be *Irish* Catholics and *Ulster* Protestants: such-plus and seen as such-plus, inherently hostile and frightening. In these poems of Seamus Heaney's, Protestants are seen as such-plus: a matter of muzzles, masks and eyes. About his own such-pluses he is neither sentimental nor apologetic. This, on their mood in (I think) the winter of 1971–2:

> As the man said when Celtic won, 'The Pope of Rome
> 's a happy man this night'. His flock suspect
>
> In their deepest heart of hearts the heretic
> Has come at last to heel and to the stake.
> We tremble near the flames but want no truck
> With the actual firing. We're on the make
>
> As ever. Long sucking the hind tit
> Cold as a witch's and as hard to swallow
> Still leaves us fork-tongued on the border bit:
> The liberal papist note sounds hollow

> When amplified and mixed in with the bangs
> That shake all hearts and windows day and night.
> ('Whatever You Say Say Nothing')

Seamus Heaney is being compared with Yeats, and this is unavoidable, since his unmistakable emergence as the most important Irish poet since Yeats. Yet to call them both 'Irish poets'
would be more misleading than illuminating, unless the Protean
nature of 'Irishness' is remembered. It would be wrong to say that
'Southern Protestant' and 'Northern Catholic' have nothing in
common, but to state what they do have in common, which they
do not have in common with the British, would be an enterprise
requiring delicate discriminations within the concept of
'Irishness'. One such common characteristic is an uneasy but
fruitful relation to the English language in surprising ways, yet
without individualist eccentricity.

Seamus Heaney's writing is modest, often conversational, apparently easy, low-pitched, companionably ironic, ominous, alert,
accurate and surprising. An Irish reader is not automatically reminded of Yeats by this cluster of characteristics, yet an English
reader may perhaps see resemblances that are there but overlooked by the Irish – resemblances coming, perhaps, from certain
common rhythms and hesitations of Irish speech and non-speech.
One may, of course, be reminded, by the subject-matter, of
Yeats's 1916 poems and of 'Nineteen Hundred and Nineteen' and
'Meditations in Time of Civil War'. Again, I am more struck with
the differences than the resemblances. Yeats was free to try, and
did splendidly try, or try on, different relations to the tragedy:
Heaney's relation to a deeper tragedy is fixed and pre-ordained;
the poet is on intimate terms with doom, and speaks its language
wryly and succinctly:

> I am neither internee nor informer;
> An inner émigré, grown long-haired
> And thoughtful: a wood-kerne
> Escaped from the massacre...

As I read and re-read *North*, I was reminded, not so much of any
other Irish poet, as of one of Rudyard Kipling's most chilling fairy-
stories, 'Cold Iron'. It is a story in which bright and tender hopes
are snuffed out by ineluctable destiny, the hand of Thor. And the

way in which Thor makes his presence felt is always 'a slow north-east wind'.

From *The Listener*, 25 September 1975, pp. 204–5.

NOTES

[Conor Cruise O'Brien, a prolific writer on political topics, suggests in another essay that what he has to say about contemporary Ireland should be 'considered less as a theoretical analysis than as a report from ... an informant: a person otherwise ignorant, but familiar with a particular local situation' ('An Unhealthy Intersection', *The Irish Times*, 22 August 1975, p. 10). Interestingly, Heaney in his view is this and more: poetry, he says elsewhere, may 'attempt to reveal, through metaphorical insight, what is actually happening and even, in a broad sense, what is about to happen' ('Passion and Cunning', *In Excited Reverie* [ed. A. Norman Jeffares and K.G.W. Cross, London, 1965], p. 278). In this sense, he reads Heaney's poetry directly into the troubles of Ireland. Quotations not identified by O'Brien in this review are from 'Grauballe Man' ('bruised like a forceps baby'), 'Whatever You Say Say Nothing' ('in a wooden horse', 'besieged within the siege') and 'Exposure' ('I am neither internee nor informer ...'). Ed.]

3

'Inner Emigré' or 'Artful Voyeur'? Seamus Heaney's *North*

EDNA LONGLEY

Seamus Heaney himself sees *North* (1975) as a culmination: 'I'm certain that up to *North*, that that was one book; in a way it grows together and goes together.'[1] While broadly agreeing that the collection indeed crowns Heaney's previous poetry – in terms of merit as well as development – British and Irish commentators have diverged in their emphases. Anthony Thwaite, for instance, praises both style and content:

> These new poems have all the sensuousness of Mr Heaney's earlier work, but refined and cut back to the bone. They are solid, beautifully wrought, expansively resonant. They recognise tragedy and violence without despairingly allowing them to flog human utterance into fragments.[2]

But he does not probe the content more particularly or more politically, falling back on the blurb ('Seamus Heaney has found a myth which allows him to articulate a vision of Ireland' etc.). Five years later Blake Morrison was to note: 'with the exception of Conor Cruise O'Brien in the *Listener*, hardly anyone seemed interested in what it was that Heaney had to "say" about Northern Ireland'.[3] There is nothing new in divergent perceptions on either side of the Irish Sea. (Or, conversely, in Irish writers simultaneously transmitting different messages to different audiences.) Still, O'Brien's informed response established a native line of comment on *North*, including contributions by its author, that raises the most fundamental questions about the relationship between literature and politics. He begins: 'I had the uncanny feeling, reading these poems, of listening to the thing itself, the actual substance of historical agony and dissolution, the tragedy of a people in a place: the Catholics of Northern Ireland.'[4] Being so locally tuned in, O'Brien can dismiss simplistic comparisons between Heaney and Yeats: 'Yeats was free to try, and did splendidly try, or try on, different relations to the tragedy: Heaney's relation to a deeper tragedy is fixed and pre-ordained.'[5]

Is Heaney then, like 'The Tollund Man', 'Bridegroom to the goddess'? His reaction to the Man's photograph deserves the much-abused term 'epiphany', with its full Joycean connotations: a revelation of personal and artistic destiny expressed in religious language. Glossing the poem, he figures as pilgrim-acolyte: 'My sense of occasion and almost awe as I vowed to go to pray to the Tollund Man and assist at his enshrined head';[6] or as initiate into an order:

> when I wrote that poem I had a sense of crossing a line really, that my whole being was involved in the sense of – the root sense – of religion, being bonded to something, being bound to do something. I felt it a vow.[7]

The three parts of the poem itself might be tabulated as evocation ('his peat-brown head,/ The mild pods of his eye-lids'), invocation ('I could ... pray/ Him to make germinate/ The scattered, ambushed/ Flesh of labourers'), and vocation ('Something of his sad freedom ... Should come to me'). If nothing else, 'The Tollund Man' certainly germinated *North*. In so far as Heaney's own role in the poems parallels that of the bridegroom-victims, does he really attain 'sad freedom', or in fact sacrifice some imaginative liberty to that 'dark-bowered queen', Cathleen Ní Houlihán? Has tribal pre-ordination, or ordination, any petrifying effect on poetic life?

Part of the answer must lie in the distinctive strengths of Heaney's earlier poetry: in whether certain approaches to 'historical agony' go against the grain of these strengths. From the outset his poems have travelled a rich boundary between conscious and unconscious, or instinctual, experience; between the farm and 'The great slime kings' of wild Nature. His imaginative adventures take place upon the brink that 'Personal Helicon' leans over:

> I loved the dark drop, the trapped sky, the smells
> Of waterweed, fungus and dank moss.

Symbolically summarising *Death of a Naturalist*, the wells with their varying depths and contents represent different entries into different parts of the hidden self. The poem evokes both Robert Frost's 'For Once, Then, Something', and Heaney's comment on another Frost poem, 'The Most of It':

> a poem housing power of some kind. It's not discourse, analysis, judgment, display, it moves by instinct, moves itself, moves the reader; a sense of connection and perhaps not much deliberation.[8]

'Personal Helicon' partly exemplifies, partly describes such strategic semi-consciousness. Key-verbs – savour, hover, pry, finger – fuse physical and metaphysical exploration. John Wilson Foster criticises the continuation of these methods in *Door into the Dark*: 'the dark remains unchallenged by the end of the book. Heaney has a marked reluctance to strike inwards, to cross the threshold, to explore the emotional and psychological sources of his fear'.[9] But many of the best poems in the language depend on signs, hints, mysteries. Indeed 'The Most of It' refuses to go further than 'and that was all'. Heaney 'rhymes ... to set the darkness echoing', rather than switch on lights. It will be part of my further argument that his poetry suffers when he forsakes the hovering suggestiveness of thresholds, the actual process of discovery, a slowly opening door, and comes to or from political conclusions. In *Door into the Dark* 'The Plantation', like Thomas's 'Lights Out', implies the poet's mystery-tour:

> You had to come back
> To learn how to lose yourself,
> To be pilot and stray – witch,
> Hansel and Gretel in one.

When Heaney evolved this productive strategy his Helicon was still largely personal. Interviewed (1977) by Seamus Deane about the relationship of the Ulster poets 'to the Northern crisis', he first volunteers the wise minimum: 'The root of the troubles may have something in common with the root of the poetry'; then adduces some revealing autobiography:

> the very first poems I wrote, 'Docker' and one about Carrickfergus Castle for instance, reveal this common root. The latter had William

of Orange, English tourists and myself in it. A very inept sort of poem but my first attempts to speak, to make verse, faced the Northern sectarian problem. Then this went underground and I became very influenced by Hughes and one part of my temperament took over: the private county Derry childhood part of myself rather than the slightly aggravated young Catholic male part.[10]

The 'slightly aggravated young Catholic male' did, however, occasionally surface before *Wintering Out* and his complete emergence from hibernation in *North*. As well as 'Docker' ('That fist would drop a hammer on a Catholic'), *Death of a Naturalist* contains two poems, 'At a Potato Digging' and 'For the Commander of the "Eliza"', written in reaction to Cecil Woodham-Smith's *The Great Hunger*. The Commander, obliged by orders to withhold food from starving men in a rowing-boat, is haunted by an image that anticipates the boneyard of *North*: 'Next day, like six bad smells, those living skulls/ Drifted through the dark of bunks and hatches.' Heaney's private imagery of rot and smells spills over into the public domain, perhaps also sniffing something rotten in the state of Northern Ireland. In 'At a Potato Digging' a rather awkward metamorphosis changes potatoes as 'live skulls, blind-eyed' into the real thing:

> Live skulls, blind-eyed, balanced on
> wild higgledy skeletons
> scoured the land in 'forty-five,
> wolfed the blighted root and died.

This transition is the hinge on which the poem turns from present to past (a better-oiled process in *North*). 'At a Potato Digging' starts out like an echo of Patrick Kavanagh's *The Great Hunger*: 'Clay is the word and clay is the flesh/ Where the potato-gatherers like mechanised scarecrows move/ Along the side-fall of the hill' (Kavanagh); 'A mechanical digger wrecks the drill,/ Spins up a dark shower of roots and mould./ Labourers swarm in behind ...' (Heaney). But Kavanagh's title symbolises the starvation of the spirit in twentieth-century rural Ireland; his perspective on servitude to the land is local in place and time, whatever historic deprivations lurk in the background. As Heaney says, 'The "matter of Ireland", mythic, historical or literary forms no significant part of [Kavanagh's] material.'[11] And again, 'At the bottom of Kavanagh's imagination there is no pagan queen, no mystique of the national, the mythic or the tribal.'[12] (Does this make Kavanagh paradoxically more forward-looking than Heaney – a function of the North–South timelag?) Heaney's potato-diggers undoubtedly guide him towards 'the matter of Ireland', and towards his first embry-onic fusion of Catholic experience in the North with the longer na-tional history: 'A people hungering from birth'; 'and where potato diggers are/ you still smell the running sore' (rottenness in the state again). In another portent of the procedures of *North*, Heaney re-solves the poem by drawing on a mixture of Christian and pagan ritual. The diggers who make 'a seasonal altar of the sod', finally propitiate 'the famine god' by spilling 'Libations of cold tea'.

'Requiem for the Croppies', the historical poem in *Door into the Dark*, joins the centuries more seamlessly and achieves a more organic, indeed germinal, resolution: 'And in August the barley grew up out of the grave'.

> [It] was written in 1966 when most poets in Ireland were straining to celebrate the anniversary of the 1916 Rising. That rising was the harvest of seeds sown in 1798, when revolutionary republican ideals and national feeling coalesced in the doctrines of Irish republicanism and in the rebellion of 1798 – itself unsuccessful and savagely put down. The poem was born of and ended with an image of resurrec-tion based on the fact that some time after the rebels were buried in common graves, these graves began to sprout with young barley, growing up with barley corn which the 'croppies' had carried in their pockets to eat while on the march. The oblique implication was that the seeds of violent resistance sowed in the Year of Liberty had flowered in what Yeats called 'the right rose tree' of 1916. I did not realise at the time that the original heraldic murderous encounter between Protestant yeoman and Catholic rebel was to be initiated again in the summer of 1969, in Belfast, two months after the book was published.[13]

Heaney speaks in the poem as one of the 'fatal conclave', a more ef-fective tactic than his use of the Commander's voice as a semi-ironic filter. However, in 'Bogland', a threshold-poem like 'The Tollund Man' ('I wrote it quickly ... revised it on the hoof'[14]), he abandons both straight history and the dramatic monologue. He opens his proper door into 'the matter of Ireland', by imagining history as an experience rather than a chain of events, by dramatising his own imaginative experience of history, by discovering within his home-ground a myth that fits the inconclusiveness both of memory and of Irish history, and by fusing the psychic self-searching of poet and nation:

> Our pioneers keep striking
> Inwards and downwards ...

The qualities and contents of bog, as before of wells and plantation, represent an unconscious – this time collective. But it is the movement of the poem, in Heaney's Frostian sense, that counts. Metre, sound, and rhythms enact a descent through layers. The poem alternates ampler development with sharp insertions. Thus the abrupt 'They'll never dig coal here' interrupts assonances which imitate the wet softness of bog 'Melting and opening underfoot'. 'Bogland' might be called not so much 'a prospect of the mind' (to use Heaney's favourite Wordsworthian phrase for poetic landscape) as a prospecting of the mind.

1969 thus coincided with Heaney's readiness to pioneer the frontiers of Irish consciousness: 'From that moment the problems of poetry moved from being simply a matter of achieving the satisfactory verbal icon to being a search for images and symbols adequate to our predicament.' Again, 'those language and place-names ... poems [in *Wintering Out*] politicise the terrain and the imagery of the first two books.'[15] The poem that most literally, and perhaps most richly, 'politicises the terrain' is 'The Other Side', in which Heaney intertwines land, religion, and language to characterise, and tentatively close, the distance between Catholic and Protestant neighbours in Ulster:

> I lay where his lea sloped
> to meet our fallow,
> nested on moss and rushes,
>
> my ear swallowing
> his fabulous, biblical dismissal,
> that tongue of chosen people.

This new kind of exploratory relation to Mossbawn complements the Belfast terrain of 'A Northern Hoard', a sequence that puts the question to which the surrounding poems respond: 'What do I say if they wheel out their dead?' 'Tinder', whose prehistoric imagery connects with that of 'The Tollund Man', might be described as Heaney's 'Easter, 1916'. But his before-and-after contrast displays little even of Yeats's qualified excitement. The underprivileged 'tribe' who have lit the tinder of revolution, wonder what to do with their 'new history', while the poet simultaneously wonders about his role:

> Now we squat on cold cinder,
> Red-eyed, after the flames' soft thunder
>
> And our thoughts settle like ash.
> We face the tundra's whistling brush ...

Both the rhetorical questions of 'A Northern Hoard', and the answering probes into rural local history, develop the prospecting of 'Bogland'. Heaney's 'Inwards and downwards' strike also turns up anonymous ancestors, deprived even of 'scraggy acres': servant boy ('Old work-whore, slave-/ blood'), mummer (though this model of the vanishing tribal artist has English origins), 'mound-dwellers', Spenser's 'geniuses who creep/ "out of every corner/ of the woodes and glennes"'. Occasionally such figures convey a thinner, more romantic, more literal version of history: not so much active prospecting as nostalgic retrieval: 'how/ you draw me into/ your trail'. 'The Tollund Man' himself and two poems with no explicit historical ties, 'Limbo' and 'Bye-Child', embody more powerfully the same structure of feeling. 'Bye-Child', which might symbolise 'A people hungering from birth', expresses Heaney's most intense empathy with deprivation:

> Little henhouse boy,
> Sharp-faced as new moons
> Remembered, your photo still
> Glimpsed like a rodent
> On the floor of my mind.

The 'language and place-names poems' too sometimes resort to ready-made history. 'Traditions', for instance, exchanges the multi-layered socio-linguistics of 'The Other Side' for a narrower focus: 'Our guttural muse/ was bulled long ago/ by the alliterative tradition.' However these poems excitingly pioneer, in the context of Ulster English, the kind of resonance that Edward Thomas's parallel researches found more traditionally latent. And they give Heaney a valid 'political' role within his profession of poet. An aesthetic brand of revolutionary action, perhaps more linguistic reclamation than decolonisation, takes on the English language itself, with mixed declarations of love and war:

> But now our river tongues must rise
> From licking deep in native haunts

To flood, with vowelling embrace,
Demesnes staked out in consonants.
('A New Song')

As a group the poems insinuate that the ghost of Gaelic, local idiom, the sound of the land itself, all united in Heaney's own utterance, are compelling the tradition of Shakespeare and Spenser to go native.

He puts this, and other things, more bluntly in Part II of *North*:

Ulster was British, but with no rights on
The English lyric

– or so they thought. Perhaps Heaney's poetry was always a form of revolution, like negro jazz:

Between my finger and my thumb
The squat pen rests; snug as a gun.

In Berkeley (1970–1) he became aware 'that poetry was a force, almost a mode of power, certainly a mode of resistance'.[16] To Seamus Deane he says: 'I think that my own poetry is a kind of slow, obstinate, papish burn, emanating from the ground I was brought up on.'[17] 'Obstinate' is a favourite and favourable word of Heaney's, signifying the immovable object or objection that reverses 'No Surrender'. (John Hewitt's oft-repeated 'stubborn' may represent the Protestant cultural equivalent.) Up to and including *Wintering Out* his poetry may have been poetry-as-protest or protest-as-poetry in an extraordinarily profound sense: unjust Ulster 'hurt' him into poetry. However, in *North* this subtext whereby Heaney makes up for the lost time of those lost 'geniuses', the mute inglorious Spensers, coarsens as it becomes text. 'The Ministry of Fear' and 'Freedman' turn the tables with too much relish for the effect to be wholly ironic:

Those hobnailed boots from beyond the mountain
Were walking, by God, all over the fine
Lawns of elocution ...

Then poetry arrived in that city –
I would abjure all cant and self-pity –
And poetry wiped my brow and sped me.
Now they will say I bite the hand that fed me.

Such speaking-out by the 'slightly aggravated young Catholic male', or poet, accords with Heaney's view elsewhere in Part II, that artificial balance distorts: '"One side's as bad as the other," never worse' ('Whatever You Say Say Nothing'). Much of the aggravation continues as a portrait of the artist, especially in the sequence 'Singing School' which begins with 'The Ministry of Fear'. The third poem, 'Orange Drums, Tyrone, 1966', was written before the Troubles – a pointer to how throughout *North* Heaney's creative maturity catches up on his youthful pieties and impieties. Combining aural and visual menace, the drums define Unionist hegemony in terms of 'giant tumours', of a claustrophobic violence that afflicts its inflictor:

> The pigskin's scourged until his knuckles bleed.
> The air is pounding like a stethoscope.

'A Constable Calls' (the second poem) lacks the same ultimate impact, the caller's bike becoming, even from the child's eye view, an implausibly melodramatic time-bomb: 'His boot pushed off/ And the bicycle ticked, ticked, ticked.' However, both poems explore their own subjects; we infer the effect on Heaney's developing sensibility. 'The Ministry of Fear' and 'Summer 1969' (4) seem written largely for the sake of the sequence, and to fill in a poetic curriculum vitae (down to the provision of dates). Again, the nods to Yeats and Wordsworth in Heaney's titles and epigraphs (one of which is 'Fair seedtime had my soul') look self-conscious as well as satirical. 'The Ministry of Fear' veers from the sharply specific:

> In the first week
> I was so homesick I couldn't even eat
> The biscuits left to sweeten my exile.
> I threw them over the fence one night
> In September 1951 ...

to the archly literary: 'It was an act/ Of stealth.' Heaney's theme may contrast the boy and the 'sophisticated' author ('Here's two on's are sophisticated'), but his language need not divide them. Also sophisticated, 'Summer 1969' forces home-thoughts from Spain: 'stinks from the fishmarket/ Rose like the reek off a flaxdam'; cites Lorca and Goya as exemplars in the context of trying 'to touch the people'; and finally applies too much local colour to the latter's portrait:

> He painted with his fists and elbows, flourished
> The stained cape of his heart as history charged.

This is elementary stuff from the proven matador of *Wintering Out*.

The two remaining poems, 'Fosterage' (5) and 'Exposure' (6), withdraw towards the centre of Heaney's own art. The former quotes the anti-heroic advice of Ulster short-story writer Michael McLaverty ('Don't have the veins bulging in your biro'), although the manner and content of the last line partially disregard it: 'and sent me out, with words/ Imposing on my tongue like obols'. 'Exposure' (to which I shall return) sets up a much more genuine inner conflict than 'Summer 1969', and falls a long way short of confidently identifying the artist with the man of action:

> I walk through damp leaves,
> Husks, the spent flukes of autumn,
>
> Imagining a hero
> On some muddy compound,
> His gift like a slingstone
> Whirled for the desperate.

This truly is the doubtful mood and mode of Yeats's 'Meditations in Time of Civil War':

> I turn away and shut the door, and on the stair
> Wonder how many times I could have proved my worth
> In something that all others understand or share.

But if 'Exposure' casts second thoughts back over *North* as a whole, most of Part II underwrites Part I – in the sense of para-phrase as well as of explaining its motivation. A few critics indeed have found Heaney's personal and documentary explicitness more to their taste than the mythic approach of Part I. Colin Falck con-siders it 'a relief ... that he can still call on some of his old direct-ness in dealing with the Ulster conflicts'.[18] But is the directness of 'Whatever You Say Say Nothing' either equal or equivalent to the sensuous immediacy of Heaney's first three books?

> The times are out of joint
> But I incline as much to rosary beads
> As to the jottings and analyses
> Of politicians and newspapermen

> Who've scribbled down the long campaign from gas
> And protest to gelignite and sten,
>
> Who proved upon their pulses 'escalate',
> 'Backlash' and 'crack down', 'the provisional wing',
> 'Polarisation' and 'long-standing hate'.
> Yet I live here, I live here too, I sing,
>
> Expertly civil tongued with civil neighbours
> On the high wires of first wireless reports,
> Sucking the fake taste, the stony flavours
> Of those sanctioned, old, elaborate retorts:
>
> 'Oh, it's disgraceful, surely, I agree,'
> 'Where's it going to end?' 'It's getting worse' ...

Heaney too seems to practise a kind of shorthand: 'gas/ And protest to gelignite and sten' cannot be offloaded on to 'newspaper-men', while 'the provisional wing' is a hasty reference that carries its own 'backlash'. His subsequent anatomy of Ulster evasiveness ('Smoke-signals are loud-mouthed compared with us .../ O land of password, handgrip, wink and nod,/ Of open minds as open as a trap'), labours the point in comparison with Derek Mahon's bleak earlier indictment:

> [We] yield instead to the humorous formulae,
> The spurious mystery in the knowing nod.
> Or we keep sullen silence in light and shade,
> Rehearsing our astute salvations under
> The cold gaze of a sanctimonious God.
> ('In Belfast')

The mood of Heaney's poem comes over as irritation, impatience, rather than grand indignation (perhaps partly a result of his difficult gear change from poetic smoke-signaller to loud-speaker). The concluding vision of a petty society leaves a sour taste, because it admits empathy but excludes sympathy: 'Coherent miseries, a bite and sup,/ We hug our little destiny again.' His blanket dismissal of cliché is more palatable, indeed a cliché itself. Yet it may have something to do with the fact that Heaney's own poetry – unlike, say, MacNeice's *Autumn Journal* – has among its many rich resources no means of accommodating, transforming, criticising such idiom. The inadequacy of media jargon, or of everyday commonplace, invalidates neither the political process nor 'civilised outrage'. However, 'Whatever You Say Say Nothing' – which Heaney did not include in his *Selected Poems* – essentially voices the same sentiment as Edward Thomas's 'This is No Case of Petty Right or Wrong'. Just as Thomas during the First World War insisted on expressing England in his own way ('I hate not Germans, nor grow hot/ With love of Englishmen, to please newspapers'), so Heaney is justifying the language, aesthetic and perspective of the greater part of his book.

The lecture 'Feeling into Words', from which I have already quoted, coincided with the completion of *North*. By 'a search for images and symbols adequate to our predicament', Heaney

> [does] not mean liberal lamentation that citizens should feel compelled to murder one another or deploy their different military arms over the matter of nomenclatures such as British or Irish. I do not mean public celebrations or execrations of resistance or atrocity – although there is nothing necessarily unpoetic about such celebration, if one thinks of Yeats's 'Easter, 1916'. I mean that I felt it imperative to discover a field of force in which, without abandoning fidelity to the processes and experience of poetry ... it would be possible to encompass the perspectives of a humane reason and at the same time to grant the religious intensity of the violence its deplorable authenticity and complexity. And when I say religious, I am not thinking simply of the sectarian division. To some extent the enmity can be viewed as a struggle between the cults and devotees of a god and goddess. There is an indigenous territorial numen, a tutelar of the whole island, call her Mother Ireland, Cathleen Ní Houlihán, the poor old woman, the Shan Van Vocht, whatever; and her sovereignty has been temporarily usurped or infringed by a new male cult whose founding fathers were Cromwell, William of Orange and Edward Carson, and whose god-head is incarnate in a rex or caesar resident in a palace in London. What we have is the tail-end of a struggle in a province between territorial piety and imperial power.
>
> Now I realise that this idiom is remote from the agnostic world of economic interest whose iron hand operates in the velvet glove of 'talks between elected representatives', and remote from the political manoeuvres of power-sharing; but it is not remote from the psychology of the Irishmen and Ulstermen who do the killing, and not remote from the bankrupt psychology and mythologies implicit in the terms Irish Catholic and Ulster Protestant. The question, as ever, is 'How with this rage shall beauty hold a plea?' And my answer is, by offering 'befitting emblems of adversity'.[19]

My contention will be that 'this idiom' can represent as unreal an extreme as the other: that Part I of *North* (unlike *Wintering Out*) often falls between the stools of poetry and politics instead of building a mythic bridge.

After the passage quoted above, Heaney tells how he found 'befitting emblems' in P.V. Glob's *The Bog People*, and swore his vow to the Tollund Man. What is the precise 'emblematic' relevance of these mummified figures to the 'man-killing parishes' of Northern Ireland? The prototype developed by 'The Tollund Man' is a scapegoat, privileged victim and ultimately Christ-surrogate, whose death and bizarre resurrection might redeem, or symbolise redemption for,

> The scattered, ambushed
> Flesh of labourers,
> Stockinged corpses
> Laid out in the farmyards ...

Here Heaney alludes particularly to Catholic victims of sectarian murder in the 1920s. His comment to James Randall interprets the amount of family as well as religious feeling in the poem: 'The Tollund Man seemed to me like an ancestor almost, one of my old uncles, one of those moustached archaic faces you used to meet all over the Irish countryside.'[20] Thus related to 'the moustached/ dead, the creel-fillers' elsewhere in *Wintering Out*, the Man becomes the logical conclusion, the terminal case, the *reductio* of ancestral dispossession and oppression. In 'Feeling into Words', having summarised Glob's account of 'ritual sacrifices to the Mother Goddess' for the sake of fertility, Heaney asserts: 'Taken in relation to the tradition of Irish political martyrdom for that cause whose icon is Cathleen ní Houlihán, this is more than an archaic barbarous rite: it is an archetypal pattern. And the unforgettable photographs ... blended in my mind with photographs of atrocities, past and present, in the long rites of Irish political and religious struggles.'[21] Heaney does not distinguish between involuntary and voluntary 'martyrdom', and the nature of his 'archetype' is such as to subsume the latter within the former.

If 'The Tollund Man' and its glosses lay down a 'pattern' for *North*, as it seems reasonable to suppose, how do the later Bog poems compare with the original model? 'The Grauballe Man' obviously invites such a comparison; even the inference that the poems typify successive books (after the manner of 'Sailing to Byzantium' and 'Byzantium', or 'Toads' and 'Toads Revisited'). Whereas 'The

Tollund Man' varies its angle of approach and moves with the dynamic of a pilgrimage, 'The Grauballe Man' has more the air of a set-piece, arrival, its subject celebrated because he's there, rather than summoned into being by the poet's need:

> As if he had been poured
> in tar, he lies
> on a pillow of turf
> and seems to weep
>
> the black river of himself.
> The grain of his wrists
> is like bog oak,
> the ball of his heel
>
> like a basalt egg.

A difference in quality issues from the difference in stance; emotion anticipated in excitement gives way to tranquil contemplation; the intensity of conversion to ritual observance; crucifixion to resurrection. Almost too dutifully the poem venerates wrists, heel, instep, hips, spine, chin, throat, hair – inclining to rosary beads indeed. The chain of inventive similes reinforces the point that the Man has been translated into the element of the bog, and is thus at one with faintly healing nature, but the Tollund Man somehow remains the *human* face of the Bog People. The less elaborate physical detail in the first poem counts for more, especially 'The mild pods of his eyelids'. 'Mild' combines physical suggestiveness with a subliminal reference to Jesus ('Gentle Jesus, meek and mild'), while its last three letters set up a soothing assonance within the line, which ratifies the union. The two humanising images in 'The Grauballe Man': 'And his rusted hair,/ a mat unlikely/ as a foetus's', 'bruised like a forceps baby', compete with each other and retain a chiefly visual quality. (Again, the simple 'stained face' of 'The Tollund Man' says more.) The climax of the poem, following on the latter simile, appears unduly self-referring, pointed towards the 'perfection' with which the rosary has been told:

> but now he lies
> perfected in my memory,
> down to the red horn
> of his nails,
>
> hung in the scales
> with beauty and atrocity ...

Beauty on the whole has outweighed atrocity by the time we reach 'the actual weight/ of each hooded victim, slashed and dumped'. In fact the poem almost proclaims the victory of metaphor over 'actuality':

> Who will say 'corpse'
> to his vivid cast?
> Who will say 'body'
> to his opaque repose?

Possibly someone should. The ultimate difference between the two poems is that between Christ on the Cross and a holy picture: the urgent presence of 'The Tollund Man' worked 'to a saint's kept body'. Heaney may have mistaken his initial epiphany for a literal signpost, when it was really a destination, a complete emotional curve that summed up profound feelings and wishes about the situation in Northern Ireland. The ambiguous resolution – 'lost,/ Unhappy and at home' – may be as far as he can genuinely go, and it resembles other reactions in his poetry to tragic circumstances. 'Elegy for a Still-born Child' (*Door into the Dark*), for instance, ends: 'I drive by remote control on this bare road ... White waves riding home on a wintry lough.'

Heaney's contracted or 'perfected' perception of the Bog People in *North* renders their emblematic function, as well as his poetry, less complex. If what was hypothetical in 'The Tollund Man' – the consecration of 'the cauldron bog' – has hardened into accepted doctrine, do these later images imply that suffering on behalf of Cathleen may not be in vain, that beauty can be reborn out of terror: 'The cured wound'? The females of the species also attain a 'leathery beauty'. For the girl in 'Punishment', the wind 'blows her nipples/ to amber beads', and the tone of love-making compensates for any deficiencies:

> Little adulteress,
> before they punished you
>
> you were flaxen-haired,
> undernourished, and your
> tar-black face was beautiful.

As women cannot be 'bridegrooms', Heaney must find them a different place in the 'archetypal pattern'. The final moral twist of 'Punishment' has attracted a good deal of comment:

I who have stood dumb
when your betraying sisters,
cauled in tar,
wept by the railings,

who would connive
in civilised outrage
yet understand the exact
and tribal, intimate revenge.

This is all right if Heaney is merely being 'outrageously' honest about his own reactions, if the paradox 'connive ... civilised' is designed to corner people who think they have risen above the primitive, if the poem exposes a representative Irish conflict between 'humane reason' and subconscious allegiances. But can the poet run with the hare ('I can feel the tug/ of the halter') and hunt with the hounds? Ciarán Carson observes:

> Being killed for adultery is one thing; being tarred and feathered is another ... [Heaney] seems to be offering his 'understanding' of the situation almost as a consolation ... It is as if he is saying, suffering like this is natural; these things have always happened; they happened then, they happen now, and that is sufficient ground for understanding and absolution. It is as if there never were and never will be any political consequences of such acts; they have been removed to the realm of sex, death and inevitability.[22]

Perhaps the problem is one of artistic, not political, fence-sitting. The conclusion states, rather than dramatises, what should be profound self-division, one of Heaney's most intense hoverings over a brink. In any case it remains unresolved, unless the poem does in a sense make a political point by endorsing the 'idiom', of something deeper than politics. (Although today's anthropology may only be yesterday's politics.) Blake Morrison argues:

> It would be going too far to suggest that 'Punishment' in particular and the Bog poems generally offer a defence of Republicanism; but they are a form of 'explanation'. Indeed the whole procedure of *North* is such as to give sectarian killing in Ulster a historical respectability which it is not usually given in day-to-day journalism.[23]

In fact Heaney grants no licence to the latter. He excludes the intersectarian issue, warfare *between* tribes, by concentrating on the Catholic psyche as bound to immolation, and within that immolation to savage tribal loyalties. This is what he means by 'slaughter/ for the common good' ('Kinship'), and by 'granting the religious intensity of the violence its deplorable authenticity and complexity' – and, of course, no apologia for the 'male cult' of imperial power. 'Kinship' defines the battlefield in astonishingly introverted Catholic and Nationalist terms:

> Our mother ground
> is sour with the blood
> of her faithful,
>
> they lie gargling
> in her sacred heart
> as the legions stare
> from the ramparts.

If *North* doesn't cater for 'liberal lamentation', neither does it offer a universal, Wilfred Owen-style image of human suffering. It is a book of martyrs rather than of tragic protagonists. Only 'Strange Fruit' questions its own attitude, challenges inevitability:

> Murdered, forgotten, nameless, terrible
> Beheaded girl, outstaring axe
> And beatification, outstaring
> What had begun to feel like reverence.

The frank adjectives capsize what has previously been rather a decorative dawdle of a sonnet ('Pash of tallow, perishable treasure'; 'Diodorus Siculus confessed/ His gradual ease among the likes of this'). They also capsize a good deal else in *North*. Heaney told John Haffenden: '['Strange Fruit'] had ended at first with a kind of reverence, and the voice that came in when I revised was a rebuke to the literary quality of that reverent emotion.'[24]

'Bog Queen' has the advantage of dealing directly with the goddess herself, so that questionable behaviour on the part of her acolytes may be ignored. The female figures in the poems, perhaps understandably, bear a family resemblance to one another: 'The pot of the skull,/ The damp tuck of each curl'; 'My skull hibernated/ in the wet nest of my hair'; 'They unswaddled the wet fern of her hair'; 'my brain darkening'; 'your brain's exposed/ and darkened combs'. However 'Bog Queen', although over-amplified like 'The Grauballe Man', renews that well-worn genre the aisling by presenting Ireland as her landscape, weather, geography, and history, and by pushing her 'old hag' incarnation to an extreme:

> My diadem grew carious,
> gemstones dropped
> in the peat floe
> like the bearings of history.

Since this is the one Bog poem with true Irish antecedents,[25] it can begin with an apt analogue of dormant nationhood ('I lay waiting/ between turf-face and demesne wall'), and end with an equally plausible 'rising':

> and I rose from the dark,
> hacked bone, skull-ware,
> frayed stitches, tufts,
> small gleams on the bank.

These lines, and the poem's clearly shaped symbol, speak for themselves. But Heaney sometimes asks too much of his myth, as if all statement has been shunted off to Part II, as if 'archetypes' remain above or below argument. ('Punishment' suggests the contrary.) A number of his comments on poetry nudge it towards the visual arts – a surprising development from such a rhythmic prodigy: 'the verbal icon'; 'a search for images and symbols'; 'The poetry I love is some kind of image or visionary thing'; 'a painter can lift anything and make an image of it'.[26] The notion of 'befitting emblems' also requires examination. Their original context is section II of 'Meditations in Time of Civil War', where Yeats defines the purpose of his art in terms of 'founding' his Tower:

> that after me
> My bodily heirs may find,
> To exalt a lonely mind,
> Befitting emblems of adversity.

Yeats's 'emblems' are the many facets of the Tower and of his poetry as a whole. Heaney seems to regard a symbol or myth as sufficiently emblematic in itself: 'beauty' pleading with 'rage' within the icon of 'The Grauballe Man' – Man and poem synonymous – rather than through any kind of dialectic. Nor does the myth, as the resemblances between the poems suggest, undergo much evolution.

Before the publication of *North*, John Wilson Foster said of the language poems in *Wintering Out*: 'Heaney's conceit (landscape = body = sex = language) and the way it sabotages emotion leads him into ... difficulties'.[27] In *North* the addition of = Ireland, of the aisling element, makes it still harder to determine which level is primary, or whether they are all just being ingeniously translated into each other. Presumably 'Come to the Bower' signifies the poet's imaginative intercourse with his country, but does the conceit do more than consummate itself?

> I reach past
> The river bed's washed
> Dream of gold to the bullion
> Of her Venus bone.

When England participates in the landscape–sex–Ireland poems, Heaney's edifice and his artifice wobble. In 'Bone Dreams' the poet's lady uneasily assumes foreign contours:

> I have begun to pace
> the Hadrian's Wall
> of her shoulder, dreaming
> of Maiden Castle.

'Ocean's Love to Ireland' overworks phallic symbolism: Ralegh 'drives inland'; 'his superb crest ... runs its bent/ In the rivers of Lee and Blackwater'; 'The Spanish prince has spilled his gold/ / And failed her'. Love poetry in political language risks even more than the reverse:

> And I am still imperially
> Male, leaving you with the pain,
> The rending process in the colony,
> The battering ram, the boom burst from within.
> The act sprouted an obstinate fifth column
> Whose stance is growing unilateral.

This poem, 'Act of Union', pursuing the parallel between sexual and political union, and between imperialism and maleness, casts the speaker in a role which fits uneasily. And the allegory could apply to begetting Loyalism as much as 'obstinate' Republicanism. In any case, the poem hardly persuades as a man's emotion towards his wife or child: 'parasitical/ And ignorant little fists'.

Given Heaney's previous successful explorations of landscape, water, femaleness, what has gone wrong this time? His prose comments support the view that an obsession with stacking up parallels has replaced flexible 'soundings'. And in the case both of sex-and-landscape and of Bogland regions, Ireland is the straw that breaks the poems' backs. The Jutland connection does achieve certain archetypal dimensions but, as 'Punishment' indicates, the moral and political ground beyond the self-contained emblem is boggy indeed. With reference to the process in 'Kinship', whereby the poet finds 'a turf-spade' and quickly ends up 'facing a goddess', Ciarán Carson points out:

> The two methods are not compatible. One gains its poetry by embodiment of a specific, personal situation; the other has degenerated into a messy historical and religious surmise – a kind of Golden Bough activity, in which the real differences between our society and that of Jutland in some vague past are glossed over for the sake of the parallels of ritual.[28]

Whereas 'Bogland' enacted the stages of the poet's thrust into the past, he now obtains ready access: 'Kinned by hieroglyphic peat ... to the strangled victim' ('Kinship');

> To lift the lid of the peat
> And find this pupil dreaming
> Of neolithic wheat!
>   ('Belderg')

That exclamation (at quernstones) represents a kind of elementary archaeological awe, borne out by the poem's Irish, Planter, and Norse 'growth rings' which express simply 'A congruence of lives'. In *Wintering Out* Heaney worked from present to past, interpreting (the historic congruence and incongruity of 'The Other Side'); in *North* he works from past to present – equating. The book appears fascinated more by bones, fossils, relics, archaisms – 'antler combs, bone pins,/ coins, weights, scale-pans' – than by those things which they are emblems of. 'Bone Dreams', as perhaps its title candidly admits, loses all contact with the thing itself: 'I wind it in/ / the sling of mind/ to pitch it at England'. An ecumenical gesture, despite the metaphor, but 'England' soon becomes an amalgam of history, geography, literary and linguistic tradition ('Elizabethan canopies./ Norman devices'; '*ban-hus* ... where the soul/ fluttered a while'; 'I am ... a chalk giant'; 'Hadrian's Wall'; etc.). Apart from section VI, a beautifully exact poem about a mole – and moles do focus differences between the Irish and English terrains – the poem turns the tables on Romantic versions of Ireland in English literature.

But the real costume-drama imports into *North* are the Vikings. The title-poem begins with the poet searching for a kindred revelation to that of 'The Tollund Man':

> I returned to a long strand,
> the hammered shod of a bay,
> and found only the secular
> powers of the Atlantic thundering.
>
> I faced the unmagical
> invitations of Iceland,
> the pathetic colonies
> of Greenland, and suddenly
>
> those fabulous raiders ...

The somewhat abstract adjectival sequence – 'secular', 'unmagical', 'fabulous' – gives the show away. Why not write a 'secular' or nature poem about the sea? (Like 'Shoreline' in *Door into the Dark*, where the Danes are a notional and mysterious 'black hawk bent on the sail'.) Why dismiss Iceland as 'unmagical', unless because Heaney is not Auden? 'Suddenly' (at the end of a stanza) introduces 'fabulous raiders' to a fable-hungry poet too much on cue. They also open communication with remarkable speed, and the word 'epiphany', deeply implicit in 'The Tollund Man', is actually used:

> ocean-deafened voices
> warning me, lifted again
> in violence and epiphany.
> The longship's swimming tongue
>
> was buoyant with hindsight –
> it said Thor's hammer swung
> to geography and trade,
> thick-witted couplings and revenges,
>
> the hatreds and behindbacks
> of the althing, lies and women,
> exhaustions nominated peace,
> memory incubating the spilled blood.

This is Heaney's own 'hindsight', a 'relevant' historical summary which hardly requires such elaborate sponsorship. (May he be for-

given the zeugma 'lies and women'!). And does the idea of the
North really provide an umbrella for the not very Nordic north of
Ireland, fertility rites and capital punishment in prehistoric
Denmark, and the conquests of the Vikings in Ireland – coming to
or from the north? Although all these different places, time-zones
and moral worlds clearly strike genuine imaginative chords in
Heaney, why attempt to unify them into a mythic confederation?
Perhaps again in order to stress the obvious: 'these things have
always happened', as Carson says, and as Morrison finally puts it:
'His allusions to former cultures amount to a sort of historical
determinism.'[29] Yet determinism, the plundering of the past for
parallels, circular thinking (all incidentally features of Republican
and Loyalist ideology) once more insist on 'territorial piety', on a re-
ligious-anthropological, even slightly glamorous way of apprehend-
ing the conflict, beside which 'talks between elected representatives'
indeed look dull. In the last three quatrains of 'North' the longship
adds an aesthetic to the subject-matter it has already supplied:

> It said, 'Lie down
> in the word-hoard, burrow
> the coil and gleam
> of your furrowed brain.
>
> Compose in darkness.
> Expect aurora borealis
> in the long foray
> but no cascade of light.
>
> Keep your eye clear
> as the bleb of the icicle,
> trust the feel of what nubbed treasure
> your hands have known.'

This self-dedication hints at a purpose – 'long foray' – beyond
'befitting emblems', and to which Heaney's sensuous intimacy with
his world ('nubbed treasure') might contribute a value as well as an
'explanation'. Like D.H. Lawrence and Ted Hughes before him, he
edges towards turning his instinctive sureties into a philosophy.

Ritual is undoubtedly a value and a method, as well as a subject,
in *North*. It sets and sets off the emblems. While of course aware
that some rituals have more in their favour than others, Heaney
employs the term a little oddly at times: 'the long rites of Irish political and religious struggles'. A struggle is not a rite, just as murder
like that at Vinegar Hill is not 'heraldic' when it happens. The

decorative tinge that Heaney imparts to violence and to history derives from a ritualising habit, which itself derives from his religious sensibility. The continual catalogues in *North* – whether details of the Bog People, inventories of objects like 'antler-pins', or historical summaries as in the message of the longship – level disparate experience into a litany, a rosary, a faintly archaic incantation: 'neighbourly, scoretaking/ killers, haggers/ and hagglers, gombeen-men,/ hoarders of grudges and gain'. In those lines from 'Viking Dublin' alliteration swamps meaning. 'Funeral Rites' declares Heaney's love for the positive function of ritual:

> Now as news comes in
> of each neighbourly murder
> we pine for ceremony,
> customary rhythms ...

(An echo of Yeats there.) Carson praises the poem's initial evocation of remembered funerals:

> their eyelids glistening,
> their dough-white hands
> shackled in rosary-beads

but then comments: 'all too soon, we are back in the world of megalithic doorways and charming, noble barbarity'.[30] The worthy root-emotion of 'Funeral Rites' is that of 'The Tollund Man' – Heaney's passionate desire to 'assuage'[31] – but he goes to such ritualistic lengths as to obliterate his starting-point:

> I would restore
>
> the great chambers of Boyne,
> prepare a sepulchre
> under the cupmarked stones ...
>
> Somnambulant women,
> left behind, move
> through emptied kitchens
>
> imagining our slow triumph
> towards the mounds.

An affirmation of 'custom' and 'ceremony' – especially as a kind of mass trance – cannot in itself earn 'the cud of memory/ allayed for

once'. Heaney's 'rites', ancient, modern or imagined, are profoundly 'Catholic' in character:

> My sensibility was formed by the dolorous murmurings of the rosary,
> and the generally Marian quality of devotion. The reality that was
> addressed was maternal, and the posture was one of supplication ...
> Irish Catholicism, until about ten years ago, had this Virgin Mary
> worship, almost worship. In practice, the shrines, the rosary beads, all
> the devotions were centred towards a feminine presence, which I
> think was terrific for the sensibility. I think that the 'Hail Mary' is
> more of a poem than the 'Our Father'. 'Our Father' is between chaps,
> but there's something faintly amorous about the 'Hail Mary'.[32]

The sense in *North* that something is to be gained by going through
the ritual, telling the beads, adopting a posture of supplication or
worship, curiously aligns Heaney with the early rather than the
later Yeats (the Catholic ethos of the Rhymers' Club). 'A Prayer for
my Daughter', on the other hand, is not only a prayer but a contest
in which 'custom' and 'ceremony' engage with their opposites.

The whole design of *North*, including its layout, proclaims a
more punctilious patterning than that of Heaney's first three books:
'I had a notion of *North*, the opening of *North*: those poems came
piecemeal now and again, and then I began to see a shape. They
were written and rewritten a lot.'[33] In contrast with the fecund
variety of *Wintering Out* there is system, homogenisation. Certain
poems seem dictated by the scheme (rather than vice versa), com-
missioned to fill in the myth or complete the ritual. Conspicuous
among these are three first-person quatrain sequences, all in six
parts: 'Viking Dublin: Trial Pieces', 'Bone Dreams' and 'Kinship'.
Neatly spanning the Vikings, England and Bogland, the sequences
present the poet in a somewhat self-conscious physical and imaginative relation to each mythic territory: 'a worm of thought/ / I follow
into the mud'; 'I push back/ through dictions'; 'I step through
origins'. Such announcements seem again a substitute for action,
for genuine prospecting. 'Land' and 'Gifts of Rain' in *Wintering
Out* began this kind of open quest, which owes a debt to the Ted
Hughes of *Wodwo*. But the further back Heaney pushes, in default
of a specific impulse, the more specialised or specialist he in fact
becomes; so that the sequences exaggerate the book's anthropologi-
cal, archaeological and philological tendency. The evolution since
Wintering Out of the theme of language typifies other contractions.
The place-name poems, if occasionally too calculated, stir mutual

vibrations between landscape and language. But in 'Viking Dublin' Heaney's phonetic fantasy drives a huge wedge between word and thing: a longship's 'clinker-built hull' is 'spined and plosive/ as *Dublin*'. 'Kinship', already off to a sign-posting start ('Kinned by hieroglyphic/ peat') that has travelled far from 'We have no prairies' ('Bogland'), eventually goes into a swoon of synonyms:

> Quagmire, swampland, morass:
> the slime kingdoms,
> domains of the cold-blooded,
> of mud pads and dirtied eggs.

> But *bog*
> meaning soft,
> the fall of windless rain ...

'Bone Dreams', perhaps because of the poet's outsider position, relies more heavily on linguistic keys to unlock England: 'Elizabethan canopies,/ Norman devices,/ / the erotic mayflowers/ of Provence/ and the ivied latins/ of churchmen', 'the scop's/ twang, the iron/ flash of consonants/ cleaving the line'. This comes uncomfortably close to the way Heaney talks about English in his lecture 'Englands of the Mind' (1976). In Geoffrey Hill's poetry: 'The native undergrowth, both vegetative and verbal, the barbaric scrollwork of fern and ivy, is set against the tympanum and chancel-arch, against the weighty elegance of imperial Latin';[34] '[Hughes's] consonants ... take the measure of his vowels like calipers, or stud the line like rivets.'[35] That the gap has narrowed between Heaney's creative and critical idioms, while widening between word and thing, underlines the extent to which the artist's own specialism also figures in these poems. Every poet worth his salt imprints his poetry with a subtext about poetry itself – as Heaney does, profoundly and skilfully, in 'The Forge' or 'Bogland'. A minority, because of the particular nature of their art, go public like Yeats as the poet-artist, taking on all comers. The protagonist's high profile in the *North* sequences, however, reveals him almost incestuously involved with the contents of his own imagination:

> My words lick around
> cobbled quays, go hunting
> lightly as pampooties
> over the skull-capped ground.
>   ('Viking Dublin')

> I grew out of all this
> like a weeping willow
> inclined to
> the appetites of gravity.
> ('Kinship')

(Contrast: 'As a child, they could not keep me from wells' in 'Personal Helicon'.) Heaney's appetite for abstraction has certainly grown: 'ceremony', 'history', 'violence and epiphany', 'memory', 'dictions', 'the cooped secrets/ of process and ritual'. Several commentators on *North* have headlined 'Hercules and Antaeus' as symbolising the different approaches of Parts II and I. Mark Patrick Hederman follows up such an attribution with this analysis:

> Hercules and Antaeus represent two different kinds of poet: the first composes his own poetry; the second is composed by his own poetry. The first is the self-assertive poet, the political poet, who has a definite vision of things, who chooses his style and his words, who decides what kind of poet he is going to be. The second kind of poet is he whom Martin Heidegger calls the 'more daring' ... because he works from the heart and ... articulates a song 'whose sound does not cling to something that is eventually attained, but which has already shattered itself even in the sounding ...'[36]

The poem certainly dramatises a conflict in Heaney (amply evidenced by *Preoccupations*) between an instinctive, 'feminine' artesian procedure ('the cradling dark,/ the river-veins, the secret gullies/ of his strength'), and an ordering, 'male' architectonic 'intelligence' ('a spur of light,/ a blue prong graiping him/ out of his element'). However, Hercules may be quite as responsible for the prescribed rituals of Part I as for the outbursts of Part II: telling yourself to 'Lie down/ in the word-hoard' makes it less likely that you have done so. Stylistic examination suggests that Heaney has upset his strategic brinkmanship, his former complex creative balance, by applying architectonic methods to artesian matters, by processing his rich organic resources into hard-edged blocks, by forgetting 'They'll never dig coal here'.

Heaney should have been the last poet to turn 'the word-hoard' into a dragon-hoard: 'the coffered/ riches of grammar/ and declensions'. The burnishing by repetition of certain words is an allowable consequence of recurrent subjects; other instances serve the grand design, as in the shot-gun marriages of berg and bog: 'the black glacier/ of each funeral'; 'gemstones dropped/ in the peat floe/ like

the bearings of history./ / My sash was a black glacier/ wrinkling';
'floe of history'. But repeated rhythms and constructions do more
than words to reinforce the ritual or cement the architecture. Metre,
the skinny quatrain, is the most obvious formal unifier: 'those thin
small quatrain poems, they're kind of drills or augers for turning in
and they are narrow and long and deep'.[37] The narrowness of the
line, in conjunction with that of the stanza, makes immense
demands on both local variation and overall rhythm, if pre-
fabricated cadences are to be prevented. As Heaney himself said
later, 'The shortness of a line constricts, in a sense, the breadth of
your movement'.[38] In fact, the quatrain often falls into two iambic
pentameters, each harshly severed at the caesura:

> Come back past
> philology and kennings,
> re-enter memory
> where the bone's lair ...

It can dwindle to mere layout unjustified by stress or sense:

> ... is a love-nest
> in the grass.

The method really amounts to a ribbon-developed sentence where
the enjambement of line and stanza quickly becomes itself a convention, and the basic unit must be a phrase that will fit into something more like a passive receptacle than an active drill. This form
blurs climaxes and by-passes terminuses, while also letting the sequences divide too tidily into equal sections. Nevertheless Heaney
stiffens the backbone of the poems by drawing on the 'alliterative
tradition'. His comments on its importance to Ted Hughes interpret his own motives: 'Hughes relies on the northern deposits, the
pagan Anglo-Saxon and Norse elements, and he draws energy also
from a related constellation of primitive myths and world-views.
The life of his language is a persistence of the stark outline and vitality of Anglo-Saxon that became the Middle English alliterative
tradition ...'[39] The 'iron/ flash of consonants' undoubtedly strikes
sparks, as in the dedicatory 'Sunlight' ('the scone rising/ to the tick
of two clocks'), but can also be overdone ('haggers/ and hagglers')
and pepper a poem with hard little pellets, for which the Anglo-
Saxon compound word is the model: 'Earth-pantry, bone-
vault,/sun-bank', 'oak-bone, brain-firkin' (an empty interchange of

images). Consonantal monosyllables are conspicuous – taking their cue from 'bone' and 'skull' – especially those with an archaic cast: shod, scop, bleb, coomb, crock, glib (as a noun), nubbed. Heaney's fondness for the hard -ed ending as participle/ adjective (often with a co-opted noun) has developed into infatuation: 'the tomb/ Corbelled, turfed and chambered,/ Flored with dry turf-coomb'; 'Their puffed knuckles/ had unwrinkled, the nails/ were darkened, the wrists/ obediently sloped'. Sometimes the participles seem to involve a shortcut as well as shorthand: 'the cud of memory/ allayed'. The ending of 'The Grauballe Man', 'each hooded victim,/ slashed and dumped', is less poignantly precise than 'the scattered, ambushed/ Flesh of labourers' and 'Stockinged corpses' of 'The Tollund Man'. Constant asyndeton helps to compress the pellets, but the conjunction 'and' sets up its own syntactical orthodoxy: 'geography and trade,/ thick-witted couplings and revenges'; 'ancestry and trade'; 'pinioned by ghosts/ and affections,/ / murders and pieties'. The prominence of paired abstractions in the Viking poems underlines their anxiety to connect. Thus the form and sound of the quatrain exert pressure on syntax and meaning to the point where 'customary rhythms' may indeed take over.

And yet *North* is framed by three poems that avoid or transcend such mannerisms. 'Mossbawn: Two Poems in Dedication' occupies a truly timeless zone within which 'calendar customs' of domesticity and agriculture inoculate against the more barbaric 'rites' to come. Two emotionally and rhythmically expansive endings emphasise how much Part I cuts down, and cuts out, in pursuit of 'the matter of Ireland':

> And here is love
> like a tinsmith's scoop
> sunk past its gleam
> in the meal-bin.
> ('Sunlight')

> O calendar customs! Under the broom
> Yellowing over them, compose the frieze
> With all of us there, our anonymities.
> ('The Seed Cutters')

The first stanza of 'Sunlight' does contain 'helmeted', 'heated' and 'honeyed', but their varied physicality shows up 'slashed and dumped'; just as the last four lines show up the periphrastic sensu-

ousness of 'Kinship': 'The mothers of autumn/ sour and sink,/ fer-
ments of husk and leaf/ / deepen their ochres'. Consummating a sequence of diversely rendered 'customary rhythms', the subtle
chiastic assonance 'gleam' – 'meal' dramatises the complete subjugation both of 'love' and the poem – and the poem because of its
love – to what they work in. These poems are Heaney's real,
unceremonious assertions of 'custom' and humanity, his most important refusal to let 'human utterance' be flogged 'into fragments'.
Carson observes that in the opening of 'The Seed Cutters':

> They seem hundreds of years away. Brueghel,
> You'll know them if I can get them true ...

'the apostrophe works perfectly; we realise how Brueghel's realism,
his faithfulness to minutiae, are akin to Heaney's, and what could
have been portentousness takes on a kind of humility'.[40] Compare
the strained self-introduction to Tacitus in 'Kinship': 'And you,
Tacitus,/ observe how I make my grove/ on an old crannog/ piled by
the fearful dead' – this he doesn't know and doesn't get true. *Field
Work* makes a significant return to Mossbawn, to 'that original
townland', for visionary renewals.

From composure to 'Exposure', from sunlit suspended moment
or Grecian Urn 'frieze' to 'It is December in Wicklow'. With day,
season, Nature, the weather, the heavens all in a state of exhausted
flux – 'Alders dripping, birches/ Inheriting the last light', Heaney
wonders about the lasting usefulness of his own enterprise, about
perfection of the life or of the work. The poem asks why he sits

> weighing and weighing
> My responsible *tristia*.
> For what? For the ear? For the people?

Anguished dialectic, recalling that of 'A Northern Hoard', banishes
both the polished icon of Part I, and the top-of-the-head arguments
in the rest of 'Singing School'. The contrast between images of dripping, falling, darkening, 'let-downs and erosions', and 'The
diamond absolutes', dramatises a profound self-searching, a 'sad
freedom', which goes beyond the aesthetic politics of 'Hercules and
Antaeus' into the moral and emotional priorities of the artist.
Fundamentally, the poem asks whether departure from Ulster, for
which the writing of *North* may be an over-compensation ('blowing
up these sparks'), has precluded some personal or poetic revelation
(akin to that of 'The Tollund Man', perhaps):

> Who, blowing up these sparks
> For their meagre heat, have missed
> The once-in-a-lifetime portent,
> The comet's pulsing rose.

In 'Exposure' the poet earns the label he gives himself – 'inner émigré', inwardly examining his emigration – which conflicts with another, bestowed not quite self-critically enough in 'Punishment':

> I am the artful voyeur
>
> of your brain's exposed
> and darkened combs ...

Is this objective correlative, or substitute, for an interior journey?

Heaney's move South between *Wintering Out* and *North* must indeed have shifted the co-ordinates of his imagination: distanced some things, brought others closer. In an essay of 1975 Seamus Deane found Heaney (and Derek Mahon) apolitical in comparison with John Montague, whose *The Rough Field* (1972) had 'politicised the terrain' of his native Tyrone: 'it is in Montague, with his historical concentration, that this fidelity [to the local] assumes the shape of a political commitment'.[41] Interviewing Heaney after *North*, Deane encourages him to 'commit' himself: 'Do you think that if some political stance is not adopted by you and the Northern poets at large, this refusal might lead to a dangerous strengthening of earlier notions of the autonomy of poetry and corroborate the recent English notion of the happy limitations of a "well-made poem"?' Heaney replies:

> I think that the recent English language tradition does tend towards the 'well-made poem', that is towards the insulated and balanced statement. However, major poetry will always burst that corseted and decorous truthfulness. In so doing, it may be an unfair poetry; it will almost certainly be one-sided.[42]

('One side's as bad as the other, never worse.') This interchange logically, but oddly, ties in the espousal of a Nationalist attitude with divorce from 'English' modes. The combination marks a step across the border, away from 'vowelling embrace'. Similarly, whereas *Wintering Out* was written from the perspective of Belfast/South Derry, Heaney's hinterland interpreting the 'plague'-ridden city, *North* was written from the perspective of Wicklow/Dublin, and a broader Nationalism:

> I always thought of the political problem – maybe because I am not really a political thinker – as being an internal Northern Ireland division. I thought along sectarian lines. Now I think that the genuine political confrontation is between Ireland and Britain.[43]

The vision of 'The Other Side' is absent from *North*: 'the legions stare/ from the ramparts'. The 'Mossbawn' poems (though not the learned debate about the place-name's origin in 'Belderg') prove the local textures that Heaney's panoptic view omits. 'The Seed Cutters' also shows how the English dimension of his technique lives on in a concreteness and empiricism reminiscent of nothing so much as Edward Thomas's 'Haymaking' (written during the First World War): 'All of us gone out of the reach of change – / Immortal in a picture of an old grange'. *Preoccupations* salutes the varied influences that have fertilised Heaney's imagination, and which render irrelevant the false distinction between 'well-made' and 'major' poetry, rather than good and bad. (No *real* poem is 'well-made' in any limited sense; no major poem ill-made.) Heaney here seems to join ranks with Montague and Thomas Kinsella, who in different ways, and often too self-consciously, have stressed the European and transatlantic alliances which should be reflected in the outlook and technique of Irish poetry.

The Deane interview epitomises the intensive pressure on Heaney, including his own sense of duty: to be more Irish, to be more political, to 'try to touch the people', to do Yeats's job again instead of his own. Printed in the first issue of the journal *Crane Bag*, it heralds successive, obsessive articles on the relevance of his poetry to the Northern conflict. Again, Deane sets the tone with an attack on Conor Cruise O'Brien:

> But surely this very clarity of O'Brien's position is just what is most objectionable. It serves to give a rational clarity to the Northern position which is untrue to the reality. In other words, is not his humanism here being used as an excuse to rid Ireland of the atavisms which gave it life even though the life itself may be in some ways brutal?[44]

Heaney demurs ('O'Brien's ... real force and his proper ground is here in the South'[45]); nor is he responsible for the conscription of his poetry to bolster pre-set Nationalist conceptual frameworks, to endorse 'an Irish set of Archetypes, which form part of that collectivity unearthed by Jung, from which we cannot escape'.[46] But one of O'Brien's 'clarities' is his distrust of the 'area where literature and politics overlap'.[47] If they simply take in one another's mytho-logical laundry, how can the former be an independent long-term agent of change? *North* does not give the impression of the urgent 'matter of Ireland' bursting through the confines of 'the well-made poem'. Heaney's most 'artful' book, it stylises and distances what was immediate and painful in *Wintering Out*. It hardens a highly original form of procedure ('pilot and stray') into a less original form of content ('imperial power' *versus* 'territorial piety'). By plucking out the heart of his mystery and serving it up as a quasi-political mystique, Heaney temporarily succumbs to the goddess, to the destiny feared in Derek Mahon's 'The Last of the Fire Kings'[48] where the people desire their poet-king

> Not to release them
> From the ancient curse
> But to die their creature and be thankful.

From Edna Longley, *Poetry in the Wars* (Newcastle, 1986), pp. 140–69, 253–4 (An earlier version appeared in Tony Curtis (ed.), *The Art of Seamus Heaney* [Bridgend, 1982].)

NOTES

Edna Longley's piece combines the New Critical concern with the poetry's canonical worth and formal qualities which we saw in Ricks's review (essay 1) and the political preoccupations visible in O'Brien's essay (no. 2). It makes wide reference to English poets (Edward Thomas, Lawrence, Auden, Larkin, Ted Hughes, Geoffrey Hill) as well as those from south (Yeats, Kavanagh) and north (Hewitt, Montague, Mahon) of the Irish border. It assumes knowledge of Burntollet where Loyalist groups attacked Civil Rights marchers in 1969 and Vinegar Hill where the Wexford rising was brutally crushed in 1798 (pp. 34, 51).

Certain terms of traditional 'rhetoric' are used: 'zeugma' (p. 51) is a figure in which two words are yoked together although only one of them is strictly appropriate to the intended meaning; 'asyndeton' (p. 57) is the omission of normally expected conjunctions; 'chiastic' (p. 58) usually indicates a figure in which the order of words in one clause is reversed in the next but is here used about a similar reversal of *letters* in juxtaposed words. Ed.]

1. John Haffenden, *Viewpoints: Poets in Conversation* (London, 1981), p. 64.

2. Anthony Thwaite, *TLS*, 3829, 1 August 1975, p. 866.

3.   Blake Morrison, 'Speech and Reticence: Seamus Heaney's *North*', *British Poetry since 1970: A Critical Survey*. ed. Peter Jones and Michael Schmidt (Cheadle Hulme, 1980), p. 103.

4.   Conor Cruise O'Brien, *The Listener*, 25 September 1975, pp. 404–5.

5.   Ibid.

6.   Seamus Heaney, 'Feeling into Words', *Preoccupations: Selected Prose 1968–1978* (London, 1980), p. 59.

7.   James Randall, 'An Interview with Seamus Heaney', *Ploughshares*, 5:3 (1979), 18.

8.   Haffenden, *Viewpoints*, p. 71.

9.   John Wilson Foster, 'The Poetry of Seamus Heaney', *Critical Quarterly*, 16 (1974), 40.

10. Seamus Deane, '"Unhappy and at Home", Interview with Seamus Heaney', *The Crane Bag*, 1:1 (Spring 1977), 61.

11. Seamus Heaney, '"From Monaghan to the Grand Canal", the Poetry of Patrick Kavanagh', *Preoccupations*, p. 115.

12. Heaney, 'The Sense of Place', ibid., p. 142.

13. Heaney, 'Feeling into Words', ibid., p. 56.

14. Ibid., p. 55.

15. Randall, *Ploughshares*, 17.

16. Ibid., p. 20.

17. Seamus Heaney, *The Crane Bag*, 1:1 (Spring 1977), 62.

18. Colin Falck, *The New Review*, 2:17 (August 1975), 61.

19. Heaney, *Preoccupations*, pp. 56–7.

20. Randall, *Ploughshares*, 18.

21. Heaney, *Preoccupations*, pp. 57–8.

22. Ciarán Carson, 'Escaped from the Massacre?' review of *North*, *The Honest Ulsterman*, no. 50 (Winter 1975), 184–5.

23. Morrison, *British Poetry since 1970*, pp. 109–10.

24. Haffenden, *Viewpoints*, p. 61.

25. P.V. Glob, *The Bog People* (London, 1971), pp. 77–8. The body, probably of a Danish Viking, was found in 1781 on Lord Moira's estate in Co. Down.

26. Haffenden, *Viewpoints*, pp. 61, 66.

27. John Wilson Foster, *Critical Quarterly*, 16 (1974), 45.

28. Carson, *The Honest Ulsterman*, no. 50, 184.

29. Morrison, *British Poetry since 1970*, p. 110.

30. Carson, *The Honest Ulsterman*, no. 50, 185.

31. Haffenden asks: *'The word "assuaging" seems a favourite with you; can you say why?'* Heaney replies: 'It's possible to exacerbate ... I believe that what poetry does to me is comforting ... I think that art does appease, assuage' (p. 68).

32. Haffenden, *Viewpoints*, pp. 60–1.

33. Ibid., p. 64.

34. Heaney, *Preoccupations*, p. 160.

35. Ibid., p. 154.

36. Mark Patrick Hederman, 'Seamus Heaney, The Reluctant Poet', *The Crane Bag*, 3:2 (1979), 66.

37. Randall, *Ploughshares*, 16.

38. Ibid.

39. Heaney, *Preoccupations*, p. 151.

40. Carson, *The Honest Ulsterman*, no. 50, 185–6.

41. Seamus Deane, 'Irish Poetry and Irish Nationalism', in *Two Decades of Irish Writing*, ed. Douglas Dunn (Cheadle Hulme,1975), p. 16.

42. Deane, *The Crane Bag,* 1:1 (Spring 1977), 62–3.

43. Ibid.

44. Ibid., 63–4.

45. Ibid.

46. Hederman, '"The Crane Bag" and The North of Ireland', *The Crane Bag*, 4:2 (1980), 98–9. Quotation from a letter of his to Conor Cruise O'Brien, which continues: 'Your desire to demythicise us is, perhaps, an impossibility, and one which can only serve to drive the "reality" even more deeply and dangerously underground.'

47. 'An Unhealthy Intersection', *Irish Times*, 21 August 1975; quoted by Richard Kearney in 'Beyond Art and Politics', *The Crane Bag*, 1, no. 1 (Spring 1977), 9. [The quotation is actually from the continuation of O'Brien's essay in *Irish Times*, 22 August 1975, p. 10. Ed.]

48. Derek Mahon, *The Snow Party* (London, 1975), p. 10.

4

Seamus Heaney: The Timorous and the Bold

SEAMUS DEANE

As he tells us in his essay 'Feeling into Words', Seamus Heaney signed one of his first poems 'Incertus', 'uncertain, a shy soul fretting and all that'.[1] Feeling his way into words so that he could find words for his feelings was the central preoccupation of his apprenticeship to poetry. In a review of Theodore Roethke's *Collected Poems* he declares that 'An awareness of his own poetic process, and a trust in the possibility of his poetry, that is what a poet should attempt to preserve'.[2] The assurance of this statement is partly undercut by the last phrase. It strikes that note of uncertainty, of timorousness which recurs time and again both in his poetry and in his prose. His fascination with the fundamentals of music in poetry, his pursuit of the central energies in another writer's work, his inspection of the experiences, early and late, which guarantee, validate, confirm his perceptions, his admiration of the sheer mastery of men like Hopkins or Yeats, all reveal a desire for the absolute, radical certainty. But this boldness has caution as its brother. For all its possibilities and strengths, poetry is a tender plant. Heaney dominates a territory – his home ground, the language of Hopkins, an idea of poetry – in a protective, tutelary spirit. Images of preservation are almost as frequent as those of nourishment. The occlusions of life in the Northern state certainly contributed to this. It was not only a matter of saying nothing, whatever you say. For him, there is no gap between enfolding and unfolding. It is a deep instinct, the reverence of an acolyte before a

64

mystery of which he knows he is also the celebrant. Hence the allegiance to the mastery of other writers is indeed that of an apprentice. But he is indentured, finally, to the idea of poetry itself and is awed to see it become tactile as poems in his own hands. His boldness emerges as he achieves mastery, but his timorousness remains because it has been achieved over mystery.

This duality is visible in his first two books. Writing in a medley of influence – Frost, Hopkins, Hughes, Wordsworth, Kavanagh, Montague – he emerges from the struggle with them with a kind of guilt for having overcome them. This sense of guilt merges with the general unease he has displayed in the face of the Northern crisis and its demands upon him, demands exacerbated by the success of his poetry and the publicity given to him as a result. Although political echoes are audible in *Death of a Naturalist* and in *Door into the Dark*, there is no consciousness of politics as such, and certainly no political consciousness until *Wintering Out* and *North*. It would be easy, then, to describe his development as a broadening out from the secrecies of personal growth in his own sacred places to a recognition of the relations between this emergent self and the environing society with its own sacred, historically ratified, places. This would not be seriously inaccurate, but it is unsatisfactory because it misses one vital element – the source of guilt in Heaney's poetry and the nature of his search for it.

His guilt is that of the victim, not of the victimiser. In this he is characteristic of his Northern Irish Catholic community. His attitude to paternity and authority is apologetic – for having undermined them. His attitude to maternity and love is one of pining and also of apology – for not being of them. Maternity is of the earth, paternity belongs to those who build on it or cultivate it. There is a politics here, but it is embedded in an imagination given to ritual. That which in political or sectarian terms could be called nationalist or Catholic, belongs to maternity, the earth itself; that which is unionist or Protestant, belongs to paternity, the earth cultivated. What Heaney seeks is another kind of earth or soil susceptible to another kind of cultivation, the ooze or midden which will be creative and sexual (thereby belonging to 'art') and not barren and erotic (thereby belonging to 'society' or 'politics'). Caught in these tensions, his Ireland becomes a tragic terrain, torn between two forces which his art, in a healing spirit, will reconcile. Thus his central trope is marriage, male power and female tenderness conjoined in ceremony, a ritual appeasement of their opposition. One

source of appeasement is already in his hands from an early age –
the link between his own, definitively Irish experience and the experience of English poetry. There was a reconciliation to be further
extended by Kavanagh and Montague in their domestication of the
local Irish scene in the English poetic environment. But what was
possible, at one level, in poetry, was not possible at another, in politics. Part of the meaning of Heaney's career has been in the pursuit
of the movement from one level to another, always postulating the
Wordsworthian idea of poetry as a healing, a faith in qualities of relationship which endure beyond the inclinations towards separa-
tion. Yet such has been the impact of the Troubles in the North,
that Heaney's central trope of marriage has been broken, and in
Field Work (1979) a new territory has been opened in pursuit of a
reconciliation so far denied, although so nearly achieved.

In the early volumes, poems commemorated activities and trades
which were dying out – thatchers, blacksmiths, water-diviners,
threshers, turf-cutters, ploughmen with horses, churners, hewers of
wood and drawers of water. These, along with the victims of historical disasters, the croppies of 1798, the famine victims of 1845–7,
are, in one light, archaic figures; in another, they are ancestral presences, kin to parents and grandparents, part of the deep hinterland
out of which modern Ireland, like the poet, emerged. These figures
have skills which are mysterious, even occult. Banished, they yet
remain, leaving their spoor everywhere to be followed, like 'Servant
Boy' who leaves his trail in time as well as on the ground:

> Your trail
>
> broken from haggard to stable,
> a straggle of fodder
> stiffened on snow,
> comes first-footing
>
> the back doors of the little
> barons: resentful
> and impenitent,
> carrying the warm eggs.

In commemorating them, Heaney is forming an alliance between his
own poetry and the experience of the oppressed culture which they
represent (the Catholic Irish one) and also between his poetry and
the communal memory of which their skills, as well as their misfor-
tune, are part. *Death of a Naturalist* and *Door into the Dark* are not

simply threnodies for a lost innocence. They are attempted recoveries of an old, lost wisdom. The thatcher leaves people 'gaping at his Midas touch'; the blacksmith goes in from the sight of motorised traffic 'To beat real iron out'; the diviner 'gripped expectant wrists. The hazel stirred'. And the Heaneys had a reputation for digging:

> By God, the old man could handle a spade.
> Just like his old man.

For the inheritor, the poet, his matching activity is the writing of verse, a performance which has to be of that virtuoso quality that will make people stare and marvel at this fascinating, almost archaic, skill, still oddly surviving into the modern world. The sturdy neatness of Heaney's verse forms in the first two volumes and the homely vocabulary emphasise this traditional element, enabling us to treat them as solid, rural objects, authentically heavy, not as some fake version of pastoral. But the alliance I spoke of has yet deeper implications.

In Part 2 of 'A Lough Neagh Sequence' (from *Door into the Dark*) we are given what, for want of a better word, may be called a description of an eel:

> a muscled icicle
> that melts itself longer
> and fatter, he buries
> his arrival beyond
> light and tidal water,
> investing silt and sand
> with a sleek root

That sibilant sensuousness, however spectacular, is not devoted entirely to description. It gives to the movement of the eel an almost ritual quality, converting the action into a mysterious rite, emphasising the sacral by dwelling so sensuously on the secular. This mysterious and natural life-force becomes the root of the soil into which it merges before it is disturbed again by something like 'the drainmaker's spade'. Heaney's fascination with the soil, for which he has so many words, all of them indicating a deliquescence of the solid ground into a state of yielding and acquiescence – mould, slime, clabber, muck, mush and so on – ends always in his arousal of it to a sexual life. Quickened by penetration, it responds. A spade opens a canal in which the soil's juices flow. A turf-cutter strips it bare. It converts to water as a consonant passes into a vowel. Even there, there is a sexual differentiation, the vowel being female, the consonant male; and in the sexual differentiation there is a political distinction, the Irish vowel raped by the English consonant. Thus a species of linguistic politics emerges, with pronunciation, the very movement of the mouth on a word being a kiss of intimacy or an enforcement. Variations on these possibilities are played in *Wintering Out* in poems like 'Anahorish', 'Gifts of Rain', 'Broagh', 'Traditions', 'A New Song', 'Maighdean Mara', and in 'Ocean's Love to Ireland' and 'Act of Union' in *North*. It might be said that the last two poems from the later volume go too far in their extension of the subtle sexual and political tensions of the others, turning into a rather crude allegory what had been a finely struck implication. However, the close, intense working of the language in all these poems derives from his activation of the words in terms of sexual and political intimacies and hatreds. In addition, many poems display an equal fascination for decomposition, the rotting process which is part of the natural cycle but which signals our human alienation from it. Fungoid growth, frog-spawn, the leprosies of decay in fruit and crop, are symptoms of 'the faithless ground' ('At a Potato Digging') and this extends to encompass soured feelings, love gone rancid, as in 'Summer Home' (from *Wintering Out*):

> Was it wind off the dumps
> or something in heat
>
> dogging us, the summer gone sour,
> a fouled nest incubating somewhere?
>
> Whose fault, I wondered, inquisitor
> of the possessed air.
>
> To realise suddenly,
> whip off the mat
>
> that was larval, moving –
> and scald, scald, scald.

The language of Heaney's poetry, although blurred in syntax on occasion, has extraordinary definition, a braille-like tangibility, and yet also has a numinous quality, a power that indicates the existence of a deeper zone of the inarticulated below that highly articulated surface:

As if he had been poured
in tar, he lies
on a pillow of turf
and seems to weep

the black river of himself.
('The Grauballe Man', *North*)

When myth enters the poetry, in *Wintering Out* (1972), the process of politicisation begins. The violence in Northern Ireland reached its first climax in 1972, the year of Bloody Sunday and of assassinations, of the proroguing of Stormont and the collapse of a constitutional arrangement which had survived for fifty years. Heaney, drawing on the work of the Danish archaeologist P.V. Glob, began to explore the repercussions of the violence on himself, and on others, by transmuting all into a marriage myth of ground and victim, old sacrifice and fresh murder. Although it is true that the Viking myths do not correspond to Irish experience without some fairly forceful straining, the potency of the analogy between the two was at first thrilling. The soil, preserving and yielding up its brides and bridegrooms, was almost literally converted into an altar before which the poet stood in reverence or in sad voyeurism as the violence took on an almost liturgical rhythm. The earlier alliance with the oppressed and archaic survivors with their traditional skills now became an alliance with the executed, the unfortunates who had died because of their distinction in beauty or in sin. The act of digging is now more ominous in its import than it had been in 1966. For these bodies are not resurrected to atone, in some bland fashion, for those recently buried. They are brought up again so that the poet might face death and violence, the sense of ritual peace and order investing them being all the choicer for the background of murderous hate and arbitrary killing against which it was being invoked. In 'The Digging Skeleton (after Baudelaire)' we read:

Some traitor breath

Revives our clay, sends us abroad
And by the sweat of our stripped brows
We earn our deaths; our one repose
When the bleeding instep finds its spade.

Even in this frame of myth, which has its consoling aspects, the violence becomes unbearable. The poet begins to doubt his own reverence, his apparent sanctification of the unspeakable:

> Murdered, forgotten, nameless, terrible
> Beheaded girl, outstaring axe
> And beatification, outstaring
> What had begun to feel like reverence.
> ('Strange Fruit', *North*)

The sheer atrocity of the old ritual deaths or of the modern political killings is so wounding to contemplate that Heaney begins to show uneasiness in providing it with a mythological surround. To speak of the 'man-killing parishes' as though they were and always would be part of the home territory is to concede to violence a radical priority and an ultimate triumph. It is too much. Yet how is the violence, so deeply understood and felt, to be condemned as an aberration? Can an aberration be so intimately welcomed?

> I who have stood dumb
> when your betraying sisters,
> cauled in tar,
> wept by the railings,
>
> who would connive
> in civilised outrage
> yet understand the exact
> and tribal, intimate revenge.
> ('Punishment', *North*)

Heaney is asking himself the hard question here – to which is his loyalty given: the outrage or the revenge? The answer would seem to be that, imaginatively, he is with the revenge, morally, with the outrage. It is a grievous tension for him since his instinctive understanding of the roots of violence is incompatible with any profound repudiation of it (especially difficult when 'the men of violence' had become a propaganda phrase) and equally incompatible with the shallow, politically expedient denunciations of it from quarters not reluctant to use it themselves. The atavisms of Heaney's own community are at this stage in conflict with any rational or enlightened humanism which would attempt to deny their force. Heaney's dilemma is registered in the perception that the roots of poetry and of violence grow in the same soil; humanism, of the sort mentioned here, has no roots at all. The poems 'Antaeus' and 'Hercules and Antaeus' which open and close respectively the first part of *North*, exemplify the dilemma. Antaeus hugs the ground for strength. Hercules can defeat him only by raising him clear of his mothering soil.

the challenger's intelligence

is a spur of light,
a blue prong graiping him
out of his element
into a dream of loss

and origins ...

This is surely the nub of the matter – 'a dream of loss/and origins'. Origin is known only through loss. Identity and experience are inevitably founded upon it. Yet Heaney's loss of his Antaeus-strength and his Herculean postscript to it (in Part II of *North*) is only a brief experiment or phase, leading to the poem 'Exposure' which closes the volume. In 'Exposure', the sense of loss, of having missed

The once-in-a-lifetime portent,
The comet's pulsing rose ...

is created by the falseness of the identities which have been enforced by politics. This is a moment in Heaney's work in which he defines for himself a moral stance, 'weighing/My responsible *tristia*', only to lose it in defining his imaginative stance, 'An inner émigré, grown long-haired/And thoughtful', and then estimating the loss which such definitions bring. To define a position is to recognise an identity; to be defined by it is to recognise loss. To relate the two is to recognise the inescapable nature of guilt and its intimacy with the act of writing which is both an act of definition and also the commemoration of a loss. The alertness to writing as definition – the Hercules element – and the grief involved in the loss that comes from being 'weaned' from one's origins into writing – the Antaeus element – dominate Heaney's next book, *Field Work*. But it is worth repeating that, by the close of *North*, writing has itself become a form of guilt and a form of expiation from it.

In *Field Work*, all trace of at consoling or explanatory myth has gone. The victims of violence are no longer distanced; their mythological beauty has gone, the contemplative distance has vanished. Now they are friends, relations, acquaintances. The violence itself is pervasive, a disease spread, a sound detonating under water, and it stimulates responses of an extraordinary, highly-charged nervousness in which an image flashes brightly, a split-second of tenderness, no longer the slowly pursued figure of the earlier books:

> In that neuter original loneliness
> From Brandon to Dunseverick
> I think of small-eyed survivor flowers,
> The pined-for, unmolested orchid.
>   ('Triptych I, After a Killing')

In this volume, that gravid and somnolent sensuousness of the earlier work has disappeared almost completely. Absent too is the simple logic of argument and syntax which has previously distinguished the four-line, four-foot verses he had favoured. Atrocity is closer to him now as an experience and he risks putting his poetry against it in a trial of strength. In 'Sibyl', Part II of 'Triptych', the prophetic voice speaks of what is happening in this violent land:

> 'I think our very form is bound to change.
> Dogs in a siege. Saurian relapses. Pismires.
>
> Unless forgiveness finds its nerve and voice,
> Unless the helmeted and bleeding tree
> Can green and open buds like infants' fists
> And the fouled magma incubate
>
> Bright nymphs ...'

Forgiveness has to find its nerve and voice at a time when the contamination has penetrated to the most secret and sacred sources. The ground itself is 'flayed or calloused'. It is perhaps in recognition of this that Heaney's voice changes or that the tense of his poems changes from past to future. What had been the material of nostalgia becomes the material of prophecy. The monologue of the self becomes a dialogue with others. The poems become filled with voices, questions, answers, guesses. In part, the poet has gained the confidence to project himself out of his own established identity, but it is also true, I believe, that the signals he hears from the calloused ground are more sibylline, more terrifying and more public than those he had earlier received. The recent dead make visitations, like the murdered cousin in 'The Strand at Lough Beg' or as in 'The Badgers', where the central question, in a very strange poem, is:

> How perilous is it to choose
> not to love the life we're shown?

At least a partial answer is given in the poem in memory of Robert Lowell, 'Elegy':

The way we are living,
timorous or bold,
will have been our life.

Choosing one's life is a matter of choosing the bold course, that of
not being overwhelmed, not driven under by the weight of grief,
the glare of atrocious events. Among the bold are the recently dead
artists Robert Lowell and Sean O'Riada;[3] but the victims of the
recent violence, Colum McCartney, Sean Armstrong, the unnamed
victim of 'Casualty', are among the timorous, not the choosers but
the chosen. Among the artists, Francis Ledwidge[4] is one of these, a
poet Heaney can sympathise with to the extent that he can embrace
and surpass what held Ledwidge captive:

> In you, our dead enigma, all the strains
> Criss-cross in useless equilibrium ...

Perhaps the poet was playing aspects of his own choice off
against one another. Leaving Belfast and the security of a job in
the University there, he became a freelance writer living in the
County Wicklow countryside, at Glanmore. In so far as he was
leaving the scene of violence, he was 'timorous'; in so far as he
risked so much for his poetry, for the chance of becoming 'pure
verb' ('Oysters'), he was 'bold'. The boldness of writing confronted now the timorousness of being there, gun, not pen, in
hand. The flute-like voice of Ledwidge had been overcome by the
drum of war, the Orange drum. But this, we may safely infer, will
not happen to Heaney:

> I hear again the sure confusing drum
>
> You followed from Boyne water to the Balkans
> But miss the twilit note your flute should sound.
> You were not keyed or pitched like these true-blue ones
> Though all of you consort now underground.

In 'Song' we have a delicately woven variation on this theme.
Instead of the timorous and the brave, we have the mud-flowers
and the immortelles, dialect and perfect pitch, main road and by-
road, and between them all, with a nod to Fionn McCool,

> And that moment when the bird sings very close
> To the music of what happens.

This is the moment he came to Glanmore to find. It is the moment of the *Field Work* sequence itself, four poems on the vowel 'O', envisaged as a vaccination mark, a sunflower, finally a birthmark stained the umber colour of the flower, 'stained to perfection' – a lovely trope for the ripening of the love relationship here. It is the remembered moment of 'September Song' in which

> We toe the line
> between the tree in leaf and the bare tree.

Most of all, though, it is the moment of the Glanmore sonnets, ten poems, each of which records a liberation of feeling after stress or, more exactly, of feeling which has absorbed stress and is the more feeling. The sequence is in a way his apology for poetry. In poetry, experience is intensified because repeated. The distance of words from actuality is compensated for by the revival of the actual in the words. This paradoxical relationship between loss and revival has been visible in all Heaney's poetry from the outset, but in these sonnets it receives a more acute rendering than ever before. The purgation of the ominous and its replacement by a brilliance is a recurrent gesture here. Thunderlight, a black rat, a gale-warning, resolve themselves into lightning, a human face, a haven. As in 'Exposure', but even more openly, the risk of an enforced identity is examined. But the enforcement here is that desired by the poet himself, the making of himself into a poet, at whatever cost, even the cost of consequences this might have both for himself and his family. The fear of that is portrayed in the Dantesque punishments of 'An Afterwards'. But in the sonnets there is nothing apologetic, in the sense of contrite, in the apology for poetry. This is a true *apologia*. It transmits the emotion of wisdom. What had always been known is now maieutically drawn out by these potent images until it conjoins with what has always been felt. The chemistry of the timorous and the bold, the familiar and the wild, is observable in Sonnet VI, in which the story of the man who raced his bike across the frozen Moyola River in 1947 produces that wonderful final image of the final lines in which the polarities of the enclosed and the opened, the domesticated and the weirdly strange, are crossed, one over the other:

> In a cold where things might crystallise or founder,
> His story quickened us, a wild white goose
> Heard after dark above the drifted house.

In such lines the sense of omen and the sense of beauty become one. In *Field Work* violence is not tamed, crisis is not domesticated, yet they are both subject to an energy greater, more radical even, than themselves. By reiterating, at a higher pitch, that which he knows, his familiar world, Heaney braves that which he dreads, the world of violent familiars. They – his Viking dead, his dead cousin and friends, their killers – and he live in the same house, hear the same white goose pass overhead as their imaginations are stimulated by a story, a legend, a sense of mystery.

It is not altogether surprising, then, to find Heaney accompanying Dante and Vergil into the Inferno where Ugolino feeds monstrously on the skull of Archbishop Roger. The thought of having to repeat the tale of the atrocity makes Ugolino's heart sick. But it is precisely that repetition which measures the scale of the atrocity for us, showing how the unspeakable can be spoken. Dante's lines:

> Tu vuo' ch'io rinovelli
> disperato dolor che 'l cor mi preme
> gia pur pensando, pria ch'io ne favelli
> (*Inferno*, Canto XXXIII, ll. 4–6)[5]

have behind them Aeneas's grief at having to retell the tragic history of the fall of Troy:

> Infandum, regina, iubes renovare dolorem,
> Troianas ut opes et lamentabile regnum
> eruerint Danai, quaeque ipse miserrima vidi
> et quorum pars magna fui ...
> (*Aeneid*, II, ll. 3–6)[6]

The weight of a translation is important here because it demonstrates the solid ground-hugging aspect of Heaney's language and concerns, and reminds us once again, as in Kinsella,[7] of the importance of the Gaelic tradition and its peculiar weight of reference in many poems. 'The Strand at Lough Beg' is enriched in the same way by the reference to the Middle Irish work *Buile Suibhne*, a story of a poet caught in the midst of atrocity and madness in these specific areas:

> Along that road, a high, bare pilgrim's track
> Where Sweeney fled before the bloodied heads,
> Goat-bears and dogs' eyes in a demon pack
> Blazing out of the ground, snapping and squealing.

Atrocity and poetry, in the Irish or in the Italian setting, are being manoeuvred here by Heaney, as he saw Lowell manoeuvre them, into a relationship which could be sustained without breaking the poet down into timorousness, the state in which the two things limply coil. Since *Field Work*, Heaney has begun to consider his literary heritage more carefully, to interrogate it in relation to his Northern and violent experience, to elicit from it a style of survival as poet. In this endeavour he will in effect be attempting to reinvent rather than merely renovate his heritage. In his work and in that of Kinsella, Montague and Mahon, we are witnessing a revision of our heritage which is changing our conception of what writing can be because it is facing up to what writing, to remain authentic, must always face – the confrontation with the ineffable, the unspeakable thing for which 'violence' is our helplessly inadequate word.

From Seamus Deane, *Celtic Revivals* (London, 1985), pp. 174–86.

NOTES

[This is the first essay in the volume to break with both the traditional politico-literary and the New Critical approaches (represented respectively by essays 2 and 1 and combined in essay 3). Instead, we find a commitment to the ideological dimension of the poetic act influenced by both left-wing (Theodor Adorno, Raymond Williams) and conservative (Harold Bloom, René Girard) theorists. Ed.]

1. Seamus Heaney, *Preoccupations: Selected Prose 1968–1978* (London, 1980), p. 45.

2. Ibid., p. 190.

3. Sean O'Riada (b. 1931) was an Irish composer and traditional musician. [Ed.]

4. The poet, Francis Ledwidge (b. 1891), an Irish volunteer in the British Army, was killed in France on 31 July 1917. [Ed.]

5. Translated by Heaney in 'Ugolino' as '"Even before I speak/The thought of having to relive all that/Desperate time makes my heart sick"' [Ed.]

6. Deane's purpose in underpinning the Italian with some lines of Virgil may be to 'politicise' the sense of 'atrocity' in Dante (and Heaney): 'O queen, you order me to reopen the unspeakable wound so that the Greeks may bring down the Trojan wealth and their sorrowing

kingdom, pitiful events which I myself saw and in which I took a considerable part'. [Ed.]

7. On Thomas Kinsella's use of the Gaelic tradition, see Deane's *Celtic Revivals* (London, 1985), pp. 142–5. [Ed.]

5

Representation in Modern Irish Poetry

EAMONN HUGHES

The introduction to *The Penguin Book of Contemporary British Poetry* claims 'to extend the imaginative franchise'.[1] The anthology functions as a Representation of the Poet's Act, suggesting that somewhere, a poetic equivalent of Westminster, there are those who hold the power to extend the franchise. Seamus Heaney's response to the anthology, *An Open Letter*, is at root a declaration of independence, an expressed desire *not* to be represented at a poetic Westminster. But there are problems with this declaration of independence. Seamus Deane has spoken of how Heaney caresses the intimacies of the Anglo-Irish connection and we live in a world of interdependencies in which such intimacies cannot simply be rejected, constituting as they do our reality. Rejecting them does not return us to a pristine origin; it leaves us instead in a void. The usual questions which arise from such considerations are about how the Irish are (mis)represented. Instead, I want to consider how certain Irish writers represent other cultures, particularly England's.

The second section of Seamus Heaney's *North*, particularly 'Singing School', is a pivotal moment in his career. Although often dismissed,[2] it is Heaney's first sustained interrogation of his intimacy with English culture. His response is to strip his writing of the influences of that culture. His later writing shows this to have been a wrong turning, rejects the attempted nativism of 'Singing School', and returns to English culture with a new and dialectical purpose: nor is Heaney alone in this.

Paul Muldoon's volumes end with long poems influenced by the Irish language traditions of voyage and vision poetry but referring only to these neutralises him by locating him in a safe, known tradition. It implies a nativist endorsement of the methods of a modern writer. Other, equally weighty influences in Muldoon's writing, for example, the narrative songs of Bob Dylan or the detective quests of Raymond Chandler, must be acknowledged. This is not just to say that there is a need to relocate Irish poetry in a broader context, although this is no small matter. It is rather to stress that the continuous influence of local contexts is dialectically balanced by influences from the wider world. Consequently, Irish poetry is best viewed as an intertextuality which can only be understood through a consideration of both nativist and external influences. '7 Middagh Street', the bravura poem which closes *Meeting the British*[3] (hereafter in the text as *MtB*), is a deliberately intertextual debate on whether poetry can make things happen. The figure of Auden begins the sequence by quoting from Masefield's 'Cargoes', itself previously represented in the volume as a parentally recommended distraction from growing sexual and political knowledge ('Profumo', *MtB*, p. 8). The sequence ends with Louis (MacNeice) and others proclaiming that '... poetry can make things happen – /not only can, but *must* ...' (*MtB*, p. 59). Nevertheless, there are those who hold to the idea that poetry is separate from the political:

> 'MacNeice? That's a Fenian name.'
> As if to say, 'None of your sort, none of you
>
> will as much as go for a rubber hammer
> never mind chalk a rivet, never mind caulk a seam
> on the quinquereme of Ninevah.'
>
> (*MtB*, p. 60)

These lines pit a monocultural and aestheticist position against the actualities of Northern Ireland in a rewrite of 'Ulster was British, but with no rights on/ The English lyric ...'[4] and make clear the fatuity of trying to hold on to the autonomous text – whether it be 'Ulster' or 'Cargoes' – in an internationalist, multinationalist and post-imperial world.

Tom Paulin's poetry is also often read in relation to a nativist tradition. In this case it is the unionist tradition which provides a safe point of reference, on the assumption that Paulin's attitude to it is a disgust for its shabbinesss and vulgarity as apparently typified by a poem such as 'Off the Back of a Lorry':

> A zippo lighter
> and a quilted jacket.
> two rednecks troughing
> in a gleamy diner,
> the flinty chipmarks on a white enamel pail.
> Paisley putting pen to paper
> in Crumlin jail ...[5]

However, the poem, like the tradition it describes, relies on American popular culture – its 'tune' is that of 'These Foolish Things' – which alters its apparent disgust to exasperated affection. Without a sense of such external presences we are unable to appreciate the full impact of the poetry. This is especially so in Paulin's most recent collection, *Fivemiletown*,[6] which deploys a pentecostal range of tongues as it sets out Paulin's 'defiant version of *dinnseanchas*'.[7]

There are a number of reasons for considering *North* (hereafter in the text as *N*) especially Part II, in this light. It was among the first and most keenly anticipated poetical responses to the Northern political situation.[8] It is the first step in the politics of contemporary poetry in the North and is indicative of the struggle the Northern poet has to undergo in order to create a representative voice.

North, famously, is divided into two parts. In Part II, Heaney turns from the synoptic vision of Part I, which is historical and analogical in method, to a more personal and intertextual approach, particularly in 'Singing School'. Certain theoretical considerations, which bear on my opening comments, will elucidate Heaney's method throughout *North*.

Stan Smith has used Julia Kristeva's concepts of 'foreign discourses' and 'intertextuality' to assess Yeats's attitude to inheritance.[9] The issue of inheritance has a number of determinants, not the least of which is the problematic relationship of the Irish writer to English language and culture. Traditionally this gives rise to the lot of the Irish writer; alienated from language, the writer must work with language in such a way as to redefine the self in language by forcing language to come to terms with experience for which it is not fitted. The concept of 'intertextuality' is thus of central importance to modern Irish writing as the writer's 'fretting' issues in a dialogic procedure within language and his discourse becomes 'carnivalesque'. This, Kristeva defines as 'a social and political protest. There is no equivalence, but rather, identity between challenging official linguistic codes and challenging official law'.[10] The problematic nature of Irish identity required both a challenge to cultural and political preoccupations, and an attempt to comprehend, in both senses of that word, the variety of cultural experience which is available because of the split and joined nature of Irish-English. Irish writing is therefore a literature in which lived experience and linguistic performance are not necessarily matched. However, while much of this applies to contemporary writing, the historical situation for Heaney is different from that of Yeats. Volosinov has distinguished the 'native language ... one's "kith and kin"; we feel about it as we feel about our habitual attire' from the foreign language:

> Only in learning a foreign language does a fully prepared consciousness – fully prepared thanks to one's native language – confront a fully prepared language which it need only accept. People do not 'accept' their native language – it is in their native language that they first reach consciousness.[11]

His point is that active response, rather than passive understanding, is available through the native language. To acknowledge English language and culture as foreign is to be passive, to be represented. To reject English language and culture as foreign may achieve independence but does not alter those representations. To accept English language and culture as now native may be to lose a measure of independence, but it is to gain the right to be active, to represent. This is the central concern of Part II of *North* in which Heaney represents the constituents of the self and its voice.

The first three poems of Part II represent the North as a babble of voices. Throughout this welter, the poet's concern is with the possibilities of freedom and of reshaping language. 'Singing School' continues this representation of other voices with the purpose of representing the self.

The epigraphs to 'Singing School', from the autobiographical works of Wordsworth and Yeats (*N*, p. 62), signal Heaney's examination of the 'tradition of myself'.[12] The self which he presents is obviously from a Catholic background. To say this, however, is not enough. If it were, we should have to agree with O'Brien about the 'bleak conclusiveness'[13] of the volume, because we would be surrendering to the implication that the self, and its voice in these poems, is fixed, consistent, and unitary. Heaney's method in 'Singing School' does not allow that conclusion. The 'foreign discourses' within this sequence are external and determining in one way, but they are equally internal and determined presences; that is to say they exist apart from Heaney, but they are also a part of Heaney's own voice. His experience of language is both personal and social; language exists as both 'langue', the social order of language, and 'parole', the personal voice.[14] Intertextuality is, therefore, a fact of language as a whole, although it can be subject to conscious manipulation as in 'Singing School'. Heaney's voice does not exist apart from the allusions of 'Singing School'. We can recognise the voices of Wordsworth, Yeats, Kavanagh, Deane, Shakespeare, Coleridge, Hopkins, Lorca, Goya – if a painter may be allowed a voice – Michael McLaverty, Mansfield, Chekhov, Joyce, Montague, Mandelstam, and Ovid in this sequence – all voices which are themselves intertextual and informed by history – but if we removed them we would not be left with the 'pure drop' of Heaney.

Each epigraph to 'Singing School' contains an apparent opposition: 'beauty and fear' for Wordsworth, and 'Orange' and 'Fenian' for Yeats. In the autobiographical works from which the oppositions come, the impulse is for both elements to be comprehended. Wordsworth and Yeats are not simply opposed for Heaney – they are not just English and Irish – because Wordsworth was a part of Yeats's cultural 'langue' and both are a part of Heaney's cultural 'langue'. The sequence is concerned with comprehension rather than opposition even if comprehension ultimately fails.

'The Ministry of Fear' (*N*, pp. 63–5) is about Heaney's growth as a poet. Addressed to Seamus Deane, it begins with a reference to Kavanagh,[15] and goes on to school life, education and the learning of a variety of voices, but returns to the 'South Derry rhyme' (*N*, p. 64), which locates his voice. The poem matches Heaney's lived experience against an array of 'foreign discourses'. The language in which he registers experience is the language of a poetic tradition which he is constructing. Gazing into 'new worlds' from his school, he echoes Shakespeare:[16] throwing biscuits away becomes a Wordsworthian 'act of stealth':[17] his first attempts at writing poetry develop, in Kavanagh's terms, into a life (*N*, p. 63). His experiences in school – 'inferiority complexes ...' – and corporal punishment, are both Shakespearean[18] and Joycean[19] (*N*, p. 64). Certain events seemingly cannot be voiced in this way – the growth of sexuality and the encounter with the RUC (*N*, p. 64)[20] – which is consonant with the inability of the English poetic traditions perceived by Heaney to comprehend particular types of experience. He has spoken of the 'insulated and balanced statement ... that corsetted and decorous truthfulness' towards which 'recent English language' poetry has tended.[21] Although certain issues cannot, apparently, be forced into this tradition, Heaney relies on it to represent the facts of his own life. The name he gives the framework in which he grows, 'the ministry of fear', evokes both Coleridge's 'secret ministry' and Wordsworth's 'ministry/more palpable'[22] in such a way as to suggest the importance of this poetic tradition in Heaney's self-representation.

Heaney, as schoolboy, is 'shying as usual' (N, p. 64) – still indulging the reticence of his community. This is not a response to the overwhelming force of English culture. That culture represents a means of expressing himself while still remaining true to the traditions of his community. The poem is an effort to comprehend both the silence of the community and this poetic tradition. 'Ulster was British, but with no rights on/The English lyric...' (N, p. 65) is therefore a statement of the situation which Heaney is trying to redress in his very articulation of it.

The poem's 'foreign discourses' can be divided into English and Irish with the Irish voices being apparently more intimate. The latter are just as removed from Heaney as the English ones. Deane, for example, is bewildering. His 'hieroglyphics' are not easily comprehended and his 'svelte dictions' seem almost an embarrassment (N, p. 65). Deane's strangeness is balanced by Kavanagh's reminder of the importance of the local, which Heaney both endorses and alters. Heaney's balancing of these two is a mark of his confidence. English poetry, Irish poetry, Catholic schooling, sexuality, and the fear of living in a hostile state are the elements which constitute Heaney's identity in this poem. His confidence rests not in a certainty about how they fit together but in his juxtaposition of them as his identity.

> I threw them over the fence one night
> In September 1951
> When the lights of houses in the Lecky Road
> Were amber in the fog. It was an act
> of stealth.
> Then Belfast, and then Berkeley.
> Here's two on's are sophisticated.
>
> (N, p. 63)

The movement from an exact time, place and climate, to Belfast and then Berkeley – the outermost point of travel – provokes an allusion to Lear which implies both a regret at this sophistication – meaning disguise – and the sense that the wish to cast off one's 'habitual attire' is a sign of madness.[23] This is all the true voice of the poet, because it is the voice he has composed from the available components. When Blake Morrison reads 'The Ministry of Fear' as a sign of Heaney's aspiration to participate in the English poetic tradition,[24] he imposes his own provincial attitude and does not admit the complexity of Heaney's relationship, which encompasses both Kavanagh's distinction between the 'craven provincial' and the 'genuine parochial', and the duality of the self, to that tradition.

> One half of one's sensibility is in a cast of mind that comes from belonging to a place, an ancestry, a history, a culture, whatever one wants to call it. But consciousness and quarrels with the self are the result of what Lawrence called 'the voices of my education'.[25]

Heaney's attitude is not one of being Irish and wanting to be British; nor is it one of being tainted by Britishness and wanting to be pristinely Irish. Rather, he feels himself pulled in two ways. His identity and his voice are not unitary because their determinants are not unitary. This struggle for definition is specifically located in a preoccupied language.

The language issue is a common feature of any history of colonial dispossession and the reassertion of national rights:

> For any speaker of it, a given language is at once either more or less his own or more or less someone else's, and either more or less cosmopolitan or more or less parochial – a borrowing or a heritage, a passport or a citadel.[26]

What makes Heaney's case and that of Irish writers in general, so problematical is that there is only one language which can practically fulfil all the contradictory roles of a language-struggle, English. Although English is not itself unitary, the writer cannot take what he wants from it and leave the rest. The poet's search for a voice in which to express his own identity, his own 'parole', is made the more complex by the fact that all the available 'langues' are relativised within the one system. Nor is the voice wholly determined. It is also determining. The 'literary heritage' of 'The Ministry of Fear' does not exist as an absolute; it is a heritage

which Heaney himself constructs and it is biddable to his voice.
Heaney is aware of this two-way process. His analysis of poetry as
both taking and making, 'a dig for finds that end up being plants',[27]
is a description of how we construct traditions from available
materials. Poetry is both a determined activity and an act of construction. 'The Ministry of Fear' establishes the complex of factors
from which Heaney's voice arises and which that voice alters. It is
the poet's attention to voice, in a world of reticence, which sets him
apart from his community and which bestows responsibilities upon
him. 'The Ministry of Fear' is located outside common experience
because it is attentive to specifically literary concerns, but it has reminders of the world of direct experience. The next two poems turn
to experienced rather than linguistic elements of the ministry of
fear.

'A Constable Calls' and 'Orange Drums, Tyrone 1966' are both
poems of alienation. Throughout the former there is an air of
menace and a sense of guilt which is disproportionate to the knowledge of the actual wrong that has been committed. The visit is obviously routine and so too is the fear which nonetheless attaches to it.
If 'A Constable Calls' is regarded as a measured response to the
RUC, rooted in experience, then 'Orange Drums, Tyrone 1966' is
most often regarded as being far from measured.

Morrison has called 'Orange Drums ...' (N, p. 68) 'hostile carica-
ture', and has noted that Heaney did not include it in his *Selected
Poems*, although Morrison's judgement and Heaney's decision are
not necessarily related. Morrison has also pointed out the contrast
between 'exact' in 'Punishment' (N, pp. 37–8) and 'grossly' in
'Orange Drums ...'.[28] The contrast is not simply, as he implies, sectarian. 'Exact' is part of an honest effort to account for the way in
which a sense of belonging includes collusion in certain communal
emotions; it does not imply approval of those emotions but it is an
admission of the power of the communal over the individual for
which Morrison's liberal conscience does not allow. 'Grossly', primarily a description of a drum, becomes, because of what the drum
symbolises, part of the poet's confrontation of disquieting features
within his experience. Both 'grossly' and 'exact' are alike in
denoting disquiet.

'Orange Drums ...' is a carefully specific instance of the ministry
of fear: Orange drums in 1966 had a sharper edge than they had
had in previous years. In 1966 they were a response to the 50th an-
niversary celebrations in Southern Ireland of Easter 1916, as well as

being an expression of Orange triumphalism. As F.S.L. Lyons has said:

> The 1916 anniversary convinced staunch Ulster Unionists, if they needed any convincing, that the leopard had not changed his spots and that inside every nationalist there was a ravening republican waiting to get out.[29]

1966 might with some justice be seen as the pivotal year in the development of the present political situation in Northern Ireland. On the one hand Terence O'Neill's 'liberal unionism' seemed to offer hopeful signs, but Ian Paisley had already achieved some prominence. The possibilities of a North–South 'rapprochement' seemed strong, but Catholics were being shot and their businesses burned. The poem is concerned with this balance, no matter how tentatively and unsuccessfully. The fear and hostility in the poem are obvious, but there are three balancing factors which have to be ignored if the poem is to read as a simple expression of bigotry. Firstly, the poem is about a part of Heaney's own experience; it is, like everything else in this sequence, a lesson learnt in his 'singing school'. The voice describing these events is made, in part, by them and cannot deny them. Placing the poem in Heaney's work as a whole confirms that what it describes cannot be merely denied. It is one of his 'craftsman' poems in which there is an explicit or implicit comparison between a craft and poetry making. It would therefore be doubly out of character for Heaney to reject completely the drummer. Finally, the line, 'He is raised up by what he buckles under' (N, p. 68), carries the sense of how any craftsman, including Heaney, working within rules and conventions, is better for such discipline. There is a surprising allusion within the line. The only other appearance of a form of the word 'buckle' occurs in 'Fosterage' where G.M. Hopkins is 'his buckled self' (N, p. 71), a reference to 'The Windhover' and its central pun on the word 'buckle':

> Brute beauty and valour and act, oh, air, pride, plume here
> Buckle! AND the fire that breaks from thee then, a billion
> Times told lovelier, more dangerous, O my chevalier![30]

Here again rule and convention are seen as both a constriction and a spur to better craftsmanship. The line quoted from 'Orange Drums ...' paraphrases these lines from 'The Windhover' and while the allusion is tentative, it remains central to an understanding of the tensions and difficulties of this poem, as well as to the project of the sequence as a whole.

The sequence has so far moved from the confident intertextuality of 'the Ministry of Fear' to the naked, unallusive voice of 'A Constable Calls' and the awkward, hesitant allusion of 'Orange Drums ...' in such a way that it seems as if the voice which Heaney is constructing is unable to represent all aspects of the self. The 'voices of his education' have little to offer when he wishes to bring certain parts of his lived experience into his writing; the same gap appeared in 'The Ministry of Fear' when Heaney dealt with intimate or Northern Irish experiences. This monologism, as opposed to the intertextual dialogue, suggests that the project of 'The Ministry of Fear' might fail. Alternatively, the second and third poems of the sequence can be seen as precisely those aspects of the lived experience which must be accommodated by 'the voices of education', if those voices are to retain their value, and if Heaney's own voice is not to be irremediably split. In this light, the confidence of 'The Ministry of Fear' becomes an overly easy cultural ecumenism which fails to take account of the project's inherent difficulties and tensions.

'Summer 1969' addresses itself to this issue. In a kind of exile, sweating through the 'life of Joyce' (N, p. 69), Heaney is guiltily preoccupied with events in Belfast. The question at the heart of the poem is 'How should the poet respond?' In what way should he try to 'touch the people', and how should he try to represent these events? Lorca is suggested as a possible model but it is Goya who dominates this poem. If the 'life of Joyce' and superficial indifference of the first stanza suggest and then discount exile as a possible response, the second stanza acts as pivot and the references to Goya indicate two possible responses.

Those responses are mediated by an echo of Yeats' 'Municipal Gallery Revisited'.[31] In each case, the poet looks at paintings as a way of representing his circumstances. Heaney, in partial exile, cannot share Yeats' tranquillity. The first painting to which he refers, Goya's 'Shootings of the Third of May' (N, p. 69), offers engagement as a response. In both the painting and Heaney's description of it, sympathy is with the rebel rather than the military firing squad. This is an attitude Heaney had taken previously,[32] but its dangers become apparent as he turns his attention to Goya's 'Black Paintings': 'Saturn devouring his son' – 'Saturn/Jewelled in the

blood of his own children'; 'Quarrel by cudgelling' – '... that holm-
gang/ Where two berserks club each other to death/ For honour's
sake, greaved in a bog, and sinking' (N, p. 70). This is the most
pessimistic note of the entire sequence. In between these two paintings is 'Gigantic Chaos turning his brute hips/ Over the world ...'
(N, p. 70) which can only be 'The Colossus (Panic)', although it is
not a 'Black painting' nor is it in the same room as them.[33] The
order in which Heaney consciously places these paintings offers a
gruesome commentary by analogy on Ireland. The old sow eating
her farrow is evident in 'Saturn devouring his son'; a mass evacuation flees before the figure of chaos and we are left with 'two
berserks' locked in a holmgang, the almost obsolete word connot-
ing the 'anachronistic passions'[34] at large in the North. The poem
enables us to construct this analogy between Goya's paintings and
Northern Ireland, but it is only by placing the poem back in the sequence that we can evaluate it. The preceding poems in the sequence are almost entirely enmeshed in local actualities. 'Summer
1969' suffers the opposite fate. Here the cosmopolitan dominates
and Ireland is represented only by analogy. The poem's importance
in the sequence lies in Goya as a model of artistic response:

> He painted with his fists and elbows, flourished
> The stained cape of his heart as history charged.
>   (N, p. 70)

The histrionic quality does not match Heaney's reticence and
thoughtfulness in other poems in the sequence, but while this open-
ness and vulnerability amounts to engagement it also leads to the
madness and despair of the 'Black Paintings'. The analogies that we
are enabled to construct are subject to O'Brien's strictures about
determinism: the imposition of paradigms which are not responsive
to local contingencies is not worthwhile, leading only to the clichéd
response of 'Whatever you say say nothing'.

This critique of 'Summer 1969' is substantiated by the opening
words of the following poem, 'Fosterage':

> 'Description is revelation!' Royal
> Avenue, Belfast, 1962.
> A Saturday afternoon ...
>   (N, p. 71)

The opening words, spoken by the poem's dedicatee, Michael
McLaverty, are immediately responded to by the poem's exact

location in time and space, and more importantly by the fact that the poet is once again on home ground. McLaverty, in Heaney's description of him, possesses 'fidelity to the intimate' while being sensible of 'the great tradition that he works in'[35] and the virtues of patience and a sense of the value of words. He is an exemplary presence: the writer as a congruence of the forces at work in Northern Ireland. What is notable about the poem is that it not only moves the poet back to his own place but also back in time, against the flow of the sequence so far. 1962 is a time of origins: 'me newly cubbed in language' (N, p. 71), and the preceding poems are therefore partially revoked. The 'ministry of fear' is not denied, but the focus has shifted to the idea of a second ministry, and a new beginning. Other voices are present in the poem: McLaverty's voice, obviously, but it in turn is a conflation of Hopkins, Mansfield, and Chekhov.[36] Affection for McLaverty and his role as foster-father draws Heaney back into Irish history.

There are undercurrents in the poem, however, which belie this, perhaps sentimental, reading. The 'words ... like obols' (N, p. 71) may be highly valued but the simile suggests a death of the self. Nor is McLaverty's teaching straightforward. The advice, 'Go your own way./ Do your own work', is ironical, especially when followed by references to models more suited to the short-story writer than to the poet. In this way the poem distances the voices within it and suggests that the poet's own voice, while acknowledging its components, must speak for itself. The heart of the poem is the restraint proposed by McLaverty which is opposed to the violence of Goya. This restraint can be just as vulnerable and open as Goya's overstatement.

'Exposure' (N, pp. 72–3) is the consequence of the previous five poems of the sequence. It presents us with the poet at the moment of writing. As with 'Fosterage' it is located in a specific time and place: 'It is December in Wicklow' (N, p. 72). The title bespeaks the poet's sense of vulnerability away from the protection of fosterage and the question the poem poses is 'who is responsible for this exposure?'; is it the poet himself or is it a failure of the cultural traditions evident in the rest of the sequence. Those traditions are here present only as hints and traces: Yeats may be present in the diction; Joyce, Montague and Kinsella in the fire imagery.[37] Neil Corcoran identifies Osip Mandelstam as the primary presence in the poem with a secondary reference to Ovid in exile.[38] The English poetic tradition is replaced by others just as the country replaces the city, the South ironically replaces the eponymous North, and the historical replaces the contemporary:

> I am neither internee nor informer:
> An inner émigré, grown long-haired
> And thoughtful: a wood-kerne
> Escaped from the massacre.
>   (N, p. 73)

The poet, refusing the opposed contemporary terms 'internee' and 'informer', has adopted the strategy of the 'wood-kerne', whose engagements are followed by strategic withdrawals. The choice of term is important, because this reference back to the Elizabethan period is to an originary moment in the relation of Ireland and England. As Heaney withdraws to the South and engages in dialogue with Irish, Russian and Roman voices,[39] he represents himself in a term derived from Old Irish. The exposure of the poem is, in part, a stripping away of English voices. The poem offers no understanding; its tone is one of regret and puzzlement. By refusing both contemporary terms within which the self might be comprehended, there is a sense of lost opportunity and of a lost self. The suggestion of the death of the self in 'Fosterage' is continued by this poem's winter imagery and its movement from the contemporary to the historical, a time before the self. This leads us to a contradiction in the poem's title: what is being exposed if not the self?

The answer is best provided by the autobiographical impulse underlying the sequence. If the other poems are taken to be 'spots of time' – those epiphanic moments which bring the self into definition – then the 'missed comet' is the failure to comprehend the variety of selves in the other poems. The exposure is then not of the self but of the failure of self-comprehension, indicated by the absence of English voices. This is not to say that there has been a complete failure to carry out the sequence's project. Its context is not only the poems which precede it in *North* but also those which follow it in *Field Work*.[40] The autobiographical impulse has not yet been worked out. Comprehension has not yet been achieved because the representation of the self eventually lacks one of its prime constituents. The project of 'Singing School' is thus continued in *Field Work* and beyond until it can achieve, not that Irish shibboleth of independence but rather a sense of dialectical equality in *Station Island*, with a glance back to the missed comet of 'Exposure':

... 'Who cares,'
he jeered, 'any more? The English language
belongs to us. You are raking at dead fires,

a waste of time for somebody your age.
That subject people stuff is a cod's game.[41]

After this, Heaney, previously a digger and delver 'par excellence', becomes a traveller, and in *The Haw Lantern*[42] he makes English both a citadel and a passport to cross frontiers, especially the frontier of writing, and in so doing acquires the right to represent as well as being represented.

From *Aspects of Irish Studies*, ed. M. Hill and S. Barber (Belfast, 1990), pp. 55–64, 146–7.

NOTES

[Eamonn Hughes's essay is the first one in this collection to draw attention to the literary commonalty which 'Northern poets' like Paul Muldoon and Tom Paulin share with Heaney (See Further Reading, p. 268). His theoretical perspective is more coherent and less idiosyncratic than Deane's (essay 4), responding to an influential line of thinking which passed from the Russian Formalists into structuralism and poststructuralism.

Volosinov, Bakhtin, Saussure and Kristeva enable him to examine Heaney's development in *North* in terms of a sustained analogy with linguistic phenomena, thus mediating between more ideologically partisan readings like those of Longley (essay 3) and Deane. Heaney's '*An Open Letter*' (p. 78) was first published as a Field Day Pamphlet (Derry, 1983) and can be found in *Ireland's Field Day* (London, 1985). Michael McLaverty (b. 1907) was a Belfast short-story writer and novelist (p. 88). Ed.]

1. Blake Morrison and Andrew Motion, 'Introduction', *The Penguin Book of Contemporary British Poetry* (Harmondsworth, 1982), p. 20.

2. The two most recent studies of Heaney – Neil Corcoran, *Seamus Heaney* (London, 1986), and Elmer Andrews, *The Poetry of Seamus Heaney* (London, 1988) – follow the usual pattern of concentrating discussion of Part II on 'Exposure'.

3. Paul Muldoon, *Meeting the British* (London, 1987).

4. Seamus Heaney, *North* (London, 1975), p. 65.

5. Tom Paulin, *Liberty Tree* (London, 1983), p. 33.

6. Tom Paulin, *Fivemiletown* (London, 1987).

7. George Watson, 'An uncomfortable, spikey poet', *Irish Literary Supplement*, 7:2 (Fall 1988), 33.

8. Blake Morrison, *Seamus Heaney* (London, 1982), ch. 4. See also: Simon Curtis, 'Seamus Heaney's *North*', *Critical Quarterly*, 18:1 (Spring 1976), 80–3, 83; Edna Longley, 'Fire and Air', *The Honest Ulsterman*, 50 (Winter 1975), 179–83, 182; Douglas Dunn, 'Mañana is now', *Encounter*, 45 (Nov. 1975), 76–81, 76, 77; Conor Cruise O'Brien, 'A Slow North-east Wind', *The Listener* (25 Sept. 1975), pp. 404–5.

9. Stan Smith, 'Writing a Will, Yeats's Ancestral Voices in "'The Tower" and "Meditations in Time of Civil War"', *Irish University Review*, 13:1 (Spring 1983), 14–37.

10. Julia Kristeva, 'Word, Dialogue and Novel', in *Desire in Language* (Oxford, 1980), p. 65.

11. V. N. Volisinov, *Marxism and the Philosophy of Language*, trans. Ladislav Matejka and I.R. Titunik (Cambridge, MA, 1986), pp. 73–81: the direct quotations are on pp. 75, 81 and 73 respectively.

12. W.B. Yeats, *The Autobiography of William Butler Yeats* (New York, 1964), p. 312.

13. O'Brien, 'A Slow North-east Wind', p. 404.

14. Ferdinand de Saussure, *Course in General Linguistics*, trans. Wade Baskin, intro. Jonathan Culler (London, 1974), p. 9. See also Culler's 'Introduction', pp. xvii–xviii and Blake Morrison, *Seamus Heaney*, p. 15, n. 2 for Heaney's own sense of this issue.

15. Patrick Kavanagh, 'Epic', *Collected Poems* (London, 1972), p. 136. Allusions will be identified in the notes where appropriate.

16. William Shakespeare, *The Tempest* V.i.182.

17. William Wordsworth, *The Prelude, A Parallel Text*, ed. J.C. Maxwell (Harmondsworth, 1972), 1805 version, Book 1, ll.388–9. Heaney's epigraph is identifiably from the 1805 text, Book 1, ll.305–9, so I shall refer only to it.

18. William Shakespeare, *The Tempest* IV.i.148.

19. James Joyce, *A Portrait of the Artist as a Young Man* (London, 1968), pp. 51–2 – the 'pandy bat' incident.

20. The incidents with the RUC, and with the priest at school, recall Joyce's two masters, Church and State, and there is an echo of Yeats's 'The years like great black oxen tread the world' ('The

Countess Cathleen', 1892 text, in *The Variorum Edition of the Plays*, ed. Russell K. Alspach [London, 1966], p. 158) in the description of the police 'like black cattle'. Although only hints, it is significant that the writers whom Heaney calls on here are both Irish. Sexual and political knowledge are precisely those areas of self-comprehension to be repressed by reading Masefield's 'Cargoes' in *Meeting the British*.

21. Seamus Deane, 'Unhappy and at Home, an Interview with Seamus Heaney', *The Crane Bag*, 1 (Spring 1977), 61–7, 63. See also Blake Morrison, *Seamus Heaney*, p. 44, n. 42.

22. Samuel Taylor Coleridge, 'Frost at Midnight', ll.72, in *Poetical Works*, ed. E.H. Coleridge (London, 1969), p. 242; William Wordsworth, *The Prelude*, Book 1, ll.370–1. There is a slight Orwellian allusion here.

23. Shakespeare, *King Lear* III.iv.105. Michael Longley uses the same quotation as epigraph to 'Options' which pre-dates 'Singing School' and is similarly about the variety of voices available to a poet; *Poems 1953–83* (Harmondsworth, 1986), pp. 106–7.

24. Blake Morrison, *Seamus Heaney*, pp. 66–7.

25. Patrick Kavanagh, *Collected Pruse* (London, 1967), pp. 282–3, and Seamus Heaney, *Preoccupations: Selected Prose, 1968–1978* (London, 1980), pp. 29, 35; Lawrence, of course, being a 'voice of education'.

26. Clifford Geertz, *The Interpretation of Cultures, Selected Essays* (London, 1975), p. 242.

27. Seamus Heaney, *Preoccupations*, p. 41.

28. Blake Morrison, *Seamus Heaney*, p. 66.

29. F.S.L. Lyons, *Ireland since the Famine* (London, 1973), p. 761.

30. G.M. Hopkins, *Poems and Prose*, selected and introduced by W.H. Gardner (Harmondsworth, 1953), p. 30.

31. W.B. Yeats, *The Poems: A New Edition*, ed. R.J. Finneran (London, 1983), pp. 319–21. This poem's presence is felt throughout *North*.

32. Seamus Heaney, 'Old Derry's Walls', *The Listener*, 24 October 1968, pp. 521–3.

33. See Antonio J. Oneiva, *A New Complete Guide to the Prado Gallery*, trans. P.M. O'Neill, new edn rev. Miriam Finkelman (Madrid, 1966), p. 182. See also Hugh Thomas, *Goya: The Third of May, 1808* (London, 1972); F.D. Klingender, *Goya in a Democratic Tradition*, intro. Herbert Read (London, 1948); G.A. Williams, *Goya and the Impossible Revolution* (London, 1976), for accounts of the

historical and political background to Goya's work which enables Heaney's analogy.

34.   Seamus Heaney, 'Delirium of the Brave', *The Listener*, 27 November 1969, pp. 757–9.

35.   Seamus Heaney, 'Introduction' in Michael McLaverty, *The Collected Short Stories* (Dublin, 1978), p. 7.

36.   Ibid., p. 7 where 'that note of exile' is to be found in Chekhov.

37.   See *A Portrait*, pp. 189–90, John Montague, *The Rough Field*, 3rd edn (Dublin, 1979), p. 19 and Thomas Kinsella, 'Death Bed', *New Poems 1973* (Dublin, 1973).

38.   Neil Corcoran, *Seamus Heaney*, pp. 124–6; and see Seamus Heaney, *The Government of the Tongue* (London, 1989), p. 72.

39.   An echo of Yeats's 'Politics', with its rejection of Roman, Russian, and Spanish politics; Yeats, *The Poems*, p. 348.

40.   Seamus Heaney, *Field Work* (London, 1979).

41.   Seamus Heaney, *Station Island* (London, 1984).

42.   Seamus Heaney, *The Haw Lantern* (London, 1987).

6

The Mouth, the Meal and the Book: Review of *Field Work*

CHRISTOPHER RICKS

Those of us who have never swallowed an oyster have presumably never lived life to the full. The Augustan poet was not merely mocking the heroic when he said that the man must have had a palate coated o'er with brass who first risked the living morsel down his throat. Seamus Heaney offers 'Oysters ('Alive and violated') as his opening. Opened at once are the oyster, the mouth, the meal and the book. It is at the start a delicious poem, not least in its play of the obdurate against the liquid:

> Our shells clacked on the plates.
> My tongue was a filling estuary,
> My palate hung with starlight.

'Clacked', for once, does not rebuke the 'tongue' of other people; 'plates' finds itself soothed out into 'palate', rather like 'oysters' into 'estuary'.

But indignation flickers, and though it is appeased it is not expunged.

> Bivalves: the split bulb
> And philandering sigh of ocean.
> Millions of them ripped and shucked and scattered.

We are not to sigh Shucks. For even the happiest recollection is liable to be blandly tinged with snobbery, as if memory were a fine cellar:

> And there we were toasting friendship,
> Laying down a perfect memory
> In the cool of thatch and crockery.

So in the end, having next riddled the oysters (they are something of a riddle themselves) as 'The frond-lipped, brine-stung/Glut of privilege', the *poem* is stung too:

> And was angry that my trust could not repose
> In the clear light, like poetry or freedom
> Leaning in from sea. I ate the day
> Deliberately, that its tang
> Might quicken me all into verb, pure verb.

The anger is real, but is headstrong. Instead of the nouns of privilege (property and possessions), there is to be the imaginative activity that is alive only as verb. At least since Ezra Pound, this has been a lure for poets, a thrill and a delusion. For as Heaney's last line acknowledges, 'verb' is indissolubly a noun. And the word which matters most is 'trust'.

When we come to close this book which opened with 'Oysters', we have finally contemplated the hideous devouring of a living morsel through all eternity. For the book ends with 'Ugolino', Dante's insatiable avenger, gnawing undyingly and unkillingly upon the head of the man who had starved to death his children and him:

> That sinner eased his mouth up off his meal
> To answer me, and wiped it with the hair
> Left growing on his victim's ravaged skull,
> Then said ...

The 'eased' is cause of wonder; and of horror, like the serviceableness and decorum of that napkin of hair. 'Ugolino' too is in part about trust:

> how my good faith
> Was easy prey to his malignancy ...

The word 'prey' feels how intimate may be the bonds between trusting and tasting. Both the first and this last poem in the book speak of 'my tongue'.

Field Work is alive with trust (how else would field work be possible?), and it could have been created only by an experienced poet secure in the grounded trust that he is trusted. Heaney is the most trusted poet of our islands. (Larkin is now trusted not to produce bad poems, but not necessarily to produce poems.) *Field Work* is an even better book than *North*, Heaney's last collection, in that it is more profoundly exemplary. One poem is admittedly sceptical of the word 'exemplary' when applied to poets, as is clear from the question which the poet, lodged in the ninth circle of Hell, puts to his wife when ('Aided and abetted by Virgil's wife') she visits his damnation. About the poets now alive, he asks:

> whose is the life
> Most dedicated and exemplary?

But Heaney's art is urgently exemplary while being aware that urgency may easily be in collusion with violence and threats. A landscape's peace of nature, a person's peace of mind, a land's peace: '*The end of art is peace*' could be, we are told, the motto of the woven harvest bow.

North, by bending itself to deep excavations within the past of Ireland and of elsewhere, achieved a racked dignity in the face of horrors. The poems were truly enlightened. But *Field Work* shows, more variously and with high composure, that there is something more primary than enlightenment. Henry James said of Eugénie de Guérin and her piety, what could not be said of Heaney and his, that she 'was certainly not enlightened'. Yet when James went on, 'But she was better than this – she was light itself,' the respectful directness of this does itself have something of light's unarguable presence. Its presence is not sentimentalised in Heaney's poems. 'I think the candour of the light dismayed us.'

Ungullible trust will always be of value, but especially so in Ireland torn by reasonable and unreasonable distrust and mistrust. The resilient strength of these poems is in the equanimity even of their surprise at some blessed moment of everyday trust. So the book's second poem, 'After a Killing', likewise gives us food for thought, but this time the food is not outré like oysters. What hope is there, after a killing? Only this – and if we insist on prefacing it with 'only', we have already sold the pass:

> And today a girl walks in home to us
> Carrying a basket full of new potatoes,
> Three tight green cabbages, and carrots
> With the tops and mould still fresh on them.

Such an ending, in its tender hope, looks cynicism's desperation levelly in the eye. The gait with which the line itself 'walks in home to us' is simply sturdy. There are no exclamations, even of gratitude, just a sense of gratitude. What could be less novel than those new potatoes? Some may think that this is bathos, but the presence within these poems of William Wordsworth (Dorothy and he at one point make a fleeting appearance, grave comic spectres not lightly to be called up for comparison) is a reminder that after the Augustans had derided it there really was discovered to be such a thing as the art of sinking in poetry.

Art practises what it preaches, and it turns into substantial worth what might be unworthy in both of those verbs. Heaney's poems matter because their uncomplacent wisdom of trust is felt upon the pulses, his and ours, and they effect this because they themselves constitute a living relationship of trust between him and us. He trusts you not to snigger at surprising simplicities:

> trusting the gift,
> risking gift's undertow.

says Heaney of a man with a musical gift, and it is brought home that there may be as much wisdom in trusting your own gifts as in trusting those who bear gifts.

What saves the poems from cadging is their supple legitimate pre-emption, their conscious, resourceful and bracing acknowledgement of what is at stake. Braced to, not against, as in the description of the sunflower as 'braced to its pebble-dashed wall', where even 'dashed' is secure and stable and not destructively hasty. A great deal of mistrust is misconstruction, and like the acrobat half-feigning a faltering Heaney's poems often tremble with the possibilities of misconstruing and misconstruction which they openly provide but which only a predator would pounce upon.

It is there, for instance, in the play of 'mould' against 'fresh':

> and carrots
> With the tops and mould still fresh on them.

After all, one near-fetched sense of the word 'mould' would bring it into contention with 'fresh'. Heaney's sense of the word here (the brown earth, not the green mildew) is manifestly unmistakable, but the force of the line is partly a matter of the other sense's being tacitly summoned in order to be gently found preposterous. Nothing can more bring home the innocent freshness of carrots with the earth still on them than the calm rejection – utterly unutterable – of the dingier sense of 'mould'.

Heaney practises this beneficent sleight throughout the poems. It is there earlier in this same poem in the line, 'As if the unquiet founders walked again', where the faltering sense of 'founders' is felt under the feet of the line, a line which walks so differently from 'And today a girl walks in home to us'. The founder of modern Ireland may perhaps founder. Or here:

> And as forgotten water in a well might shake
> At an explosion under morning
>
> Or a crack run up a gable,
> She began to speak.

It is unthinkable that Heaney just didn't notice the subterranean ripple of 'well might'. It is not an unfortunate oversight: it is a fortunate overseeing, and its point is to 'shake' our sense of these relationships without shaking our trust. If you were to notice nothing, you well might be impervious to the unseen ripples.

The ripple has, even in this sardonic poem ('Sibyl'), an affinity to comedy. Indeed, 'well might' is a comic counterpart of Kingsley Amis's satirical shaking of the word 'just'. Amis invoked Shirley:

> Only the actions of the just
> Smell sweet and blossom in their dust.

And in doing so expressed his settled distrust:

> Which does the just about as much
> Good as a smart kick in the crotch.

Just about as much.

Heaney's comedy, like all the best comedy, is a matter of trust. So 'The Skunk' is an exquisitely comic love-poem, and you have to love your wife most trustingly, and trust in the reciprocity, before you would trust yourself to a comparison of her to a skunk. No offence meant; no offensive launched. Then the poem is at once followed by 'Homecomings', where the loved woman is a clay nest and the man is a martin. Affectionate, delicate, calmingly dark, and as confidently trusting in its own arc as is the bird in its flights nimbly and repeatedly home, the poem goes out of its way (except that this is how the martin skims and veers) to speak in ways which would lend themselves to misconstruction if it weren't that love is a nesting trust. 'Far in, feather-brains tucked in silence.' For in this sweet evocation of the bird within the nest of the woman's head, nothing could be more remote than any accusation that anyone is feather-brained. How could we appreciate such trustful remoteness except by calling up the sheer ludicrousness of its possibility?

> Mould my shoulders inward to you.
> Occlude me.
> Be damp clay pouting.
> Let me listen under your eaves.

The tucked-in pressure is there in the way in which 'mould' wants to expand into 'shoulders'; and the mouth of the clay nest may be 'pouting', but in the confidence that no other pouting is going on (pure Keats, this). Nothing could be more unmisgivingly an act of loving inclusion than the stern word 'occlude' here, just as nothing could be less furtive, more openly trusting, than the final eavesdropping.

No need of manna when the actual is marvellous, our conversation

> a white picnic tablecloth spread out
> Like a book of manners in the wilderness.

Likewise, the word 'implicated' is consciously innocent in Heaney: implicated, not in wrongdoing, but as the plaiting of the harvest bow. Heaney's resourcefulness is astonishing, not least in that astonishment is not then something which the poems incite. This pacific art has learnt from the poet to whom Heaney offers here an elegy, Robert Lowell, but the effect is altogether different from Lowell's Atlantic astonishments. But then Heaney's trust in other poets is itself part of his art, as in the rueful comfort to be divined within the conclusive line: 'Our island is full of comfortless noises'. Be not afeared, the isle is full of noises ... And that's true too.

From *The London Review of Books*, 8 November 1979, pp. 4–5.

NOTE

[An Augustan point of reference is established in Ricks's first paragraph (the quotation is from Gay's 'Trivia', Book III, ll.195–8) and this is reinforced by the invocation (p. 98) of *Peri Bathous* (largely if not entirely by Pope: see Edna Leake Steeves [ed.], The *Art of Sinking in Poetry* [New York, 1968]). This is the second review by Ricks to figure in this volume (see essay 1) and his (not quite serious?) assimilation of Heaney into an English tradition rooted in the eighteenth century shows again a New Critical canonical preoccupation. But the approach is now less analytical and more widely discursive, the tone more playful, in tune with a changing critical climate (as I suggest in my Introduction). Ricks's sharing of a literary camaraderie with the poet is very different, certainly, from the 'authoritative' stance with which Leavis took 'the line of wit' as a touchstone to judge other poetry in *Revaluation* (London, 1936). Ed.]

7

Review of *Field Work*

TERRY EAGLETON

'Soon people are going to start comparing him to Yeats', wrote Clive James of Seamus Heaney, a cunningly self-fulfilling prophecy. Actually Heaney has about as much in common with Yeats as he has with Longfellow, but he is, you see, Irish, and what more obvious to compare one Irishman to than another? Isn't there something unwittingly racist about this way of thinking? Why should a Southern Protestant pseudo-Ascendency crypto-fascist who died in 1939 be presumed to be comparable to a contemporary Northern Catholic of peasant stock, just because of the abstract fact of their shared Irishness?

There are two particular reasons, among thousands of others, why the comparison of Heaney with Yeats is inept. Yeats's conception of poetry was a fairly commonplace Romantic inspirationalism, entailing an irrationalism not unconnected with his politics. Heaney, by contrast, conceives of art as labour, craft and production, precariously analogous to manual labour, a traffic with Nature mediated by verbal rather than material instruments:

> Vowels ploughed into each other: opened ground.
> The mildest February for twenty years
> Is mist bands over furrows, a deep no sound
> Vulnerable to distant gargling tractors.
> Our road is steaming, the turned-up acres breathe.
> Now the good life could be to cross a field
> And art a paradigm of earth new from the lathe
> Of ploughs. My lea is deeply tilled.
> Old ploughsocks gorge the subsoil of each sense

And I am quickened with a redolence
Of the fundamental dark unblown rose ...
                ('Glanmore Sonnets')

Perhaps the untypical formality of this, its metrical decorum and
faint sense of intellectual conceit, is meant to alert us to the specula-
tive, rather strained quality of the writing/work metaphor, which in
Heaney's work involves a displacement in a double sense – the creative displacement of all metaphor, but also, notably in the proba-
tionary poems of *Death of a Naturalist*, a secondary substitution of
intellectual for manual labour. But Frank Ormsby is probably right,
if a little romantically uncritical, when he writes of Heaney in his
Introduction to *Poets from the North of Ireland* that 'he is constantly aware of his poetry as a craft akin to the traditional crafts of
turf-cutter, ploughman, thatcher, water-diviner, salmon-fisher,
mummer and blacksmith'.[1] Yeats has images of crafting and ham-
mering too, of course, but they are finally subordinated to an aesthetic of visionary spontaneity; it is in Blake, intriguingly, that
vision and production consort most fruitfully together.

'Verbal rather than material instruments': the semioticians lie in
wait to protest, rightly, that nothing could be more material than
language itself. The recovery of the materiality of language – the
growing refusal of Cartesian, metaphysical models which would
relegate language to a pale reflection of another pale reflection
(thought), and privilege the apparently immaterial 'voice' over the
more obstrusively material 'script' – is a precious theoretical development which Heaney's poetry in some way parallels. This doesn't
just mean that he is gnarled and densely-textured; indeed that, often
enough, has been a sort of empiricist substitute for a genuine linguistic materialism, a mistaking of words for 'things' which bases
itself on a naïve reflectionism. Heaney recognises that if language is
indeed in some sense material, it has its own specific mode of materiality, complexly related to work, Nature and human relationships.
So that if Nature can be 'textualised', its wry recalcitrance to the
'literary' can also be deftly hinted at, precisely by bringing the two a
little too neatly together:

This evening the cuckoo and the corncrake
(So much, too much) consorted at twilight.
It was all crepuscular and iambic.
Out on the field a baby rabbit
Took his bearing, and I knew the deer

(I've seen them too from the window of the house,
Like connoisseurs, inquisitive of air)
Were careful under larch and May-green spruce.
I had said earlier, 'I won't relapse
From this strange loneliness I've brought us to.
Dorothy and William –' She interrupts:
'You're not going to compare us two …?'
Outside a rustling and twig-combing breeze
Refreshes and relents. Is cadences.

('Glanmore Sonnets')

The modulations of this, all the way from the faintly mincing overtones of 'It was all crepuscular and iambic' and the calculated liter-
ariness of the last two overbred lines, to the simple unadorned
perception of the rabbit, might help to assuage certain fears about
Heaney which Jon Silkin has expressed in a review.[2] Silkin argued
roughly that the later Heaney was in danger of sacrificing the
realist force of his early work to a gathering 'deftness', a rich technical virtuosity which couldn't easily be combined with his raw
materials; and indeed there did seem a risk at one point, as
Heaney's forms grew leaner and leaner, that he would have a
problem in unifying an almost unrivalled technical resourcefulness
with the social and material taproots of his art. The relation
between different sorts of materiality is in this sense a problem of
form, not just a 'theme'. What is perhaps most impressive about
Field Work, however, is that this problem seems more out in the
open, and in the best of the volume triumphantly resolved: language can be granted its own material workings without detriment
to its status as a realist medium:

On Devenish I heard a snipe
And the keeper's recital of elegies
Under the tower. Carved monastic heads
Were crumbling like bread on water.

On Boa the god-eyed, sex-mouthed stone
Socketed between graves, two-faced, trepanned,
Answered my silence with silence.
A stoup for rain water. Anathema.

From a cold hearthstone on Horse Island
I watched the sky beyond the open chimney
And listened to the thick rotations
Of an army helicopter patrolling.

('Triptych')

The characteristics devices of the first two stanzas – the nearly excessive terseness, the austere elegance of image, the curious blend of reticence and density – open out undisruptively onto the plainer notations of the third verse.

Another way in which Heaney differs from Yeats is that, if he is indubitably a 'major' poet, he isn't *obviously* so – not major in the same way, not major in an *epoch* of major poetry. Nobody could doubt from Yeats's tone that he believes poetry to be an intrinsically superior *genre* to, say, fiction, whereas it would be difficult for Seamus Heaney to believe this. Whatever Yeats's harebrained and repellent fantasies, he wrote out of an historical crisis where the impulse to 'totalise' was urgent. Heaney, whatever evidence of global imperialist crisis he may find on his doorstep, handles that evidence in the style of an 'end-of-ideologies' writer. Most of the poems in *Field Work* are superb, but the plain truth is that Heaney doesn't really have much to 'say' which is inherently more complex or compulsive than a whole range of more 'minor' writers. A lot of what Yeats had to 'say' was nonsense, but he did after all have a lot to say. This is not, of course, just a quantitative matter: it is much more a question of historical situation, which is to say, among other things, that it isn't a matter of entirely *blaming* Heaney. But nor is it a matter of letting him off the hook by dint of some historical determinism. Heaney has been much praised, and properly so; he probably is one of the finest English-language poets of the century. But it is perhaps not surprising that he has been praised by a criticism which invests deeply in 'experience' and little in 'ideas'. On the latter score, Heaney does not show up particularly well in a comparison with much less technically accomplished writers, even if there is little to fault him on the former.

From *Stand*, 21, No. 3 (1980), 77–8.

NOTE

[Terry Eagleton's theoretical concerns are Marxist but this does not emerge strongly here (the review was written for *Stand*, a non-academic literary magazine). He does draw attention to the political implications of Heaney's poetic stance in a way that anticipates David Lloyd's essay (no. 11) below. But Eagleton's basic approach here is comparable with that of Eamonn Hughes (essay 5) in its dual awareness of the language of literature and the way that literature can be seen as functioning like a language. In *Criticism and Ideology* (1976; London, 1978, p. 79) Eagleton had made use of Barthes's distinction in *Writing Degree Zero* between the text which 'may so "foreground" its signifiers as to radically deform, distantiate and defamiliarise its signified'; and that which strictly curbs 'such excess in apparent humble conformity to the logic of its "content"'. 'This key Formalist/structuralist idea animates his debate with *Stand's* editor, Jon Silkin. Eagleton's aim is to suggest that Heaney's development is not determined by the rigour of this 'either/or' formulation: that he is increasingly able to do both these things. Ed.]

1.   Frank Ormsby, *Poets from the North of Ireland* (Belfast, 1979), p. 8. The latter part of Eagleton's review, which discusses this book, has been omitted here. [Ed.]

2.   Jon Silkin, 'Bedding the Locale', *New Blackfriars* (March 1973), pp. 130–3.

8

Writing a Bare Wire: *Station Island*

NEIL CORCORAN

> There are some lines in poetry which are like wool in texture and
> some that are like bare wires. I was devoted to a Keatsian woolly line,
> textured stuff, but now I would like to be able to write a bare wire.
>   (Seamus Heaney to Fintan O'Toole, 1984)

Station Island, by far Seamus Heaney's longest book, is in three
separate parts: an opening section of individual lyrics which take
their occasions from the occurrences and the memories of the ordinary life; the central section, the title sequence itself which nar-
rates, or dramatises, a number of encounters, in dream or in
vision, with the dead; and a concluding sequence, 'Sweeney
Redivivus', which is, as Heaney puts it in one of his notes to the
volume, 'voiced for Sweeney', the seventh-century king transformed into a bird, whose story Heaney has translated from the
medieval Irish poem *Buile Suibhne* as *Sweeney Astray*.

Despite its separate parts, the book also has a formal unity,
however, signalled by the presence, in all three parts, of the
Sweeney figure. He is there in the poem which ends Part One, 'The
King of the Ditchbacks' (which is, partly, about the act of translation itself); then in the opening section of 'Station Island', in his
manifestation as the unregenerate Simon Sweeney, one of a family
of tinkers remembered from Heaney's childhood (the introduction
to *Sweeney Astray* explicitly links this Sweeney with the legendary
character); and finally, of course, in the 'Sweeney Redivivus' sequence itself. What 'The King of the Ditchbacks' calls Sweeney's

'dark morse' is therefore tapped throughout the volume; and what the code spells out is an extraordinarily rigorous scrutiny by Seamus Heaney of his own commitments and attachments to his people, and of his responsibilities as a poet. This self-scrutiny proceeds through all three parts of *Station Island* in different models. In Part One, it is pursued, sometimes implicitly, in separate lyrics originating in autobiographical experience; in 'Station Island', this contemporary self undergoes a penitential exercise in self-examination on a mythologised purgatorial pilgrimage; and in 'Sweeney Redivivus', the newly steadied self is released from its *Purgatorio* into the freedom of a kind of anti-self or parallel-self, as Heaney's voice is twinned with that of the character whose name rhymes with his own, 'Sweeney'.

The different voices of the volume – the lyric; the narrative and dramatic; the disguised or ventriloquial – are perhaps designed partly to offset the dangers of self-importance in this very self-involved book. They are, nevertheless, all chosen modalities of the voice of Seamus Heaney himself; and, in this sense, the shortest poem in *Station Island*, and one of its most perfect, 'Widgeon', may be read as an allegory of the book's procedure:

> It had been badly shot.
> While he was plucking it
> he found, he says, the voice box –
>
> like a flute stop
> in the broken windpipe –
>
> and blew upon it
> unexpectedly
> his own small widgeon cries.

This tiny anecdote about the shot wild duck is a story already told ('he says') – like the already much written-over pilgrimage to Station Island, like the *Buile Suibhne* – which Heaney now tells again, in his own words. The bird is 'badly shot', as some of the shades in 'Station Island' have been badly (wickedly, cruelly) shot, in Northern sectarian murders. 'He' in 'Widgeon' blows his own cries on the dead bird's voice box, just as Heaney briefly and poignantly returns a voice to the dead in the 'Station Island' sequence, a voice which remains, nevertheless, entirely his own voice too; and as, in 'Sweeney Redivivus', his own voice sounds through the 'voice box' of Sweeney, the bird-man.

In this dartingly implicit allegory of the way the individual poetic voice speaks through the real and the legendary dead – through biographical experience and through literary tradition – it is the word 'unexpectedly', given a line to itself, which carries the greatest charge of implication: the poet who would properly – without sentimentality, without self-importance – articulate his own small widgeon cries through encounters with the dead must seem uncalculatingly preoccupied with his subject or with the form of his own poem, having something of the intent self-forgetfulness of one who would, testingly and probingly, attempt to blow upon a dead bird's voice box. The preoccupation may then release, 'unexpectedly', and almost distractedly, a genuine self-illumination or self-definition, just as 'Widgeon' releases allegorical implications most 'unexpectedly' too.

It is precisely this unexpectedness which makes the best work of *Station Island* so bracing. The scheme of the volume is an ambitious one, and, in my opinion, the book is not equally successful in all its parts. Nevertheless, *Station Island* gives notice that Heaney's poetry, in its dissatisfied revision of earlier attitudes and presumptions, and in its exploratory inventiveness as it feels out new directions for itself, is now in the process of successfully negotiating what is, for any poet, the most difficult phase of a career – the transition from the modes and manners which have created the reputation, to the genuinely new and unexpected thing. It is a poetry, in *Station Island*, bristling with the risks and the dangers of such self-transformation but, at its high points, triumphantly self-vindicating too.

I want to spend most of the space available to me in this chapter discussing the two long sequences in *Station Island*, since they present particular difficulties which may be aided by sustained consideration. However, the individual lyrics of Part One also represent something new in Heaney's poetic voice: they have a harsher, more astringent quality than the richly sensuous music of *Field Work*. This is impelled by the preoccupations which they share with the book's sequences, as Heaney's rueful self-scrutiny is pursued in poems in which the objects and occasions of the ordinary world (rather than, as in 'Station Island', the visitations of ghosts) insist their moral claims on the poet.

In 'An Aisling in the Burren' there are, literally, sermons in stones – 'That day the clatter of stones / as we climbed was a sermon / on conscience and healing'; and in poem after poem Heaney listens to similar, if less explicit, sermons, as the natural world offers instances of the exemplary. Sloe gin, in the marvellous poem it gets to itself, is 'bitter / and dependable'; a lobster is 'the hampered one, out of water, / fortified and bewildered'; a granite chip from Joyce's Martello tower is 'a Calvin edge in my complaisant pith'; old pewter says that 'Glimmerings are what the soul's composed of'; the Pacific in Malibu is an instruction in how one is indissolubly wedded to the ascetic Atlantic; visiting Hardy's birthplace is an education in displacement; flying a kite is to know 'the strumming, rooted, long-tailed pull of grief'; listening in to 'the limbo of lost words' on a loaning is to hear how

> At the click of a cell lock somewhere now
> the interrogator steels his *introibo*,
> the light-motes blaze, a blood-red cigarette
> startles the shades, screeching and beseeching.

These instructive moralities make Part One of *Station Island* severe and self-admonitory, and the astringent lyric voice, if it is willing to be counselled, is also chastened, restrained and wearied. As a result, a number of these poems sustain a sad note of diminishment and loss, a sense of transience and of the perilous fragmentariness of memory. 'What guarantees things keeping / if a railway can be lifted / like a long briar out of ditch growth?', Heaney asks in 'Iron Spike'; and the pathos attaching to what has disappeared is one of the essential marks of these poems: they are, I think, Heaney's first real exercises in nostalgia. If the newly tart lyric manner is a departure of the kind recommended in 'Making Strange' by the voice of poetry itself – 'Go beyond what's reliable/in all that keeps pleading and pleading' – the departure is nevertheless fully conscious of how much must be left behind: 'The Loaning' confesses that 'When you are tired or terrified/your voice slips back into its old first place/and makes the sound your shades make there …'

Despite the new departures of these lyrics, however, what nevertheless keeps pleading at some level in a number of them is the political reality of the North. In 'Sandstone Keepsake', another stone acts as the spur to a meditation in which Heaney paints a wry self-portrait of the artist as political outsider which is characteristic in its shrug of uneasy self-depreciation. The poem remembers how the stone was 'lifted' from the beach at Inishowen. At the northern tip of Co. Donegal, Inishowen is at the opposite side of Lough Foyle from the Magilligan internment camp. Heaney is therefore prompted into mythologising the stone in the terms of a Dantean analogy, imagining it as 'A stone from Phlegethon,/bloodied on the bed of hell's hot river'; but he rejects the grandiose comparison in deflating embarrassment ('but not really'), before concluding the poem in the self-deflating contemplation of how he might appear to the Magilligan guards:

> Anyhow, there I was with the wet red stone
> in my hand, staring across at the watch-towers
> from my free state of image and allusion,
> swooped on, then dropped by trained binoculars:
>
> a silhouette not worth bothering about,
> out for the evening in scarf and waders
> and not about to set times wrong or right,
> stooping along, one of the venerators.

The incapacity for the political role is subtly rebuked in those lines by the pun which makes over the 'Irish Free State' into a phrase for the disengagement of poetry, and by the allusion itself which refuses the obligation Hamlet finds so overwhelming, to 'set right' the times that are 'out of joint'. 'Sandstone Keepsake' inherits, it may be, the guilt and anxiety of 'Exposure', but seems more ironically assured of the poet's peripheral status: the most the poem may aspire to is the 'veneration' of the political victim. This self-presentation, with its let-downs and erosions, casts its shadow far into *Station Island*.

'STATION ISLAND'

Station Island, or St Patrick's Purgatory, is a small rocky isle in the middle of Lough Derg in Co. Donegal which, since early medieval times, has been a place of pilgrimage for Irish Catholics. The three-day pilgrimage (which Seamus Heaney himself made three times in his youth) involves a self-punitive routine of prayer, fasting and barefoot walking around stone circles or 'beds', thought to be the remains of ancient monastic cells. From the very earliest times, Lough Derg has inspired popular legend and literature, in particular medieval accounts of miracles and visions, and historical narratives about the suppression of the pilgrimage in the eighteenth century, under the anti-Catholic Penal Laws. As a result, 'Station Island' is the name for a nexus of Irish Catholic religious, historical and cultural affiliations.

Since the nineteenth century, it has also been the subject of more specifically literary treatments: William Carleton's mocking but fascinated prose account, 'The Lough Derg Pilgrim' (1828); Patrick Kavanagh's lengthy *Lough Derg: A Poem* (written in 1942, but only published posthumously in 1978); Denis Devlin's characteristically portentous and frenzied poem, *Lough Derg* (1946); and Sean O'Faolain's well-known short story, 'The Lovers of the Lake' (1958), a story about the uneasy coexistence of sexuality and the Irish Catholic conscience. In a published talk touching on 'Station Island', 'Envies and Identifications: Dante and the Modern Poet', Heaney says that it was partly the anxiety occasioned by these numerous earlier literary versions of the pilgrimage which turned him to Dante's meetings with ghosts in the *Purgatorio* as a model for his own poem: Dante showed him how to 'make an advantage of what could otherwise be regarded as a disadvantage'. Inheriting from *Field Work's* interest in Dante, Heaney therefore makes his imaginary pilgrimage to the island a series of meetings with ghosts of the type Dante meets in the *Purgatorio* – friendly, sad, self-defining, exemplary, admonitory, rebuking.

A central passage from 'Envies and Identifications' illuminates the relationship between Heaney and Dante in the sequence:

> What I first loved in the *Commedia* was the local intensity, the vehemence and fondness attaching to individual shades, the way personalities and values were emotionally soldered together, the strong strain of what has been called personal realism in the celebration of bonds of friendship and bonds of enmity. The way in which Dante could place himself in an historical world yet submit that world to scrutiny from a perspective beyond history, the way he could accommodate the political and the transcendent, this too encouraged my attempt at a sequence of poems which would explore the typical strains which the consciousness labours under in this country. The main tension is between two often contradictory commands: to be faithful to the collective historical experience and to be true to the recognitions of the emerging self. I hoped that I could dramatise these strains by meeting shades from my own dream-life who had also been inhabitants of the actual Irish world. They could perhaps voice the claims of orthodoxy and the necessity to recognise those claims. They could probe the validity of one's commitment.

The shades Heaney meets in the poem, then, have all been 'inhabitants of the actual Irish world', whether personally known friends and acquaintances, or writers known from their work; and their conversations turn, in some way, on the living of a proper life or on the production of a proper work. The revenants are advisers, from beyond the grave, on the poet's responsibilities in the realms of morality and of art.

In I, a prelude to the pilgrimage itself, the encounter, on a Sunday, is with the unregenerate 'sabbath-breaker', Simon Sweeney, a figure of fascination as well as fear, with his advice to 'Stay clear of all processions'. The advice is set against the orthodox pieties of a crowd of women on their way to mass, in a scene which contains (in 'the field was full/of half-remembered faces') a sudden echo of the opening of the medieval poem of vision and pilgrimage, *Piers Plowman*, and its 'field full of folk' – a reminder that poetry in English, as well as in Italian, has its tradition of the dream-vision, and that 'Station Island' self-consciously inherits from it. In II, the ghost is William Carleton, encountered appropriately on the road to Lough Derg, and not on the island itself, since, after visiting Station Island in his youth, he subsequently renounced Catholicism and wrote 'The Lough Derg Pilgrim' as a denunciation of its barbarities and superstitions (hence the reference to 'the old fork-tongued turncoat'). The 'ghost' of III is the inanimate 'seaside trinket' which, for Heaney as a child, had been redolent of the death of the girl who owned it (she was, in fact, Agnes, the sister of Heaney's father, who died of TB in the 1920s).

In Section IV Heaney meets a priest who had died on the foreign missions shortly after his ordination. (This was a man called Terry Keenan, still a clerical student when Heaney knew him.) The section meditates on the ratifying role of the priesthood in Irish society, and its effect on the priest himself, 'doomed to the decent thing'. V includes three separate encounters with teachers or mentors of Heaney's, including his first teacher at Anahorish School, Barney Murphy, and – interestingly in this context – Patrick Kavanagh. VI recalls, with affectionate tenderness, a very early sexual experience and, after 'long virgin/Fasts and thirsts' under the dominion of Catholic doctrine on sexual morality, a later satisfying and fulfilling one. The ghost of VII is a man Heaney had played football with in his youth, the victim of a sectarian murder in Northern Ireland. (Heaney is remembering William Strathearn, killed by two off-duty policemen in a particularly notorious

incident in Co. Antrim.) The victim's description of the circumstances of his death impels Heaney into a confession of what he
regards as his own evasive, uncommitted politics. VIII confronts
Heaney with two further ghosts whose challenges provoke self-
rebuke – Tom Delaney, an archaeologist friend who died tragically
young at thirty-two, towards whom Heaney feels 'I had somehow
broken/covenants, and failed an obligation', and Colum
McCartney, the subject of 'The Strand at Lough Beg' in *Field Work*,
who utters the most unrelenting accusation in the sequence, '"for
the way you whitewashed ugliness and drew/the lovely blinds of the
Purgatorio/and saccharined my death with morning dew"'.

Section IX gives a voice to one of the ten IRA hunger-strikers
who died in Long Kesh between March and September 1981.
(Heaney is actually thinking of the second of them to die, Francis
Hughes, who came from his own district, Bellaghy, and whose
family he knows.) The certitude which could lead to that kind of
political suicide is juxtaposed with a dream of release and revival in
which the extraordinary symbol of a 'strange polyp' ('My softly
awash and blanching self-disgust') appears, to be supported and illuminated by a candle, and is followed by a further symbol of possibility, an 'old brass trumpet' remembered from childhood. X has
another inanimate ghost, a drinking mug removed from Heaney's
childhood home by actors for use in a play, and returned as
Ronan's Psalter is miraculously returned from the lake by an otter
at the opening of *Sweeney Astray* – a further symbol for the unexpected translations the known, ordinary and domestic may
undergo.

In XI the ghost is a monk to whom Heaney once made his confession and who, suggesting that Heaney should 'Read poems as
prayers', asked him to translate something by St John of the Cross,
the sixteenth-century Spanish mystic, as a penance. Heaney responds now, belatedly, with his version of '*Cantar del alma que se
huelga de conoscer a Dios por fe*', the 'Song of the soul that is glad
to know God by faith', a hymn to the 'fountain' of the Trinity to be
discovered within the sacrament of the Eucharist, that sign of the
believing Church in harmonious community. Finally, in the concluding section of the poem, Heaney, back on the mainland, meets
the ghost of James Joyce, who recommends a course antithetical to
that of orthodox Catholic pilgrimage, a striking-out on one's own
in an isolation which, Joyce claims, is the only way the poet's
proper work can be done.

These individual encounters find their basic structural shape in the nature of the pilgrimage itself – leaving the ordinary social world, crossing the waters of Lough Derg, and then returning to that world with some kind of refreshment and new clarity. The irony of 'Station Island', however, is that this pilgrimage leads to no confirmation in the religion and values of the tribe, but to something very like a renunciation of them. It is possible to read the sequence as a kind of reverse palinode, directed at some of the innate assumptions and attitudes of Heaney's own earlier work – a palinode which actually rejects the orthodox communal doctrine and morality, rather than giving final assent to them. When Heaney does 'repent' in IX, it is the old tribal complicities which are imagined as immature and self-restricting: '"I repent / My unweaned life that kept me competent/To sleepwalk with connivance and mistrust."' Heaney is tentative about his repentance, ironically aware of all the ways in which one must remain permanently 'unweaned' from such powerful formative influences and experiences, and the poem has, throughout, the poignancy of anxiety and misgiving. Nevertheless, 'Station Island' uses the metaphor of its Irish Catholic pilgrimage to define some of the constrictions which that religion and culture have imposed on one individual consciousness, and to suggest how, under alternative mentors, and through art, a newly enabling freedom might be gained.

It is possible to read out of the earlier parts of the poem a subtext of accusations against Catholicism: in I, where Heaney is set, behind the pious women, on a 'drugged path', that it acts as a mere opiate, numbing the obedient conscience with its claims of authority; in II, where the radical Ribbonmen of Carleton's day have become, by the time of Heaney's childhood, a drunken band who 'played hymns to Mary', that it keeps you patient and enduring, incapable of the anger of action; in III, where the child's death, held in pious memory, is juxtaposed with the brute animal reality of a dog's death, that, in attempting to account for death, it in fact refuses to face its reality, and sentimentalises it; and in IV, with its 'doomed' priest, that Irish clericalism thwarts the lives of those who represent it, and bolsters the platitudinous pieties of those it 'serves'. In the latter sections of the poem, Catholicism is heavily implicated in Heaney's adolescence of sexual dissatisfaction and guilt, and in his unease and regret about his lack of any firmer political commitment – the 'timid circumspect involvement' for which he begs forgiveness of Strathearn, and that confusion of 'evasion and artistic tact' of which McCartney accuses him. All of these charges generate the outburst of rejection in section IX – '"I hate how quick I was to know my place. / I hate where I was born, hate everything / That made me biddable and unforthcoming"' – where knowing his place is both establishing an identity with a particular territory (celebrated as a virtue often enough in the earlier work) and also meekly accepting a servitude to the mores of a community (where to 'know your place' is to stay put).

Even though it quickly undercuts itself with rueful qualifications, the venom of that climactic attack makes it unsurprising that, despite appearances, no true pilgrimage is actually undertaken in the poem. In IV, Heaney is 'ready to say the dream words *I renounce ...*', the renunciation of worldliness which is the essential prelude to repentance, when he is interrupted by the priest wondering if Heaney is on Station Island only to take the 'last look', and suggesting that, for him, the pilgrimage is without its essential point – 'the god has, as they say, withdrawn'. No orthodox praying is done on the pilgrimage: when he kneels in III, it is only 'Habit's afterlife'; and the poem-prayer in XI could be thought to undermine its song of faith with its constant refrain, 'although it is the night'. In John of the Cross this is the 'dark night of the soul', in which the mystic feels himself temporarily abandoned by God; but, to a more secular consciousness, it could equally well be the sheer inability to believe.

Heaney is also sometimes in physical positions which dissociate him from the other pilgrims: in V, he is 'faced wrong way/into more pilgrims absorbed in this exercise', and in VI, the others 'Trailed up the steps as I went down them/Towards the bottle-green, still/Shade of an oak'. That same section goes so far as to appropriate, from the beginning of the *Divine Comedy*, the moment when Dante is impelled on his journey by learning from Virgil of Beatrice's intercession, in order to describe Heaney's own sexual awakening after the enforced virginity of his Irish Catholic adolescence. The truant which Heaney is playing from the pilgrimage there turns the tradition of the vision-poem on its head, making sexual not divine love the object of the exercise; but it reminds us too that Dante's great poem of Christian quest discovers its images of heavenly bliss in a transfigured human woman.

At the centre of Heaney's pilgrimage, however, there is not presence but absence, figured frequently as a 'space'. It is 'a space utterly empty,/utterly a source, like the idea of sound' in III; 'A stillness far away, a space' in VI; 'the granite airy space/I was staring into' in VIII; and, in XII, after the pilgrimage. 'It was as if I had stepped free into a space/alone with nothing that I had not known/already'. This final linking of the blank space with freedom comes after Heaney has been counselled by Joyce; and the whole of 'Station Island' discovers its enabling and releasing alternative in its exemplary artist figures. Joyce is, implicitly, the repository of a new kind of personal and cultural health when Heaney takes his hand 'like a convalescent' and feels an 'alien comfort' in his company. In this sense, the pilgrimage to the island in the poem is a large parenthesis, the brackets of which are closed by William Carleton at one end, and by James Joyce at the other – artists offering, on the mainland, their alternatives to the orthodoxies of the island, alternatives which ironically echo the very first advice Heaney is given in the poem, the unregenerate Simon Sweeney's 'Stay clear of all processions'.

Carleton's essential significance for the poem is clarified by Heaney's essay, 'A tale of two islands', where 'The Lough Derg Pilgrim', with its portrait of a culturally and materially deprived Ireland, is opposed to Synge's much better known account, in his plays and prose, of the Aran Islands – in Heaney's opinion, a glamorising of the reality in the interests of the Irish Literary Revival. The 'two islands', 'Station' and 'Aran', represent two different Irelands, realities put to virtually opposed literary and ideological uses. Carleton, in fact, is regarded very much as a nineteenth-century equivalent of Patrick Kavanagh – a teller of the true tale, from the inside, but also from a position of estrangement, of Irish rural life ('not ennobling but disabling'). In his appearance in 'Station Island', he counsels Heaney in a righteous anger (of which Heaney knows himself – it seems, shamefully – incapable) and also in the redemptive necessity, for the Irish writer, of a memory and sensibility schooled by politics as well as by the natural world: '"We are earthworms of the earth, and all that/has gone through us is what will be our trace"'. The word associated with Carleton in 'Station Island' is 'hard'. Defining his 'turncoat' politics, Heaney has him say, '"If times were hard, I could be hard too"'; and when he departs in the final line, he 'headed up the road at the same hard pace'.

His hardness is matched by Joyce's 'straightness'. In XII, 'he walked straight as a rush/upon his ash plant, his eyes fixed straight ahead'; and when he departs, 'the downpour loosed its screens

round his straight walk'. This is the straightness of his decisiveness
and authority, as he counsels the more pliable Heaney in a course
opposed to tribal and local fidelities. This account of Joyce spells
out more clearly some of the implications of Leopold Bloom's appearance at the end of 'Traditions' in *Wintering Out*. What Heaney
jokingly calls the 'Feast of the Holy Tundish' is a very secular feast,
constructed from Stephen's diary entry for 13 April, at the end of *A
Portrait of the Artist*. The entry is 'a revelation // set among my
stars' because 13 April is Heaney's birthday. In the passage referred
to, Stephen is remembering an earlier conversation with an English
Jesuit about the word 'tundish'. The priest has never heard the word
before, but it is a common usage for 'funnel' in Stephen's Dublin:

> That tundish has been on my mind for a long time. I looked it up
> and find it English and good old blunt English too. Damn the dean
> of studies and his funnel! What did he come here for to teach us his
> own language or to learn it from us? Damn him one way or the
> other!

The damnation of the Englishman is a register of Joyce's supreme
confidence in his own language, and this is a releasing and enabling
moment, a 'password', for Heaney, who inherits in his own art the
necessity of conveying uniquely Irish experience in the English language as it is spoken in Ireland. Hence Heaney's addressing Joyce as
'old father', as Stephen addresses the mythical Daedalus at the end
of the *Portrait* (and as Heaney had already addressed the Vikings in
North).

The confidence is combined, in Joyce, with that arrogant pride
and disdain which enabled him, as Heaney has put it in *Among
Schoolchildren*, to 'deconstruct the prescriptive myths of Irishness'.
Hence Joyce's concluding advice to Heaney, in this poetic undertaking which may be said similarly to deconstruct such myths, to 'keep
at a tangent', to

> 'swim
> out on your own and fill the element
> with signatures on your own frequency,
> echo soundings, searches, probes, allurements,
>
> elver-gleams in the dark of the whole sea.'

Given the interest and complexity of its conception, and the personal urgency of its themes, it is unfortunate that, in my opinion,

'Station Island' is far from entirely successful. There are some excellent things in it. Section III, for instance, with its extraordinarily inward and intimate evocation of the way the young Heaney is almost erotically possessed by the child's death, is as good as anything he has written. And the poem's most Dantean moments – McCartney's rebuke, and the fading of some of the shades – have the kind of heartbreaking poignancy which shows the lessons learnt from the 'Ugolino' translation in *Field Work*.

Nevertheless, it seems to me that the narrative and dramatic structure of the sequence is peculiarly inhibiting to Heaney's truest poetic gifts and touch. The encounters come to seem predictable and over-schematic. The dialogue is sometimes very heavy handed: 'Open up and see what you have got' and 'Not that it is any consolation, / but they were caught' are jaw-breakingly unlikely from people in any kind of passion. The symbols seem over-insistent, particularly when one remembers the great grace and delicacy with which the literal slips into the symbolic in some of the earlier work. There are moments of distinct bathos: when, in IX, after seeing the vision of the trumpet, Heaney tells us he 'pitched backwards in a headlong fall', and we are suddenly closer to slapstick than to symbolic reverie; and, more subtly perhaps, when the Joycean voice of XII seems so much more accommodating, concerned and hortatory than anything Joyce ever wrote himself – for the good reason, perhaps, that its marine imagery is much more Heaney-like than Joycean, much closer to 'Casualty' and 'Oysters' than to the *Portrait*. Finally, there are some uncertainties in the handling of verse form, particularly in Heaney's rather ragged variations on the Dantean *terza rima*. The form is notoriously difficult in English, but Heaney's variations on it are bound to summon much too closely for comfort Eliot's tremendous imitative approximation of it in the second section of 'Little Gidding', and Yeats's use of it in a poem Heaney admires in *Preoccupations*, 'Cuchulain Comforted'.

All of this is perhaps to say, in another way, that Seamus Heaney's true distinction as a poet is a lyric distinction, and that the successful larger forms he has so far found are forms which accommodate, even while they provoke and extend, his lyricism. While I cannot think that 'Station Island' with its narrative and dramatic exigencies, is such a form, it is clearly a necessary poem for Heaney to have written, one that defines a painful realignment between himself and his own culture, and brings him to that point of newly steadied illumination where it might be said of his work, as it is said of its symbol, the polyp supported by a candle, that 'the whole bright-masted thing retrieved/A course and the currents it had gone with/Were what it rode and showed.'

'SWEENEY REDIVIVUS'

Seamus Heaney's engagement with the figure of Sweeney from the medieval Irish poem *Buile Suibhne* lasted over ten years – from his earliest attempts at a translation in 1972 until its eventual publication, as *Sweeney Astray*, in 1983 in Ireland and in 1984 in England. Sweeney, in the poem, is a possibly real seventh-century Ulster king who offends the cleric St Ronan, and is punished by being cursed after the Battle of Moira in 637. Driven mad and transformed into a bird, he flies, exiled from family and tribe, over Ireland and as far as Scotland. The poem's narrative is frequently interrupted by Sweeney's poignant lyric expressions of his own misery, and by his equally sharp and tender celebrations of the Irish landscape, particularly its trees. Sweeney is therefore, as well as being a mad, exiled king, a lyric poet; and in Robert Graves's account of *Buile Suibhne* in *The White Goddess* he describes it as 'the most ruthless and bitter description in all European literature of an obsessed poet's predicament'.

Heaney recognises in the poem a crucial point in the changeover from a pagan to a Christian culture in Ireland, and he is also interested in it for political and topographical reasons; but in the introduction to his version, he spells out too some of the implications of a recognition similar to Graves's:

> ... insofar as Sweeney is also a figure of the artist, displaced, guilty, assuaging himself by his utterance, it is possible to read the work as an aspect of the quarrel between free creative imagination and the constraints of religious, political and domestic obligation.

A further aspect, in fact, of that 'quarrel' already evident in 'Station Island'; and it is difficult to read far into Heaney's version of *Buile Suibhne* without sensing some of the ways in which Sweeney's voice is harmonised with, or subdued to, Heaney's own. Sweeney uses a vocabulary familiar from Heaney's own poems – 'visitant', 'casualties', 'recitation', 'trust', 'philander', 'teems of rain', 'A sup of water. Watercress', as well as employing the thin quatrain as his most frequent lyric form. At one point, indeed, the original is 'translated' in lines which are wryly self-referential: at the conclusion of section 67, Sweeney says:

> I have deserved all this:
> night-vigils, terror,
> flittings across water,
> women's cried-out eyes.

This is another version of a sentence which concludes 'The wanderer', one of the prose-poems in *Stations*, which mythologises Heaney's departure from his first school – 'That day I was a rich young man, who could tell you now of flittings, night-vigils, letdowns, women's cried-out eyes.'

That 'rich young man' reappears in the final poem of the 'Sweeney Redivivus' sequence, 'On the Road'. In the gospel narrative of Matthew XIX, the man asks Christ what he must do to be saved, and the answer is the uncompromisingly absolute one which Heaney repeats in his poem, 'Sell all you have and give to the poor and follow me.' The demand, whether it is made in the realm of religion or of art, and whether a response to it is a real possibility or a chimera, is one that haunts the sequence, and in a sense encloses it, since 'The King of the Ditchbacks' in Part One ends in lines which bind Heaney, Sweeney and the rich young man together. That poem has brilliantly evoked the mesmerised and obsessive process of poetic translation ('He was depending on me as I hung out on the limb of a translated phrase .... Small dreamself in the branches') before its final section effects this further 'translation' which carries Heaney over, in an imagined magical rite, into Sweeney:

> And I saw myself
> rising to move in that dissimulation,
>
> top-knotted, masked in sheaves, noting
> the fall of birds: a rich young man
>
> leaving everything he had
> for a migrant solitude.

Heaney translates himself into Sweeney, then, in the context of a biblical allusion which summons to the metamorphosis notions of urgent demand, of striking out on one's own, of exile, of attempting to go beyond what is recognised and known. They make it clear why Heaney told Seamus Deane in 1977 that he thought he had discovered in Sweeney 'a presence, a fable which could lead to the discovery of feelings in myself which I could not otherwise find words for, and which would cast a dream or possibility or myth across the swirl of private feelings: an objective correlative'.

It is clear that this 'migrant solitude' is akin to the 'tangent' recommended by Joyce at the end of 'Station Island', and the actual form of the poems of 'Sweeney Redivivus' seems to bear some relation to Heaney's description of Joyce's voice, 'definite/as a steel nib's downstroke' (in *Ulysses*, Stephen refers to 'the cold steelpen' of his art). There is a definiteness, a hard edge, a sense of the thing suddenly and speedily, but finally, articulated in Heaney's free forms in these poems. They have something of the quick cut and sharpness of a trial piece, compared to what seems to me the worked over and occasionally congealed finish of 'Station Island'. In this, their forms clearly also inherit from Heaney's view of medieval Irish lyric, as he expresses it in 'The God in the Tree' in *Preoccupations*. In that essay, he compliments Flann O'Brien (who had made his own use of Sweeney in his novel, *At Swim-Two-Birds*) for his characterisation of the 'steel-pen exactness' of Irish lyric; and he also describes such lyric himself in terms appropriate to his own sequence – its 'little jabs of delight in the elemental', its combination of 'suddenness and richness', and its revelation of the writer as 'hermit' as much as 'scribe' ('Sweeney Redivivus' includes poems called 'The Hermit' and 'The Scribes').

I think it is worth adducing this larger context for 'Sweeney Redivivus', a context in which a hard and sharp kind of Irish literature puts its pressure on Heaney, since the Sweeney of *Buile Suibhne* is really only one chord of Heaney's voice in the sequence; and, despite the description, in a note, of the poems as 'glosses' on the original story, there are in fact remarkably few obvious points of correspondence. 'Sweeney' in 'Sweeney Redivivus' is the name for a personality, a different self, a congruence of impulses, a mask antithetical to much that the name 'Seamus Heaney' has meant in his previous books. In 'Envies and Identifications', Heaney defines the Yeatsian mask in terms which seem relevant to 'Sweeney':

> Energy is discharged, reality is revealed and enforced when the artist strains to attain the mask of his opposite; in the act of summoning and achieving that image, he does his proper work and leaves us with the art itself, which is a kind of trace element of the inner struggle of opposites, a graph of the effort of transcendence.

Yeats himself is, I presume, 'The Master' in the poem of that title in the sequence, which could be written almost as an allegory of what the critic Harold Bloom has called the 'anxiety of influence': the 'master' as the precursor, the poet against whom Heaney's own art must struggle in order properly to define and articulate itself. Heaney imagines Yeats as a 'rook' in the 'tower' of, presumably, his art and of his Protestant Ascendancy culture (just as Yeats did live in a tower, and entitled one of his major books *The Tower*); and the gradual coming to terms with him is the discovery that 'his book of withholding/... was nothing/arcane, just the old rules/we all had inscribed on our slates', the discovery that Yeats's notoriously private mythology conceals an apprehensible human and political meaning and relevance. Heaney's measuring of himself against this magisterial authority, which has sounded the Sweeney note of enterprising, wily self-assertion, is also, however, combined with an envious humility –

> How flimsy I felt climbing down
> the unrailed stairs on the wall,
> hearing the purpose and venture
> in a wingflap above me.

– and the poem is the trace not so much of a struggle, as of a bold but wary inspection, a revelation of how to be unafraid which is the measure of one's own authority.

That this poem is an allegory is typical of the sequence, in which allegory and parable, the puzzling and the hermetic, are the constant modes. In fact, one of Heaney's major derivations from the original source is – as the master-as-rook suggests – a series of ornithological correspondences. 'The First Flight', for instance, views Heaney's move from Belfast to Glanmore as a bird's migration; 'Drifting Off', a version of a medieval 'Boast' poem, ascribes different human (or poetic) qualities to birds; 'A Waking Dream' imagines poetic composition as the attempt to catch a bird by throwing salt on its tail (as the popular recommendation has it), but in fact being transported into flight oneself; and 'On the Road' actually locates the moment when Heaney, previously behind the wheel of a car, is lofted into flight ('I was up and away'). Apart from this system of analogy, what the original story offers 'Sweeney Redivivus' is little more than a medieval-anchorite colouring in some poems, and a tolerant hospitality to others which could just as easily have appeared without its support-system – 'In the Beech', for instance, which imagines the young Heaney in a tree, and the brilliant 'Holly'. Indeed, three poems which appear towards the end of the sequence – 'An Artist' (on Cézanne), 'The Old Icons' (on republican politics) and 'In Illo Tempore' (on the loss of religious faith) seem written more straightforwardly in Heaney's own voice, though by now clearly schooled into a 'Sweeney' scepticism and distrust.

Although the mask, then, is not worn consistently in the sequence, 'The Master' suggests its usefulness to Heaney. There it allows him the opportunity to articulate in a parable what would otherwise be virtually impossible without pretension or overweening vanity, the measuring of himself against Yeats. Elsewhere, it allows him a similar pride in his own achievement, and a tangential, dubious, sideways-on inspection of some matters already handled more straightforwardly in his earlier work. This is why 'The First Gloss' steps from its 'justified line/into the margin' only after recalling, in the metaphor, 'the shaft of the pen', the first poem in Heaney's first collection, 'Digging'. And it is why, in the poem, 'Sweeney Redivivus', and in 'Unwinding', Heaney pursues the metaphor of his head as 'a ball of wet twine/dense with soakage, but beginning/to unwind'. The 'twine' – the string made by joining together, 'twinning', two separate strands – is both Heaney and Sweeney. Its 'unwinding' is Heaney's studied attempt to dry out the 'soakage' of his heritage and, perhaps, of his more acceptable, pliable social self.

The sequence as a whole may be thought to define different stages in this process of unwinding as, in a newly suspicious perspective, Heaney reviews his life and reputation. 'In the Beech' and 'The First Kingdom' suggest how selective his earliest accounts of his first world were. 'In the Beech' sets the young Heaney in a 'boundary tree' between the old rural ways and modern military industrialism (he is thinking, I presume, of the British airforce bases in Northern Ireland during the Second World War): the latter, of course, made no appearance in *Death of a Naturalist*. 'The First Kingdom' takes a more jaundiced view of the inhabitants of that world than one would have believed possible from the author of Heaney's first book: 'And seed, breed and generation still/they are holding on, every bit/as pious and exacting and demeaned' – where 'exacting' perhaps looks back rebukingly to the 'exact' revenge of 'Punishment'.

Similarly, 'The First Flight', 'Drifting Off' and 'The Scribes' imply a more unapologetic confidence in his own work than is apparent in anything Heaney has previously written. 'The First Flight' celebrates, with a Joycean disdain, his outwitting of adverse criticism ('they began to pronounce me/a feeder off battlefields' leaps out of the parable into contemporary literary battlefields for anyone who remembers some Northern accounts of *North*); 'Drifting Off' ends with Heaney not as the Joycean 'hawklike man', but as the hawk himself, 'unwieldy/and brimming,/my spurs at the ready'; and 'The Scribes' is an almost contemptuous jousting with, again, his critics (or his peers?), which culminates when Heaney/Sweeney throws this poem itself in their faces: 'Let them remember this not inconsiderable/contribution to their jealous art.' That 'not inconsiderable' is finely judged, keeping its temper along with its *hauteur*, utterly certain that it is 'considerable'; and the poem has something of that insolence Heaney once admired in Nadezhda Mandelstam's treatment of the Soviets, 'the unthinking authority of somebody brushing a fly from her food'. This is the reverse of accommodating, it is dangerous, and one would not like to get on the wrong side of it; but its tone allies Heaney with an Irish tradition to which he has not previously given great allegiance, one that includes eighteenth-century Gaelic poetry and Austin Clarke, for instance, as well as Joyce. Heaney has chosen – temporarily, perhaps – to call this tradition 'Sweeney'; but, under whatever name, it is a salutary guard against certain kinds of sweetness and lushness which have whispered at the edge of earshot in some of his styles.

These asperities of tone are softened by a certain regretfulness in those poems in the sequence which once again review Heaney's attitude to religion and to politics. 'The Cleric', on Catholicism, seems to acknowledge, ruefully, at its close that, having once placed faith in all of that, any future sense of freedom from it will be defined by it – the familiar enough double-bind of the devout lapsed Catholic, but phrased here, in the tones of the still-pagan Sweeney reflecting on St Ronan, in a way which gives genuinely new life to the old song:

> Give him his due, in the end
>
> he opened my path to a kingdom
> of such scope and neuter allegiance
> my emptiness reigns at its whim.

'In Illo Tempore' – its title taken from the words which introduced the reading of the gospel in the old Latin mass – is perhaps Heaney's most straightforward and personal rehearsal of the theme (released, it may be, by the Sweeney mask, but not much indebted to it). Imagining Catholicism as a language one has lost the ability to speak, consigning it to '*illo tempore*', 'that time', the poem is sadly resigned rather than gratefully released; and in this it is at one, perhaps, with the reverence still felt, at some level, for the outgrown republican images in 'The Old Icons' – 'Why, when it was all over, did I hold on to them?' In these poems, which are among the best in 'Sweeney Redivivus', resolve and regret merge to create a peculiarly chastened tone, which is also peculiarly honest.

The poem which closes 'Sweeney Redivivus', and the whole of *Station Island*, 'On the Road', may be read as a kind of summary of Heaney's career to date, and the statement of an intention for the future, as it inherits and brings to fulfilment the volume's imagery of journeying, pilgrimage, quest and migration. The poem opens with that figure common in the earlier work, Heaney-as-driver, but now with the driver behind the steering wheel's 'empty round'. This is an emptiness, a space suddenly filled with the rich young man's question about salvation. Christ's invitation, accompanied by the sudden 'visitation' of the last bird in *Station Island*, provokes a response in which Heaney is translated out of that early figure and its present emptiness, into Heaney-as-Sweeney. The flight which follows, with its swooping and dipping rhythms, seems similarly to translate Christ's injunction out of the realm of religion – Heaney/Sweeney migrating from 'chapel gable' and 'churchyard wall' – into the realm of art, as it ends inside a 'high cave mouth' beside the prehistoric cave drawing of a 'drinking deer'. This is presumably related to that 'deer of poetry .../in pools of lucent sound' which appears in 'A Migration' in Part One; but in 'On the Road', its nostril is 'flared // at a dried-up source'. It is a source, nevertheless, which provides Heaney with at least the possibility of some arid renewal:

> For my book of changes
> I would meditate
> that stone-faced vigil
>
> until the long dumbfounded
> spirit broke cover
> to raise a dust
> in the font of exhaustion.

The 'font' in a church usually contains holy water, used to make the sign of the cross; but this dry 'font of exhaustion' is perhaps Seamus Heaney's equivalent of Yeats's 'foul rag-and-bone shop of the heart' at the end of 'The Circus Animals' Desertion', that point of desolation from which, alone, the new inspiration may rise. In that poem, Yeats reviews the stages of his career in some detail, and in 'On the Road', Heaney may be thought to review his own, more glancingly, in little verbal echoes of his earlier work. The road 'reeling in' remembers the roads that 'unreeled, unreeled' in that other poem of flight, 'Westering', at the end of *Wintering Out*; 'soft-nubbed' and 'incised outline' recall the archaeological diction of *North*, as the poem's chain of optatives ('I would roost ...', 'I would migrate ...', 'I would meditate ...') make again one of the characteristic grammatical figures of *North*; the 'undulant, tenor/black-letter latin' recalls the 'sweet tenor latin' of 'Leavings', and the phrase 'broke cover' recalls the badger that 'broke cover in me' in 'The Badgers', both in *Field Work*. This unobtrusive self-allusiveness makes it plain how much in Heaney's earlier 'source' is now 'dried-up', and how much directed energy and effort must go into the construction of any new 'book of changes'.

This is the final stage of self-knowledge and self-declaration to which the Sweeney mask has brought Heaney; and I find the sequence of exceptional originality and authority. Sweeney has been a more subtle, responsive and intimate means of self-dramatisation than the sometimes creaking machinery and over-earnestness of 'Station Island'. The mask has provided the opportunity for a new kind of autobiographical poetry – not 'confessionally' flat and presumptuous, not as edgily invisible as the Eliotic *personae*, not risking the sometimes histrionic grandiloquence of Yeats. Sweeney is, above all, the name for a restless dissatisfaction with the work already done, a fear of repetition, an anxiety about too casual an assimilation and acclaim, a deep suspicion of one's own reputation and excellence. He is, therefore, also an instruction to the critic, ending his account of a poet still in mid-career, against too definitive a conclusion. As Sweeney's creator and *alter ego* reminded John Haffenden, 'the tune isn't called for the poet, he calls the tune'.

From Neil Corcoran, *Seamus Heaney* (Faber Student Guides, London, 1986), pp. 153–80.

NOTES

[Taken from one of the two most useful and influential 'introductory' studies of Heaney (Blake Morrison's [London, 1982; new edition 1993] is the other one), it is in the nature of this essay largely to explain itself as it goes along. It is essentially another piece of New Criticism seeking to present Heaney as a major poet and to emphasise his authority as a significant living writer. Other writers (Dante, Carleton, Joyce, Denis Devlin, Sean O'Faolain, Austin Clarke) and works (*Buile Suibhne, Piers Plowman*, Graves's *White Goddess*) tend to be here for their intertextual significance for Heaney rather than as touchstones in evaluating his poetry. Only Eliot and Yeats are used in this latter way. *Stations* (p. 121) was a pamphlet published in Belfast in 1975. 'Envies and Identifications: Dante and the Modern Poet' (pp. 112–13) appeared in the *Irish University Review* (15:1, Spring 1985, 5–19); 'A tale of two islands: reflections on the Irish Literary Revival' (p. 117) in P.J. Drudy (ed.), *Irish Studies*, 1 (Cambridge, 1980), 1–20. For the interviews with Heaney by Deane (pp. 121–2) and Haffenden (p. 128) see Further Reading, p. 267 below. Ed.]

9

The Government of the Tongue

SEAMUS HEANEY

Reading T.S. Eliot and reading about T.S. Eliot were equally formative experiences for my generation. One of the books about him
which greatly appealed to me when I first read it in the 1960s was
The New Poetic[1] by the New Zealand poet and critic, C.K. Stead.
The title referred to that movement, critical and creative, which was
instituted in the late nineteenth century against discursive poetry,
and which Stead judged to have culminated in England with the
publication of *The Waste Land* in 1922. One of his purposes was to
show how in *The Waste Land* Eliot made a complete break with
those popular poets of the day whom Eliot's contemporary, the
Russian poet Osip Mandelstam, would have called 'the purveyors
of ready-made meaning'[2] – bluff expositors in verse of arguments or
narratives which could have been as well conducted in prose. Stead
also provided instruction and delight by sussing out titles and
reviews of books which 'the new poetry' was up against: such as
Anna Bunston's *Songs of God and Man*, perceived by the literary
pages to have 'freshness and spirituality'; Augusta Hancock's
Dainty Verses for Little Folk which were 'written in the right
spirit'; and Edwin Drew's *The Chief Incidents in the Titanic Wreck*,
which 'may appeal to those who lost relatives in this appalling cata-
strophe'. These popular volumes (of February 1913) were possessed
of a strong horsepower of common-sense meaning. The verse was a
metrical piston designed to hammer sentiment or argument into the
public ear. This was poetry that made sense, and compared to its

candour and decent comprehensibility, *The Waste Land* showed up as a bewildering aberration. In fact, Eliot's poem was hardly available enough to the average reader even to be perceived as an aberration.

Stead also pointed out that the poem was therefore defended or promoted in terms of the public's expectations. Its first defenders argued that if poetry was discourse that made sense, then *The Waste Land* was indeed discourse, except that bits of it were missing. Wrong, Stead averred. This poem 'cannot be seen accurately if it is read as a discourse from which certain "links in the chain" have been omitted'. 'No critic concerned primarily with "meaning" could touch the true "being" of the early poetry.'

The Waste Land in Stead's reading is the vindication of a poetry of image, texture and suggestiveness; of inspiration; of poetry which writes itself. It represents a defeat of the will, an emergence of the ungainsayable and symbolically radiant out of the subconscious deeps. Rational structure has been overtaken or gone through like a sound barrier. The poem does not disdain intellect, yet poetry, having to do with feelings and emotions, must not submit to the intellect's eagerness to foreclose. It must wait for a music to occur, an image to discover itself. Stead thus rehabilitated Eliot as a Romantic poet, every bit as faithful to the process of dream and as susceptible to gifts of the unconscious as Coleridge was before he received the person from Porlock.[3] And so the figure of Old Possum,[4] netted for years in skeins of finely drawn commentary upon his sources, his ideas, his criticism of the modern world and so on, this figure was helped to rise again like Gulliver in Lilliput, no longer a hazy contour of philosophy and literary allusion, but a living principle, a far more natural force than had been recognised until then.

When I thought of 'the government of the tongue' as a general title for these lectures, what I had in mind was this aspect of poetry as its own vindicating force. In this dispensation, the tongue (representing both a poet's personal gift of utterance and the common resources of language itself) has been granted the right to govern. The poetic art is credited with an authority of its own. As readers, we submit to the jurisdiction of achieved form, even though that form is achieved not by dint of the moral and ethical exercise of mind but by the self-validating operations of what we call inspiration – especially if we think of inspiration in the terms supplied by the Polish poet Anna Swir, who writes of it as a 'psychosomatic phenomenon' and goes on to declare:

This seems to me the only biologically natural way for a poem to be born and gives the poem something like a biological right to exist. A poet becomes then an antenna capturing the voices of the world, a medium expressing his own subconscious and the collective subconscious. For one moment he possesses wealth usually inaccessible to him, and he loses it when that moment is over.[5]

Poetry's special status among the literary arts derives from the audience's readiness to concede to it a similar efficacy and resource. The poet is credited with a power to open unexpected and unedited communications between our nature and the nature of the reality we inhabit.

The oldest evidence for this attitude appears in the Greek notion that when a lyric poet gives voice, 'it is a god that speaks'. And the attitude persists into the twentieth century: one thinks of Rilke's restatement of it in his *Sonnets to Orpheus* and, in English, we may cite the familiar instance of Robert Frost's essay, 'The Figure a Poem Makes'. For Frost, any interference by the knowing intellect in the purely disinterested cognitions of the form-seeking imagination constitutes poetic sabotage, an affront to the legislative and executive powers of expression itself. 'Read it a hundred times,' he says of the true poem. 'It can never lose its sense of a meaning that once unfolded by surprise as it went.' 'It begins in delight, it inclines to the impulse, it assumes direction with the first line laid down, it runs a course of lucky events and ends in a clarification of life – not necessarily a great clarification, such as sects and cults are founded on, but in a momentary stay against confusion.'[6]

In this figure of the poem's making, then, we see also a paradigm of free action issuing in satisfactorily achieved ends; we see a path projected to the dimension in which, Yeats says, 'Labour is blossoming or dancing where/The Body is not bruised to pleasure soul'.[7] And just as the poem, in the process of its own genesis, exemplifies a congruence between impulse and right action, so in its repose the poem gives us a premonition of harmonies desired and not inexpensively achieved. In this way, the order of art becomes an achievement intimating a possible order beyond itself, although its relation to that further order remains promissory rather than obligatory. Art is not an inferior reflection of some ordained heavenly system but a rehearsal of it in earthly terms; art does not trace the given map of a better reality but improvises an inspired sketch of it.

My favourite instance of this revision of the Platonic schema is Osip Mandelstam's astonishing fantasia on poetic creation, entitled

– since Dante was the pretext for the thing – 'A Conversation about Dante'. A traditional approach to Dante, naturally enough, might involve some attention to the logical, theological and numerological significances which devolve from the number 3, there being three Persons in the Holy Trinity, three lines in each stanza of *The Divine Comedy*, three books in the whole poem, thirty-three cantos in each book, and a rhyme scheme called *terza rima*. All this can press upon the mind until Dante is gradually conceived of as some kind of immense scholastic computer, programmed by Aquinas, and printing out the triadic goods in response to whatever philosophical, metrical and arithmetical data it has been fed. Dante, in other words, is often studied as the great example of a poet whose tongue is governed by an orthodoxy or system, whose free expressiveness is under the strict control of a universe of rules, from the rules of metre to the commandments of the church. Now, enter Mandelstam. Nothing, he implies, could be further from the truth. The three-edged stanza is formed from within, like a crystal, not cut on the outside like a stone. The poem is not governed by external conventions and impositions but follows the laws of its own need. Its composition had all the spontaneity of a chain reaction, of an event in nature:

> We must try to imagine, therefore, how bees might have worked at this thirteen-thousand-faceted form, bees endowed with the brilliant stereometric instinct, who attracted bees in greater and greater numbers as they were required ... Their cooperation expands and grows more complicated as they participate in the process of forming the combs, by means of which space virtually emerges out of itself.

This is extraordinarily alive and persuasive, one felicity in a work of disconcertingly abundant genius, the greatest paean I know to the power which poetic imagination wields. Indeed the tongue, which I have been employing here as a synecdoche for that same power, is analogous in this context to the conductor's baton as it is reimagined by Mandelstam. His *hommage* to the baton is too long to quote in full, but this extract should suffice to show how deeply structured in all our thinking is this idea of imagination as a shaping spirit which it is wrong to disobey:

> Which comes first, listening or conducting? If conducting is no more than the nudging along of music which rolls forth of its own accord, then of what use is it when the orchestra is good in itself, when it

performs impeccably in itself? ... This baton is far from being an external, administrative accessory or a distinctive symphonic police which could be done away with within an ideal state. It is no less than a dancing chemical formula which integrates reactions perceptible to the ear. I beg of you not to regard it merely as a supplementary mute instrument, invented for greater visibility and to provide additional pleasure. In a certain sense this invulnerable baton contains within itself all the elements in the orchestra.[8]

As ever, Mandelstam writes jubilantly and persuasively. Far from being perceived as the mouthpiece of an orthodoxy, Dante becomes for him the epitome of chemical suddenness, free biological play, a hive of bees, a hurry of pigeon flights, a flying machine whose function is to keep releasing other self-reproducing flying machines, even, in one manic extended simile, the figure of a Chinese fugitive escaping by leaping from junk to junk across a river crammed with junks, all moving in opposite directions. Dante is thus recanonised as the sponsor of impulse and instinct – not an allegory-framer up to his old didactic tricks in the middle of the journey, but a lyric woodcutter singing in the dark wood of the larynx. Mandelstam brings Dante back from the pantheon to the palate, subverts the age-old impression that his work was written on official paper, and locates his authority not in his cultural representativeness, his religious vision or his sternly unremitting morality but rather in his status as an exemplar of the purely creative, intimate, experimental act of poetry itself.

All the same, as I warm to this theme, a voice from another part of me speaks in rebuke. 'Govern your tongue,' it says, compelling me to remember that my title can also imply a *denial* of the tongue's autonomy and permission. In this reading, 'the government of the tongue' is full of monastic and ascetic strictness. One remembers Hopkins's 'Habit of Perfection', with its command to the eyes to be 'shelled', the ears to attend to silence and the tongue to know its place:

> Shape nothing, lips; be lovely-dumb:
> It is the shut, the curfew sent
> From there where all surrenders come
> Which only makes you eloquent.

It is even more instructive to remember that Hopkins abandoned poetry when he entered the Jesuits, 'as not having to do with my vocation'. This manifests a world where the prevalent values and necessities leave poetry in a relatively underprivileged situation, requiring it to take a position that is secondary to religious truth or state security or public order. It discloses a condition of public and private repressions where the undirected hedonistic play of imagination is regarded at best as luxury or licentiousness, at worst as heresy or treason. In ideal republics, Soviet republics, in the Vatican and Bible-belt, it is a common expectation that the writer will sign over his or her individual, venturesome and potentially disruptive activity into the keeping of an official doctrine, a traditional system, a party line, whatever. In such contexts, no further elaboration or exploration of the language or forms currently in place is permissible. An order has been handed down and the shape of things has been established.

We have grown familiar with the tragic destiny which these circumstances impose upon poets and with the way in which 'ungoverned' poetry and poets, in extreme totalitarian conditions, can become a form of alternative government, or government in exile. I was struck, for example, to learn that lines by the poet Czeslaw Milosz are incorporated into the memorial to the Solidarity workers outside the gates of the Lenin Shipyard in Gdansk. But I was stunned by the image which Andrei Sinyavsky provides of the subversive and necessary function of writing as truth-telling, when he tells how, at the height of the Stalin terror, Alexander Kutzenov used to seal his manuscripts in glass preserving jars and bury them in his garden at night-time.[9] It is all there, the suggestion of art's curative powers, its stored goodness and its ultimate appeal to 'the reader in posterity'. The scene has the perturbing oneiric reality of an actual dream and could stand for the kind of ominous premonition which a dictator might experience, waking in the small hours and remembering the reality of the poetry he would constrain.

For the moment, however, I am concerned with states of affairs less repressive and less malign. I am thinking not so much of authoritarian censorship as of an implacable consensus in which the acceptable themes are given variously resourceful treatments, and in which the felicity or correctness of a work's execution constitutes the conspicuous focus of attention for both audience and artist. It is not right to assume that such conditions always produce inferior art. As a poet, for example, George Herbert surrendered himself to a framework of belief and an instituted religion; but in his case, it happened that his personality was structured in such a way that he could dwell in amity with doctrine, writing a poetry which was intellectually pure, emotionally robust and entirely authentic. An unconstrained, undebilitated mind measured itself against impositions and expectations which were both fundamental and contingent to it. Its discipline, however, proved equal to its challenges, so that a pun on the work *choler*, meaning both outburst of anger and emblem of submission, could hold the psychic and artistic balance; and a rhyme of 'child' with 'wild' could put the distress of his personal predicament in a divinely ordained perspective.[10]

Moreover, what holds for George Herbert also holds for the T.S. Eliot who wrote *Four Quartets*. As C.K. Stead also pointed out, this was a poet very different from the one who wrote *The Waste Land*, one who turned from an earlier trust in process and image to embrace the claims of argument and idea. To this grave and senior figure, the example of Dante was also important, although his import was significantly different for Eliot than for Mandelstam. Both men, interestingly enough, were turning to the great Florentine at a moment of mid-life crisis, Eliot's first essay appearing in 1929 and Mandelstam's being written, though not published, in the early 1930s. (One thinks again of preserving jars in the dark garden.) Mandelstam was interested primarily in vindication by language, Eliot in salvation by conversion. Eliot's essay ends with an evocation of the world of the *Vita Nuova*, of the necessary attempt to enter it, an attempt 'as difficult and hard as rebirth', and bows out with the declaration that 'there is almost a definite moment of acceptance when the New Life begins'. Here, ten years before the *Quartets* began in earnest, Eliot's writing looks forward to the concerns of those poems. What obsessed Mandelstam and shook him into heady critical song – namely, the sensuous foragings and transports of the body of poetic language – hardly seems to interest Eliot at all. He is much more preoccupied with the philosophical and religious significances which can be drawn from a work of art, its truth quotient rather than its technique/beauty quotient, its aura of cultural and spiritual force. There is a stern and didactic profile to the Dante whom Eliot conjures up and, as he embraces a religious faith, it is to this profile he would submit in order that it be re-created in his own work.

The Eliot of *The Waste Land*, on the other hand, reproduced in his poem a sense of bewilderment and somnambulism, a flow of inventive expressionist scenes reminiscent of those which Virgil and Dante encounter in *The Divine Comedy*. In the *Inferno*,

pilgrim and guide proceed among shades in thrall to the fates of
which they have become the archetypes, in much the same way as
Eliot's poem proceeds upon the eerie flood of its own inventiveness. But in the *Quartets*, Eliot has been born again out of the
romance of symbolism into the stricter exactions of *philosophia*
and religious tradition. The inspired, spontaneous, essentially
lyric tongue has been replaced as governor by an organ that functions more like a sorrowful *grand seigneur*, meditatively, author-
itatively, yet just a little wistfully aware of its lost vitality and
insouciance.

That vitality and insouciance of lyric poetry, its relish of its own
inventiveness, its pleasuring strain, always comes under threat when
poetry remembers that its self-gratification must be perceived as a
kind of affront to a world preoccupied with its own imperfections,
pains and catastrophes. What right has poetry to its quarantine?
Should it not put the governors on its joy and moralise its song?
Should it, as Austin Clarke said in another context, take the clapper
from the bell of rhyme? Should it go as far in self-denial as
Zbigniew Herbert's poem 'A Knocker' seems to want it to go? This
translation, in the Penguin Modern European Poets series, was
originally published in 1968:

> There are those who grow
> gardens in their heads
> paths lead from their hair
> to sunny and white cities
>
> it's easy for them to write
> they close their eyes
> immediately schools of images
> stream down their foreheads
>
> my imagination
> is a piece of board
> my sole instrument
> is a wooden stick
>
> I strike the board
> it answers me
> yes – yes
> no – no
>
> for others the green bell of a tree
> the blue bell of water
> I have a knocker
> from unprotected gardens

I thump on the board
and it prompts me
with the moralist's dry poem
yes – yes
no – no

Herbert's poem ostensibly demands that poetry abandon its he-
donism and fluency, that it become a nun of language and barber its
luxuriant locks down to a stubble of moral and ethical goads.
Ostensibly too, it would depose the tongue because of its cavalier
indulgence and send in as governor of the estate of poetry a
Malvolio with a stick. It would castigate the entrancements of
poetry, substituting in their stead a roundhead's plain-spoken
counsel. Yet oddly, without the fluent evocation of bells and
gardens and trees and all those things which it explicitly deplores,
the poem could not make the bleak knocker signify as potently as it
does. The poem makes us feel that we should prefer moral utterance to palliative imagery, but it does exactly that, makes us *feel*,
and by means of feeling carries truth alive into the heart – exactly
as the Romantics said it should. We end up persuaded we are
against lyric poetry's culpable absorption in its own process by an
entirely successful instance of that very process in action: here is a
lyric about a knocker which claims that lyric is inadmissible.

All poets who get beyond the first excitement of being blessed
by the achievement of poetic form confront, sooner or later, the
question which Herbert confronts in 'A Knocker' and, if they are
lucky, they end up, like Herbert, outstripping it rather than answering it directly. Some, like Wilfred Owen, outface it by living a
life so extremely mortgaged to the suffering of others that the
tenancy of the palace of art is paid for a hundredfold. Others, like
Yeats, promulgate and practise such faith in art's absolutely ab-
solved necessity that they overbear whatever assaults the historical
and contingent might mount upon their certitude. Richard
Ellmann's statement of the Yeatsian case is finally applicable to
every serious poetic life:

> He wishes to show how brute force may be transmogrified, how we
> can sacrifice ourselves ... to our 'imagined' selves which offer far
> higher standards than anything offered by social convention. If we
> must suffer, it is better to create the world in which we suffer, and
> this is what heroes do spontaneously, artists do consciously, and all
> men do in their degree.[11]

Every poet does indeed proceed upon some such conviction, even those who are most scrupulous in their avoidance of the grand manner, who respect the democracy of language, and display by the pitch of their voice or the commonness of their subjects a readiness to put themselves on the side of those who are sceptical of poetry's right to any special status. The fact is that poetry is its own reality and no matter how much a poet may concede to the corrective pressures of social, moral, political and historical reality, the ultimate fidelity must be to the demands and promise of the artistic event.

It is for this reason that I want to discuss 'At the Fishhouses'[12] by Elizabeth Bishop. Here we see this most reticent and mannerly of poets being compelled by the undeniable impetus of her art to break with her usual inclination to conciliate the social audience. This conciliatory impulse was not based on subservience but on a respect for other people's shyness in the face of poetry's presumption: she usually limited herself to a note that would not have disturbed the discreet undersong of conversation between strangers breakfasting at a seaside hotel. Without addressing a question as immense and unavoidable as whether silence rather than poetry is not the proper response in a world after Auschwitz, she implicitly condones the doubts about art's prerogatives which such a question raises.

Elizabeth Bishop, in other words, was temperamentally inclined to believe in the government of the tongue – in the self-denying sense. She was personally reticent, opposed to and incapable of self-aggrandisement, the very embodiment of good manners. Manners, of course, imply obligations to others and obligations on the part of others to ourselves. They insist on propriety, in the good large original sense of the word, meaning that which is intrinsic and characteristic and belongs naturally to the person or the thing. They also imply a certain strictness and allow the verbs 'ought' and 'should' to come into play. In short, as an attribute of the poetic enterprise, manners place limits on the whole scope and pitch of the enterprise itself. They would govern the tongue.

But Elizabeth Bishop not only practised good manners in her poetry. She also submitted herself to the discipline of observation. Observation was her habit, as much in the monastic, Hopkinsian sense as in its commoner meaning of a customarily repeated action. Indeed, observation is itself a manifestation of obedience, an activity which is averse to overwhelming phenomena by the exercise of subjectivity, content to remain an assisting presence rather than an overbearing pressure. So it is no wonder that the title of Bishop's last book[13] was that of an old school textbook, *Geography III*. It is as if she were insisting on an affinity between her poetry and text-book prose, which establishes reliable, unassertive relations with the world by steady attention to detail, by equable classification and level-toned enumeration. The epigraph of the book suggests that the poet wishes to identify with these well-tried, primary methods of connecting words and things:

> *What is geography?*
> A description of the earth's surface.
>
> *What is the earth?*
> The planet or body on which we live.
>
> *What is the shape of the earth?*
> Round, like a ball.
>
> *Of what is the earth's surface composed?*
> Land and water.

A poetry faithful to such catechetical procedures would indeed seem to deny itself access to vision or epiphany; and 'At the Fishhouses' does begin with fastidious notations which log the progress of the physical world, degree by degree, into the world of the poet's own lucid but unemphatic awareness:

> Although it is a cold evening,
> down by one of the fishhouses
> an old man sits netting,
> his net, in the gloaming almost invisible,
> a dark purple-brown,
> and his shuttle worn and polished.
> The air smells so strong of codfish
> it makes one's nose run and one's eyes water.
> The five fishhouses have steeply peaked roofs
> and narrow, cleated gangplanks slant up
> to storerooms in the gables
> for the wheelbarrows to be pushed up and down on.
> All is silver: the heavy surface of the sea,
> swelling slowly as if considering spilling over,
> is opaque, but the silver of the benches,
> the lobster pots, and masts, scattered
> among the wild jagged rocks,
> is of an apparent translucence
> like the small old buildings with an emerald moss

growing on their shoreward walls.
The big fish tubs are completely lined
with layers of beautiful herring scales
and the wheelbarrows are similarly plastered
with creamy iridescent coats of mail,
with small iridescent flies crawling on them.
Up on the little slope behind the houses,
set in the sparse bright sprinkle of grass,
is an ancient wooden capstan,
cracked, with two long bleached handles
and some melancholy stains, like dried blood,
where the ironwork has rusted.
The old man accepts a Lucky Strike.
He was a friend of my grandfather.
We talk of the decline in the population
and of codfish and herring
while he waits for a herring boat to come in.
There are sequins on his vest and on his thumb.
He has scraped the scales, the principal beauty,
from unnumbered fish with that black old knife,
the blade of which is almost worn away.

Down at the water's edge, at the place
where they haul up the boats, up the long ramp
descending into the water, thin silver
tree trunks are laid horizontally
across the gray stones, down and down
at intervals of four or five feet.

Cold dark deep and absolutely clear,
element bearable to no mortal,
to fish and to seals … One seal particularly
I have seen here evening after evening.
He was curious about me. He was interested in music;
like me a believer in total immersion,
so I used to sing him Baptist hymns.
I also sang 'A Mighty Fortress Is Our God.'
He stood up in the water and regarded me
steadily, moving his head a little.
Then he would disappear, then suddenly emerge
almost in the same spot, with a sort of shrug
as if it were against his better judgment.
Cold dark deep and absolutely clear,
the clear gray icy water … Back, behind us,
the dignified tall firs begin.
Bluish, associating with their shadows,
a million Christmas trees stand

waiting for Christmas. The water seems suspended
above the rounded gray and blue-gray stones.
I have seen it over and over, the same sea, the same,
slightly, indifferently swinging above the stones,
icily free above the stones,
above the stones and then the world.
If you should dip your hand in,
your wrist would ache immediately,
your bones would begin to ache and your hand would burn
as if the water were a transmutation of fire
that feeds on stones and burns with a dark gray flame.
If you tasted it, it would first taste bitter,
then briny, then surely burn your tongue.
It is like what we imagine knowledge to be:
dark, salt, clear, moving, utterly free,
drawn from the cold hard mouth
of the world, derived from the rocky breasts
forever, flowing and drawn, and since
our knowledge is historical, flowing, and flown.

What we have been offered, among other things, is the slow-motion
spectacle of a well-disciplined poetic imagination being tempted to
dare a big leap, hesitating, and then with powerful sureness actually
taking the leap. For about two-thirds of the poem the restraining,
self-abnegating, completely attentive manners of the writing keep
us alive to the surfaces of a world: the note is colloquial if tending
towards the finical, the scenery is chaste, beloved and ancestral.
Grandfather was here. Yet this old world is still being made new
again by the sequins of herring scales, the sprinkle of grass and the
small iridescent flies. Typically, detail by detail, by the layering of
one observation upon another, by readings taken at different levels
and from different angles, a world is brought into being. There is a
feeling of ordered scrutiny, of a securely positioned observer
turning a gaze now to the sea, now to the fish barrels, now to the
old man. And the voice that tells us about it all is self-possessed but
not self-centred, full of discreet and intelligent instruction, of the
desire to witness exactly. The voice is neither breathless nor detached; it is thoroughly plenished, like the sea 'swelling slowly as if
considering spilling over', and then, thrillingly, half-way through, it
does spill over:

Cold dark deep and absolutely clear,
element bearable to no mortal,
to fish and to seals ... One seal particularly

Just a minute ago I said that the habit of observation did not promise any irruption of the visionary. Yet here it is, a rhythmic heave which suggests that something other is about to happen – although not immediately. The colloquial note creeps back and the temptation to inspired utterance is rebuked by the seal who arrives partly like a messenger from another world, partly like a dead-pan comedian of water. Even so, he is a sign which initiates a wonder as he dives back into the deep region where the poem will follow, wooed with perfect timing into the mysterious. Looking at the world of the surface, after all, is not only against the better judgement of a seal; it is finally also against the better judgement of the poet.

It is not that the poet breaks faith with the observed world, the world of human attachment, grandfathers, Lucky Strikes and Christmas trees. But it is a different, estranging and fearful element which ultimately fascinates her: the world of meditated meaning, of a knowledge-need which sets human beings apart from seals and herrings, and sets the poet in her solitude apart from her grandfather and the old man, this poet enduring the cold sea-light of her own *wyrd*[14] and her own mortality. Her scientific impulse is suddenly jumped back to its root in pre-Socratic awe, and water stares her in the face as the original solution:

> If you should dip your hand in,
> your wrist would ache immediately
> your bones would begin to ache and your hand would burn
> as if the water were a transmutation of fire
> that feeds on stones and burns with a dark gray flame.
> If you tasted it, it would first taste bitter,
> then briny, then surely burn your tongue.
> It is like what we imagine knowledge to be:
> dark, salt, clear, moving, utterly free,
> drawn from the cold hard mouth
> of the world, derived from the rocky breasts
> forever, flowing and drawn, and since
> our knowledge is historical, flowing, and flown.

This writing still bears a recognisable resemblance to the simple propositions of the geography textbook. There is no sentence which does not possess a similar clarity and unchallengeability. Yet since these concluding lines are poetry, not geography, they have a dream truth as well as a daylight truth about them, they are as hallucinatory as they are accurate. They also possess that *sine qua non* of all lyric utterance, a completely persuasive inner cadence which is deeply intimate with the laden water of full tide. The lines are inhabited by certain profoundly true tones, which as Robert Frost put it, 'were before words were, living in the cave of the mouth',[15] and they do what poetry most essentially does: they fortify our inclination to credit promptings of our intuitive being. They help us to say in the first recesses of ourselves, in the shyest, pre-social part of our nature, 'Yes, I know something like that too. Yes, that's right; thank you for putting words on it and making it more or less official.' And thus the government of the tongue gains our votes, and Anna Swir's proclamation (which at first may have sounded a bit overstated) comes true in the sensation of reading even a poet as shy of bardic presumption as Elizabeth Bishop:

> A poet becomes then an antenna capturing the voices of the world, a medium expressing his own subconscious and the collective subconscious.

In the three lectures which follow, I shall explore the ways in which W.H. Auden, Robert Lowell and Sylvia Plath each contrived to become 'an antenna'. And in concluding this one, I want now to offer two further 'texts' for meditation. The first is from T.S. Eliot. Forty-four years ago, in October 1942, in wartime London, when he was at work on 'Little Gidding', Eliot wrote in a letter to E. Martin Browne:

> In the midst of what is going on now, it is hard, when you sit down at a desk, to feel confident that morning after morning spent fiddling with words and rhythms is justified activity – especially as there is never any certainty that the whole thing won't have to be scrapped. And on the other hand, external or public activity is more of a drug than is this solitary toil which often seems so pointless.[16]

Here is the great paradox of poetry and of the imaginative arts in general. Faced with the brutality of the historical onslaught, they are practically useless. Yet they verify our singularity, they strike and stake out the ore of self which lies at the base of every individuated life. In one sense the efficacy of poetry is nil – no lyric has ever stopped a tank. In another sense, it is unlimited. It is like the writing in the sand in the face of which accusers and accused are left speechless and renewed.

I am thinking of Jesus's writing as it is recorded in Chapter 8 of John's Gospel, my second and concluding text:

> And the scribes and Pharisees brought unto him a woman taken in adultery; and when they had set her in the midst,
>
> They say unto him, Master, this woman was taken in adultery, in the very act.
>
> Now Moses in the law commanded us, that such should be stoned: but what sayest thou?
>
> This they said, tempting him, that they might have to accuse him. But Jesus stooped down, and with his finger wrote on the ground, as though he heard them not.
>
> So when they continued asking him, he lifted up himself, and said unto them, He that is without sin among you, let him first cast a stone at her.
>
> And again he stooped down, and wrote on the ground.
>
> And they which heard it, being convicted by their own conscience, went out one by one, beginning at the eldest, even unto the last: and Jesus was left alone, and the woman standing in the midst.
>
> When Jesus had lifted up himself, and saw none but the woman, he said unto her, Woman, where are those thine accusers? hath no man condemned thee?
>
> She said, No man, Lord. And Jesus said unto her, Neither do I condemn thee: go, and sin no more.

The drawing of those characters is like poetry, a break with the usual life but not an absconding from it. Poetry, like the writing, is arbitrary and marks time in every possible sense of that phrase. It does not say to the accusing crowd or to the helpless accused, 'Now a solution will take place', it does not propose to be instrumental or effective. Instead, in the rift between what is going to happen and whatever we would wish to happen, poetry holds attention for a space, functions not as distraction but as pure concentration, a focus where our power to concentrate is concentrated back on ourselves.

This is what gives poetry its governing power. At its greatest moments it would attempt, in Yeats's phrase, to hold in a single thought reality and justice.[17] Yet even then its function is not essentially supplicatory or transitive. Poetry is more a threshold than a path, one constantly approached and constantly departed from, at which reader and writer undergo in their different ways the experience of being at the same time summoned and released.

From Seamus Heaney, *The Government of the Tongue* (London, 1988), pp. 91–108.

NOTES

[Heaney explains (*Preocccupations: Selected Prose 1968–1978* [London, 1980], pp. 13–14) that his early essays were written in the days of 'Practical Criticism' (another way of describing what I am calling New Criticism) and although later essays like this one are more discursive and allusive than those in *Preoccupations* they are still predominantly New Critical. Heaney must be aware that poststructuralists like Barthes and Foucault claim that authors don't matter; certainly he insists on seeing the value and the different modes of operation of poetry as inseparable from the strenuously committed life of the poet. Hence his attention to Eastern European poetry where this connection seems obvious.

The range of Heaney's literary reference (constantly relevant to his own poetry as his expositors are well aware) can only be represented adequately here by a sequence of editorial end-notes. Ed.]

1. C.K. Stead, *The New Poetic* (London, 1964).

2. '[T]ranslators of ready-made meaning': Heaney met this phrase (he misremembered a word) in Nadezhda Mandelstam's *Hope Against Hope* (Harmondsworth, 1979, p. 225). She locates it in Mandelstam's 'Conversation about Dante' but was probably referring to a different draft of that essay to the authorised version (See Jane Gary Harris's editorial note in *Mandelstam: The Complete Critical Prose and Letters*, trans. Jane Gary Harris and Constance Link (Ann Arbor, MI, 1979), p. 677.

3. See Coleridge's introductory note to 'Kubla Khan', *The Poems of Samuel Taylor Coleridge* (London, 1954), pp. 295–7.

4. An allusion to Eliot's book of verse for children, *Old Possum's Book of Practical Cats* (London, 1939).

5. Quoted by Czeslaw Milosz in his 'Introduction' to *Happy as a Dog's Tail: Poems by Anna Swir*, trans. Czeslaw Milosz with Leonard Nathan (New York, 1985), p. xiv.

6. *Complete Poems of Robert Frost* (New York, 1967), p. vi.

7. Yeats, 'Among Schoolchildren', ll.57–8.

8. Jane Gary Harris (ed.), *Mandelstam: the Complete Critical Prose and Letters*, trans. Jane Gary Harris and Constance Link (Ann Arbor, MI, 1979), pp. 409, 426.

9. See Terz, Abram (Andrei Sinyavsky), 'The Literary Process in Russia', *Kontinent 1 : the Alternative Voice of Russia and Eastern Europe* (London, 1976), pp. 73–4.

10. See the title and ll.35–6 of Herbert's poem 'The Collar'.

11. See Richard Ellmann, *The Identity of Yeats* (2nd edn, 1964; London, 1975), p. xxiv.

12. Elizabeth Bishop, *Complete Poems* (London, 1970), pp. 72–4.

13. Elizabeth Bishop, *Geography III* (London, 1977).

14. Word used in the Old English elegiac tradition for 'fate' or 'ordained course of events'. See B.J. Timmer, '*Wyrd* in Anglo-Saxon Prose and Poetry', *Neophilologus*, 26 (1940–1), 24–33, 213–28.

15. Frost to Walter Prichard Eaton, 18 September 1915. *Selected Letters*, ed. Lawrance Thompson (London, 1965), p. 191.

16. E. Martin Browne, *The Making of Eliot's Plays* (Cambridge, 1969), p. 158.

17. Yeats, *A Vision* (London, 1974), p. 25.

10

The Sign of the Cross: Review of *The Government of the Tongue*

THOMAS DOCHERTY

Seamus Heaney's new collection of critical pieces falls into two sections. The first brings together reviews, articles and lectures concerned with some poets who are more or less close to Heaney's own work: Kavanagh, Larkin, Walcott, all writers who problematise the notion of the poet's (literal) 'place', the poet's 'Here'-ness, as Larkin might have thought it. This is followed by considerations of a body of work which raises questions of the poet's place in language – poetry in translation – firstly from the Irish and then from the languages of the Eastern bloc. Finally, the second section of the book comprises Heaney's ruminations on 'the government of the tongue' in Auden, Lowell and Plath, the substance of his T.S. Eliot memorial lectures.

Near the end of the collection of essays, reviews and lectures, Heaney calls to mind Lowell's refusal to read at President Johnson's White House Festival of Arts in the 1960s. Lowell remarked then that 'every serious artist knows that he cannot enjoy public celebration without making subtle public commitments'.[1] Since he quotes this with approval, Heaney must have been troubled by a similar thought when invited to give the T.S. Eliot memorial lectures in 1986. Certainly, the essays gathered together here address the pressing issue of *conscience*. Indeed Heaney focuses on 'the role of the poet as conscience, one who wakens us to a possible etymology of that word as meaning our capacity to know the same thing together' (p. 130). This 'conscience' is later itself 'known together' with another term, 'confusion', which recurs in Frost's well-known phrase, much cited here, in which he suggested that poetry offers a 'momentary stay against confusion'. Heaney writes of Lowell's act of *conscientious objection* defining it as one in which 'doctrine, ancestry and politics *fused* themselves in one commanding stroke and Lowell succeeded in uniting the aesthetic instinct with the obligation to witness morally and significantly in the realm of public action' (p. 133; italics added). At this point, 'conscience' and 'confusion' are themselves conscientiously confused.

These two words, and their binding confusion with each other, alert us to the interweaving of two guiding threads in Heaney's criticism. On the one hand, there is a major concern with ethics, with the question of the relation of I to Thou, to borrow the terms from Buber favoured by Heaney;[2] on the other, there is a concern which often crosses with the first, warps its possibility of articulation, and this is the political dialectic, familiar to poststructuralist thought, of Identity and Difference. The figure made in this weft, and the real centre of Heaney's attentions here, is that of the critical poet herself or himself, the poet trapped in crisis, between the demands of what Heaney describes as two musics, one of celebration and one of suffering; or, in another troping of the same opposition, between the aesthetic demands of poetry and the historical demands of ethics and politics.

It is, perhaps, in the 'conscientious confusion' of these essays, their desire to discover some fundamental 'identity', a 'capacity to know the same thing together', between, say, the poets of Ireland and those of the Eastern bloc countries, that one finds the most productive crux in Heaney's critical thinking. There is a labyrinthine, or poetic, logic to the essays as a whole; but this logic reveals a particular limitation in Heaney's politicisation of the aesthetic or poetical 'conscience'. Theoretically, Heaney proceeds as if criticism were itself productive of such conscience, as if it aided in the understanding of poetry, in allowing the reader to know the same thing together with the writer. And yet there lingers in Heaney an element of distrust of that notion, as his lecture on Auden here makes clear. He discusses Auden's well-charted obscurities, and remarks that the poet's obscurity 'excludes' him but does not bother him: 'I am now content that Auden should practise such resistance to the reader's expectations; I take pleasure in its opacity and am ready to accept its obscurity – even if it is wilful – as a symptom of this poet's insistence upon the distance between art and life' (p. 121). Here, it is the very *denial* of 'conscience', the refusal of the postulation of 'identity', which makes Auden's poem fully operational. The problematic limitation in the politicisation of aesthetics in this collection of essays lies here, in the function of criticism itself as some supposed aid to understanding, or more precisely 'conscience'.

In terms of the political dialectic between identity and difference which is axiomatic to Heaney's understanding of conscience here, there is a fairly consistent orientation or earthy magnetism drawing Heaney towards the prioritisation of the pole of 'identity'. What this means, in short, is a rejection of 'difference', a rejection in which one can discover a 'blind spot' in Heaney's relation of politics to aesthetics. Clearly and overtly concerned with emancipation, Heaney in this collection of essays betrays in his own language a readiness to reduce alterity to identity, to commit precisely the same kind of 'imperialism of understanding' from which, Heaney reminds us, so many writers from the Eastern bloc have suffered. These writers can only be heard, are only available for poetry, in so far as they 'govern their tongue' and speak decorously, or in a mode which is 'understandable' or which can be accommodated by the ideologies under which they suffer. And yet there is also a realisation in Heaney here that this stance is not enough, and a deep awareness that a poetry which *defies* understanding is the most vital, the most politically emancipating. In other words, and contra Frost, Heaney validates here, perhaps despite himself, a poetry of confusion. This phrase, 'a poetry of confusion', is, however, ambiguous. On the one hand, it refers to a poetry in which one witnesses the reduction of difference or alterity to identity and sameness, a poetry which works through *anamnesis* to recall to the reader that which she or he has always already known, phenomenologically 'fusing' reader and writer in an instant of consciousness or 'conscience'. But on the other hand, it also refers to a poetry which operates in direct contrast with this, a poetry whose function is to stir anarchic confusion by being precisely *incomprehensible*, a poetry whose tongue is 'ungoverned' and indecorous or at odds with the dominant ideology through which a social formation understands or knows itself.

It is for this reason, clearly, that poetry in translation will play such an important role in Heaney's current critical thinking; for such poetry, almost by definition, will problematise understanding as such. The problem is set out right from the start, when Heaney indicates that:

> In the course of this book, Mandelstam and other poets from Eastern bloc countries are often invoked. I keep returning to them because there is something in their situation that makes them attractive to a reader whose formative experience has been largely Irish. There is an unsettled aspect to the different worlds they inhabit, and one of the challenges they face is to survive amphibiously, in the realm of 'the times' and the realm of their moral and artistic self-respect, a challenge immediately recognisable to anyone who has lived with the awful and demeaning facts of Northern Ireland's history over the last couple of decades.
>
> (p. xx)

The magnetic attraction of such writers draws Heaney here primarily because of their alterity, the 'different worlds they inhabit; and yet such 'different worlds' turn out to be 'immediately recognisable', always already known: 'Gdansk' is 'Derry' in a different accent; 'Voronezh' is a particular inflection of 'Belfast', and so on. Such 'confusion' or translation here allows for the production of a musical harmony, a kind of Owenesque pararhyme between, say, Heaney and Brodsky, Larkin and Esenin; or, in specific relation to the essays printed here, between Kavanagh and Lowell, writer of the *Mills of the Kavanaughs*, and so on. And yet a political harmonisation of 'different worlds' is not simply achieved through the aesthetic or poetic device of pararhyme, as Heaney is well aware; more importantly, nor is it entirely desirable. But Heaney – here at least – does not acknowledge the possibility that this kind of harmonic convergence of different worlds might be undesirable. In the claim to understand translation, poems which are uprooted from their cultural and political or historical provenance, there is at work what might be termed an 'imperialism of thought', in which the critic reduces the potential anarchic confusion produced by obscure 'foreign' writing through a reduction of that alterity to identity, through the production of 'conscience' in Heaney's terms. But it is precisely such an imperialism of thought which has made for the problems of writers such as Mandelstam, Akhmatova, Tsvetaeva, Holub and many others in the first place. It might be more conscientious to accept the radical incomprehensibility of such writings, to refuse to reduce their problems to the status of the merest aspects of our own; to refuse what is essentially a bland political identification made in the interests of the production of an aesthetic harmony.

But there is another aspect of this which is of importance in these essays. Heaney is making a radical shift in the orientation of his own writing, and these essays offer in some ways an *apologia pro poemate meo'*:

> Might we not nowadays affirm ... that the shortest way to Whitby, the monastery where Caedmon sang the first Anglo-Saxon verses, is via Warsaw and Prague?
>
> (pp. 40–1)

Magnetic North is turning here to an 'easter rising', and Heaney is conceding a secondary axis, one which was of extreme importance to his Modernist precursors, Yeats and, of course, Eliot in whose memory these lectures are written. But this is tantamount to making articulate a suggestion which haunts these texts. Heaney, concerned with criticism, finds himself here at a moment of crisis, a moment of literal self-crossing. He is caught between the desire for identity and conscience on the one hand and the awareness of the necessity of difference and the political demand for a song of discord on the other, a poetry which will stir confusion. He is also, clearly, on a metaphorical geopolitical crux between two axes. It is as if he finds a solution to his crisis by a covert theology. These essays mark the horizontal axis which complements the vertical axis of the earlier poetry (and the prose in *Preoccupations* too, of course), making a textual figure, a weaving of a sign of a cross. Heaney here seems to find some act of blessing, a theological act, as a figure for the redemption of the conflict between aesthetics and politics. When he explicitly invokes Jesus, it is as a *writer*, writing in the sand when confronted with a crowd eager to stone in hard judgement a woman caught in adultery or betrayal. And Jesus's position, as described by Heaney here, seems to be analogous to the position of crisis in which the poet/critic is located:

> The drawing of those characters is like poetry, a break with the usual life but not an absconding from it. Poetry, like the writing, is arbitrary and marks time in every possible sense of that phrase. It does not say to the accusing crowd or to the helpless accused, 'Now a solution will take place', it does not propose to be instrumental or effective. Instead, in the rift between what is going to happen and whatever we would wish to happen, poetry holds attention for a

> space, functions not as distraction but as pure concentration, a focus
> where our power to concentrate is concentrated back on ourselves.
> This is what gives poetry its governing power.
>
> (p. 108)

Poetry thus operates rather like a rest in a musical phrase, according to this, as a powerful but passive silence. There arises a somewhat mystical view of poetry here, one which pays enormous political dividends in principle, but which Heaney does not fully draw in these essays, concerned as they are with the possibility of understanding and comprehending difference by reducing it to an aspect of identity. Heaney opens the entire collection with a brief narrative, in which the singer David Hammond and himself were about to record some songs and poems for a friend in Michigan. On their way to make the recording, a contrary music, a music of discord, broke in: explosions and the sirens of ambulances and fire engines announced that a political history was going on even as Heaney and Hammond proposed to celebrate 'conscience' in the recording studio. This opening raises Heaney's fundamental problem of the relation of aesthetics to politics, a problem which, I suggest, he solves through the ghostly presence of a theology. But it also raises the whole question of understanding or hearing which seems crucial here.

In what is the most consequential critical piece here, on Plath, Heaney recounts another narrative allegory of the progress of the poet, this time from Wordsworth's great poem of deflection and deferral, *The Prelude*. The passage of 'The Boy of Winander' offers a tripartite staging for poetry. In the first stage, the poet learns, like the boy, how to whistle in the most basic of modes. Secondly, the poet then finds a mode of whistling 'in tune', in a kind of harmony with the owls or birds which surround him in nature. But there is a third stage in which the poet cannot sing at all, a stage in which the poet's task seems to be to hear the 'melodies and hieroglyphics of the world; the workings of the active universe ... are echoed far inside him' (p. 163). Here, the poem comes as a kind of gift, and it is the poet's task not to sing but to bear witness, to allow a poetry to articulate itself through the more or less unconscious body. It is here that the poet can begin to hear the alterity, the incomprehensible otherness which Heaney strives after in the political dialectic. The 'sirens' must be heard, but Heaney, as Ulysses, must also crucify himself on the mast as he hears them; there is the suggestion all the way through this collection that Heaney regards that suffering in the east as the primary condition of great poetry. It is this that he wishes to identify himself with; but this necessitates the flight from home, in every sense of the word, the flight from comfort and from the known; it requires a desire to sail into the unknown, to make the real move eastwards. In this, the reader of poetry would, perhaps for the first time, acknowledge its difficulty, would release poetry into its full incomprehensibility and obscurity. And she or he would thus find a mode of emancipation from the self and from the claim upon identity, a claim which fundamentally reposes in imperialist thinking, and in the desire not to hear the Other, not to hear the discordant music of Eliot's Keatsian nightingale whose song is a kind of 'poison in the ears', a song of discord, not a harmony: 'Jug jug'. In this way, poetry becomes not the repository of the possibility of anamnesis; rather, it opens the possibility of a future in which, to put this in Rilke's words here cited (in translation) by Heaney: 'You must change your life' (p. 14).

From *Irish Review*, No 5 (Autumn 1988), 112–16

NOTES

[Thomas Docherty's review is the clearest example in this New Casebook of 'deconstruction', a mode of analysis favoured by Jacques Derrida and other poststructuralists. It is not at first easy to follow and you might find it helpful to reread the detailed account of its linguistic ploys and reversals provided in the Introduction to this volume. Docherty detects an underlying binary opposition between 'identity' and 'alterity' in Heaney's discourse. By displaying how such terms achieve their meaning through their difference from each other, each carrying the 'trace' of the other, Docherty sets out to overturn Heaney's preferred hierarchy (in which 'identity' is privileged over 'alterity'). Docherty suggests that it is 'the ghostly presence of a theology' (the authority with which Jesus writes in the dust in Heaney's last long quotation) (p. 144 above) which prevents the poet from abandoning 'imperialist thinking' in aesthetic and ideological matters alike. This piece is like Eagleton's review of *Field Work* (essay 7) in drawing attention to the political implications of Heaney's aesthetic stance in the pages of a general literary magazine. Ed.]

1. Lowell's refusal to read at the White House in 1965 is documented by Steven Gould Axelrod (*Robert Lowell: Life and Art* [Princeton, NJ, 1978], pp. 180–1. [Ed.]

2. Heaney 'favours' the terminology of Martin Buber (*I and Thou* [1923; trans R.G. Smith, Edinburgh, 1937]) in his essay on Auden on p. 126 of *The Government of the Tongue*. He associates the obscurity of Auden's earlier poetry with Buber's 'I–Thou' relationship: the later poetry, says Heaney, is stronger on the relationship of the subject with things, of 'I' with 'It'. [Ed.]

11

'Pap for the Dispossessed':[1] Seamus Heaney and the Poetics of Identity

DAVID LLOYD

I

> I believe they are afflicted with a sense of history that was once the
> peculiar affliction of the poets of other nations who were not them-
> selves natives of England but who spoke the English language ... A
> desire to preserve indigenous traditions, to keep open the imagina-
> tion's supply lines to the past ... to perceive in these a continuity of
> communal ways, and a confirmation of an identity which is threat-
> ened – all this is signified by their language.
> (Seamus Heaney, 'Englands of the Mind', *Preoccupations*, p. 150)

The centrality of the question of identity to Irish writing and critical discussion of it since the nineteenth century is not due simply
to the contingent influence of political preoccupations. Rather, it
indicates the crucial function performed by literature in the articulation of those preoccupations, inasmuch as literary culture is
conceived as offering not merely a path towards the resolution,
but the resolution itself of the problems of subjective and political
identity. At present, the Irish poet whose work has most evidently
gained such authority is Seamus Heaney, the dust-jackets of
whose volumes of poetry since *Field Work* carry such banal assertions as 'Everyone knows by now that Heaney is a major
poet ...'[2] Heaney's quasi-institutional acceptance on both sides of the

Atlantic as a major poet and bearer of the tradition coincides with a tendency to regard his work as articulating important intuitions of Irish identity, and as uttering and reclaiming that identity beyond the divisive label, 'Anglo-Irishness'. Therefore, it is not untimely to interrogate these assumptions in the context of an historical elaboration of the principal concepts which founded and still dominate literary and political formulations of Irish identity.

An isomorphism can be traced not only between Heaney's formulations of his poetic and the poetic theories current at the inception of Irish nationalism, but furthermore, between his poetic and the aesthetic politics whose 'atavisms' and 'archetypes' it pretends to sound. This is not to suggest, with some, the uncanny 'Orphic' potential of this poet to 'lead us through that psychic hinterland which we will have to chart before we can emerge from the northern crisis', or even to substantiate the interpretative validity of his 'unwavering pursuit of a myth through which we might understand Northern Ireland today'.[3] Rather, it is to address a crucial insufficiency in the poetic itself, one which permits Heaney to pose delusory moral conflicts whose real form can better be understood as a contradiction between the ethical and the aesthetic elements of bourgeois ideology. Heaney's inability to address such contradictions stringently stems from the chosen basis of his poetic in the concept of identity. Since this concept subtends the ethical and aesthetic assumptions that his poetry registers as being in conflict, and yet thoroughly informs his work, he is unable ever to address the relation between politics and writing more than superficially, in terms of thematic concerns, or superstitiously, in terms of a vision of the poet as a diviner of the hypothetical pre-political consciousness of his race.

It is within the matrix of British Romanticism that the question of Irish identity is posed, with the result that the critique of imperialism is caught up within reflected forms of imperialist ideology. This is already apparent in the initial formulations on literature and identity of Young Ireland's ideologists in the 1840s, which in fact present the predicament they would pretend to be resolving. The nationalist critic D.F. MacCarthy provides a representative instance. Insisting that any knowledge of a people's genius is incomplete 'unless it be based upon the revelations they themselves have made, or the confessions they have uttered', MacCarthy argues that full knowledge of the ballad poetry of Ireland would furnish not only an aid to an archaeology of the Irish genius, but the very foundation on which an Irish literature might construct a distinctive identity:

> that we can be thoroughly Irish in our feelings without ceasing to be English in our speech; that we can be faithful to the land of our birth, without being ungrateful to that literature which has been 'the nursing mother of our minds'; that we can develop the intellectual resources of our country, and establish for ourselves a distinct and separate existence in the world of letters without depriving ourselves of the advantages of the widely-diffused and genius-consecrated language of England, are facts that I conceive cannot be too widely disseminated.[4]

Beneath the affirmation of MacCarthy's text persists the disturbance in which it originates, an apprehension of the real state of Ireland, its identifications split between the 'real' and the 'nursing' mother.

This passage, and its implicit resolution, is representative of Irish nationalist thinking in the nineteenth century: rather than oppose their apprehension of a real incoherence against the imperial call to union and identity, the Irish nationalists chose to seek an alternative principle of unity on which to base their opposition. Hence it is for the writer to seek beyond the evidence of disintegration for counter-evidence of the continuity of an Irish spirit in his writings. What allows him privileged access to that spirit – and here the argument is resolutely circular – is his total integration with it, 'saturated with Irish feeling ... sympathising in every beat of an Irish peasant's pulse', as an anonymous contributor in the Young Ireland journal of the 1840s, the *Nation*, phrases it.[5]

The writer, like the analogous figure of the martyr, attains 'saturation' with meaning, and hence representativeness, for nationalism by partaking of that which he represents, the spirit of the nation. Both represent the ideal resolution of the problem faced by the ideologists of the bourgeois nation state which comes into existence by deposing 'arbitrary' power: how, that is, 'to reconcile individual liberty with association'.[6] The resolution is primarily ethical, since it locates the nature and form of human liberty in identification with the spirit or *Geist* of the people. The identity of the individual, his integrity, is expressed by the degree to which that individual identifies himself with and integrates his differences in a national consciousness. This identification becomes in Ireland, as across the whole spectrum of European nationalisms, a precondition to politics rather than a political option.[7] But while the martyr provides the high points or, as the 1916 nationalist leader Patrick Pearse was later to express it, the 'burning symbols', through which the call to identity achieves its moments of intensity, it is the function of the writer to mediate the continuity of the national spirit. The distinctively Irish literature intended by nationalist theorists was to have uncovered a common ground beneath political conflicts, whether between peasant and landlord, Catholic and Protestant, or class and class, which could then be seen as mere surface phenomena of Irish society. In such a way, Irish literature was to become a 'central institution or idea', forming a 'social bond' to replace the historically evolved constitution that was thought to override and integrate social differences in England. Twenty years before Arnold's famous formulations, Irish culture is envisaged as performing the work of integration, uniting simultaneously class with class and the primitive with the evolved.[8]

Writing is accordingly endowed with the function of grounding, a term which serves to conduct the uneasy shifts between organic metaphors of the spirit and growth of the nation and architectural metaphors of the construction of an institution. The slogan of the *Nation* succinctly expresses the ramifications of the nationalist project: 'To foster public opinion and make it racy of the soil.' The act of fostering, by which a people 'separated from their forefathers' are to be given back an alternative yet equally arbitrary and fictive paternity, is renaturalised through the metaphor of grounding: through its rootedness in the primary soil of Ireland, the mind of Ireland will regain its distinctive savour. The 'root' meaning of culture is implicit here, and certainly, in so far as a literary culture is envisaged as the prime agent and ground of unification, it is literary taste which is subjected to the most rigorous 'reterritorialisation'. In an essay entitled 'Our National Language' Thomas Davis diagnosed the consequences of imposing a foreign language on a native population as a primary deterritorialisation, a decoding of the primitive relation of the Irish to their territory, 'tearing their identity from all places'.[9] That deterritorialisation is seen by Davis as occurring in three main forms: in the relation of identity to territory, in the relation of place-name to territory, in the relation of the people to their history, envisaged as the continuity of a patrimony. Language mediates each of these relations. The reterritorialisation of language as the literary language of culture is accordingly threefold. The

identification of the writer with that spirit of the nation which his researches reveal supplies his relation to the 'entail of feeling' which
links him to his patrimony; that identification similarly ensures the
revitalisation of the relation of his language to native place or
ground, despite the fact that that language will, as MacCarthy was
only too aware, be English; and thirdly, the revitalised relation of
writer to place sutures that writer's formerly ruptured identity, en-
suring, as if to complete the topology, his relation to the paternal
spirit or genius of the nation. Since nationalism offers a theory of the
integration of the individual subject with the destiny of the race, it is
not surprising that the dynamic sketched above resembles that of the
'family romance' by which, supposedly, the victory of the race over
the individual is achieved.[10] As in the family, so in the nation, as nationalist ideologists have so often stressed. Within the triangle of his
family romance, the writer mediates between his motherland and a
symbolic fatherland. He elevates his imaginary relation with the land
of his birth to an identification with a spiritual nation which is that
of his forefathers in the double sense of *their* possession and *his*
inheritance. His identity is thus assured in assuring the quasi-
procreative relationship between land and culture.

The recourse to the 'racial archetype', in the ever more
commodified and familiar images of Irish nationalism, and the manipulation of the relation of Irishness to Irish ground, linked as
these are through Kathleen Ní Houlihán, the motherland, together
produce the forms in which the aestheticisation of Irish politics is
masked. Aesthetics, understood here to be ultimately the concept
of man as producer and as producer of himself through his prod-
ucts, posits an original identity which precedes difference and
conflict and which is to be reproduced in the ultimate unity that
aesthetic works both prefigure and prepare. The naturalisation of
identity effected by an aesthetic ideology serves to foreclose historical process and to veil the constitution of subjects and issues in
continuing conflict, while deflecting both politics and ethics into a
hypothetical domain of free play.[11] This is, *par excellence*, the
domain of culture, envisaged by Arnold as the end of historical
process and as the timeless zone within time where one may cultivate one's 'best self' beyond or outside historical conflict. Aesthetic
politics in turn represents images of origin and unity to convey an
ethical demand for the political coherence which will override
whatever differences impede a unification in continuity with
original identity.

It would be generally true to say that the history of Ireland in the last seventy years – to regress no further – exemplifies both the efficacy and the disabling contradictions of the politics of identity. The peculiar and largely anomalous position of Ireland as an ex-colonial state in a Western European context has led to political and social developments which are untypical of, but by no means entirely alien to, the general political frame of recent European history. Nationalism, and the concomitant concern with racial and cultural identity, are, as has been suggested, political phenomena, oriented towards the production of a sense of popular unity and conceived within a generally oppositional framework. Under normal circumstances, the efficacy of the appeal to racial identity as a unifying principle would wither away once political victory has been achieved and consolidated in the nation state. Other modes of political organisation tend to displace nationalism in the politically stabilised nation state, although it is clear enough that at moments of crisis appeal to some form of nationalist ideology is a constant resource of both governments and their oppositions.[12]

The anomalous character of recent Irish history derives from the fact that, unlike most other Western European states, the moment of nationalist victory did not constitute a moment of apparent national unification, but rather institutionalised certain racial and sectarian divisions. The Treaty of 1922, which, after prolonged guerilla warfare, established the Irish Free State, did so only at the expense of also establishing the Northern Irish state, a self-governing enclave with a deliberately and artificially constructed majority of Protestant citizens. But although the Treaty appears thus to have instituted simply another divisive factor in Irish politics, within the two states themselves its effect was to perpetuate forms of nationalist ideology as dominant and hypothetically unifying forces.

In the Republic, it has not been hardline nationalists alone who have appealed to partition as the major block to the attainment of a full Irish identity. The doctrine of the territorial and political integrity of Ireland was enshrined in the Irish constitution and has been conceived, if only formally, as a primary political objective of any Irish government. Moreover, and more importantly, the perpetuation of partition has allowed the persistence of what is effectively a two-party system, dominated by parties whose origins lie in the initial rejection of the Treaty's provisions by one group of nationalists. Since the parties – Fine Gael and Fianna Fáil – serve urban and rural bourgeois interests respectively, the instant articulation of Irish politics in relation to the questions of the border and of Irish identity has historically been detrimental to the development of the smaller Labour party. The politics of identity, precisely by locating division and difference at the border of the Irish state, has tended to obscure another internal political reality: class difference.[13] The contradiction is, of course, that although in the short term such policies have served bourgeois interests, and even drawn working-class support for what would seem objectively unlikely policies, it has in the longer term helped to retard the development of capitalism in Ireland by dividing bourgeois interests. Ireland remains accordingly in a classical postcolonial situation in which economic underdevelopment continually undermines attempts to forge political cohesion.

In Northern Ireland, on the other hand, the figment of Protestant identity, with all its racial overtones, immediately masked certain internal differences of sect and geographical origin as well as of economic interest. More importantly, 'Protestantism' acted for bourgeois politicians as a means to divide Protestant and Catholic workers along sectarian lines. In a manner reminiscent of the ideological function of the English constitution as a barrier against Jacobinism in the late eighteenth century, the border played a crucial role in externalising the threat of difference, placing it outside the Protestant community and the ideally Protestant state, and permitting the definition of the Catholic population as alien.[14] Through the crises of recent years, those internal differences have returned with manifest political effects in the splitting of the Unionist Party and in the increasing militance of working-class loyalists. The effects of sectarian and political differences between Protestants and Catholics, unionists and republicans within Northern Ireland needs little emphasis.

What may need emphasis, however, is the role which a politics of identity has played in producing the form of the current civil war in Ireland. The combined effect of political thinking on each side of the border has been to perpetuate not only nationalist ideologies, but their articulation along sectarian and, effectively, racial grounds. The real basis of the present struggle in the economic and social conditions of a postcolonial state, and the peculiar twist given to class differences by such conditions, has consequently been systematically obscured. This obscurantism has further permitted, both within and without Ireland, a subtle knotting in popular liberal and conservative interpretations of Irish history: vociferous mystification as to the apparently insistent repetitiveness of Irish history joins with a persuasive insinuation that the reasons for repetition lie in the nature of Irish identity. It is the argument of this essay that such mystifications are inherent in the cultural and aesthetic thinking which dominates both the Irish and the English traditions, and that the apparent freedom of the aesthetic realm from politics is in itself a crucially political conception. The political function of aesthetics and culture is not only to suggest the possibility of transcending conflict, but to do so by excluding (or integrating) difference, whether historically produced or metaphysically conceived, in so far as it represents a threat to an image of unity whose role is finally hegemonic.[15] The poetics of identity is intimately involved in both the efficacy and the contradictions of aesthetic politics and political aesthetics.

II

And when we look for the history of our sensibilities I am convinced, as Professor J.C. Beckett was convinced about the history of Ireland generally, that it is to what he called the stable element, the land itself, that we must look for continuity.

(Heaney, 'The Sense of Place')

Since his earliest volumes, Seamus Heaney's writings have rehearsed all the figures of the family romance of identity, doubled, more often than not, by an explicit affirmation of a sexual structure in the worker's or the writer's relation to a land or place already given as feminine. A certain sexual knowingness accounts in part for the winsome quality of such poems as 'Digging', 'Rite of Spring', or 'Undine' in the early volumes.[16] The winsomeness and the knowingness are compounded by the neatness with which the slight *frissons* produced by the raised spectres of patricide, rape or seduction are stilled by *dénouements* which stress the felicities of analogy or cure the implied violence of labour and sexuality with a warm and humanising morality. That such knowledge should be so easily borne and contained makes it merely thematic, and renders suspect the strenuousness of that 'agon' which Harold Bloom seems to identify in Heaney's work as the effort to evade 'his central trope, the vowel of the earth'.[17] Bloom here correctly identifies a crucial theme in Heaney's work, and one which indeed organises his preoccupation with the establishment of poetic identity. The relevant question, however, is whether that 'agon' ever proceeds beyond thematic concerns, and, further, whether it could do so without rupturing the whole edifice within which the identity of the poet, his voice, is installed.

To be sure, Heaney makes much play, both in his poems and in his prose writings, with the deterritorialisation inflicted both on a national consciousness by the effects of colonialisation, and on the individual subject by acculturation. But in Heaney's writing such perceptions initiate no firm holding to and exploration of the quality of dispossession; rather, his work relocates an individual and racial identity through the reterritorialisation of language and culture. Heaney's rhetoric of compensation – 'You had to come back/To learn how to lose yourself,/To be pilot and stray' (*Door into the Dark*, p. 50) – uncritically replays the Romantic schema of a return to origins which restores continuity through fuller self-possession, and accordingly rehearses the compensations conducted by Irish Romantic nationalism. But his poetic offers constantly a premature compensation, enacted through linguistic and metaphorical usages which promise a healing of division simply by returning the subject to place, in an innocent yet possessive relation to his objects. 'Digging', an instance still cited sometimes with the authority of an *ars poetica*, finds its satisfactions in a merely aesthetic resolution, which, indeed, sets the pattern for most of the subsequent work:

> Between my finger and my thumb
> The squat pen rests; snug as a gun.
>
> Under my window, a clean rasping sound
> When the spade sinks into gravelly ground:
> My father, digging. I look down
>
> Till his straining rump along the flowerbeds
> Bends low, comes up twenty years away
> Stooping in rhythm through potato drills
> Where he was digging.

That which is posed as problematic, the irreducible difference between physical and cultural labour, and consequently the relation of the writer to his subjective history, is neatly resolved merely by reducing physical labour to a metaphor for cultural labour, while displacing the more intractable question of subjective history beyond the frame of the poem as the project of that labour. At the same time, the intimation of violence, of a will to power, carried in the opening lines already with more fashionable swagger than engagement – 'snug as a gun' – is suppressed at the end by suppressing the metaphorical vehicle:

> Between my finger and my thumb
> The squat pen rests.
> I'll dig with it.

With that suppression the writer can forget or annul the knowledge of writing's power both for dispossession and subjection – 'I look down' – and represent it instead as the metaphorical continuation of a work which has already been taken as a metaphor for writing. What assures that continuity, both across generations and across the twenty-year span of the writer's own history, is the symbolic position of the father in possession of and working the land. Standing initially as a figure for the writer's exclusion from identity with land and past, the father, by way of his own father, slides across into the position of a figure for continuity:

> By God, the old man could handle a spade.
> Just like his old man.
>
> My grandfather cut more turf in a day
> Than any other man on Toner's bog.
> Once I carried him milk in a bottle
> Corked sloppily with paper. He straightened up
> To drink it, then fell to right away
> Nicking and slicing neatly, heaving sods
> Over his shoulder, going down and down
> For the good turf. Digging.
>
> The cold smell of potato mould, the squelch and slap
> Of soggy peat, the curt cuts of an edge
> Through living roots awaken in my head.
> But I've no spade to follow men like them.

'Digging' holds out the prospect of a return to origins and the consolatory myth of a knowledge which is innocent and without disruptive effect. The gesture is almost entirely formal, much as the ideology of nineteenth-century nationalists – whose concerns Heaney largely shares – was formal or aesthetic, composing the identity of the subject in the knowing of objects the very knowing of which is an act of self-production. This description holds for the writer's relation to the communal past as well as to his subjective past: in the final analysis, the two are given as identical. Knowledge can never truly be the knowledge of difference: instead, returned to that from which the subject was separated by knowledge, the subject poses his objects (perceived or produced) as synecdoches of continuity:

> poetry as divination, poetry as revelation of the self to the self, as restoration of the culture to itself; poems as elements of continuity, with the aura and authenticity of archaeological finds, where the buried shard has an importance that is not diminished by the importance of the buried city; poetry as a dig, a dig for finds that end up being plants.[18]

Poetry as divination, poetry as dig: in both these formulations Heaney resorts to metaphors which seek to bypass on several fronts the problematic relation of writing to identity. Firstly, the objectification of the subject that writing enacts is redeemed either through the fiction of immediate self-presence, or in the form of the significant moment as synecdoche for the whole temporal sequence, in which is composed the identity of the subject as a seamless continuum. Secondly, the predicament of a literary culture as a specialised mode of labour is that it is set over against non-cultural labour, yet Heaney's writing continually rests in the untested assumption that a return is possible through writing back to the 'illiterate' culture from which it stems and with which, most importantly, it remains at all times continuous. The actual, persisting relation between the literate and the non-literate, at times antagonistic, at times symbiotic, disappears along with such attendant problems as class or ethnic stratification in a temporal metaphor of unbroken development. No irreparable break appears in the subject's relation to his history by accession to culture, nor is culture itself anything but a refined expression of an ideal community of which the writer is a part. Thirdly, given that the 'touchstone' in this context is Wordsworth, the specific relation of an 'Irish identity' to the English literary – and political – establishment provides not only the language, but the very terms within which the question of identity is posed and resolved, the terms for which it is *the* question to be posed and resolved. For it is not simply the verse form, the melody, or whatnot, that the poet takes over;[19] it is the aesthetic, and the ethical and political formulations it subsumes, that the Romantic and imperial tradition supplies.

To this cultural tradition, it is true, Heaney seeks to give an Irish 'bend', grafting it on to roots which are identified as rural, Catholic, and, more remotely, Gaelic. That grafting is enabled by the return to place, a reterritorialisation in a literal sense initially, which symbolically restores the interrupted continuity of identity and ground. An implicit theory of language operates here, for which the name is naturally integrated with place, the sign identified with the signified, the subject with the object. The putative sameness of place supplies an image of the continuity underlying the ruptures so apparent in the history of language usage in Ireland. If identity slips between belonging in and owning the land, between object and subject, between nature and culture, in unrelenting displacement, the land as 'preoccupation' furnishes the purely formal ground, the matrix of continuity, in which identity ultimately reposes. The signs of difference that compose the language are underwritten by a language of containment and synthesis, that is, 'the living speech of the landscape', which is in turn identified with the poem itself, the single, adequate vocable: a word 'with reference to form rather than meaning'.[20] In all its functions, language performs the rituals of synthesis and identity, from the mysterious identification of the guttural and the vowel with Irishness, the consonantal with Englishness, to the symbolic function of metaphor which produces those recurrent stylistic traits of Heaney's metaphors of identity born by the genitive, the copula or the compound: 'the hammered shod of a bay'; 'the tight vise of a stack'; 'the challenger's intelligence/is a spur of light,/a blue prong'; 'My body was braille'; 'Earth-pantry, bone-vault,/sun-bank'.

Place, identity and language mesh in Heaney, as in the tradition of cultural nationalism, since language is seen primarily as naming, and because naming performs a cultural reterritorialisation by replacing the contingent continuities of an historical community with an ideal register of continuity in which the name (of place or of object) operates symbolically as the commonplace communicating between actual and ideal continua. The name always serves likeness, never difference. Hence poems on the names of places must of their nature be rendered as gifts, involving no labour on the part of the poet, who would, by enacting division, disrupt the immediacy of the relation of culture to pre-culture:

> I had a great sense of release as they were being written, a joy and a devil-may-careness, and that convinced me that one could be faithful to the nature of the English language – for in some sense these poems are erotic mouth-music by and out of the anglo-saxon [sic] tongue – and, at the same time, be faithful to one's own non-English origin, for me that is County Derry.

The formulation renovates the concerns, even the rhetoric, of early nationalist critics.

Thus the name 'Anahorish' resides as a metonym for the ancient Gaelic culture that is to be tapped, leading 'past the literary mists of a Celtic twilight into that civilisation whose demise was effected by soldiers and administrators like Spenser and Davies' (*Preoccupations*, p. 36). 'Anahorish', 'place of clear water', is at once a place-name and the name of a place-name poem in *Wintering Out*. The name as title already assures both continuity between subject and predicate and the continuity of the poet's identity, since titular possession of this original place which is itself a source guarantees the continuity of the writing subject with his displaced former identity:

> Anahorish
>
> My 'place of clear water',
> the first hill in the world
> where springs washed into
> the shiny grass ...

The writer's subjective origin doubles the Edenic and absolute origin, the untroubled clarity of his medium allowing immediacy of access to the place and moment of original creation, which its own act of creation would seem to repeat and symbolise, knowledge cleansed and redeemed to graceful polish. The poem itself becomes the adequate vocable in which the rift between the Gaelic word and its English equivalent is sealed in smooth, unbroken ground, speech of the landscape:

> *Anahorish*, soft gradient
> of consonant, vowel-meadow.

The rhetoric of identity is compacted not only in these metaphors, representative again of Heaney's metaphors of identity, but in the two sentences that compose the first and most substantial part of the poem, where no main verbs fracture the illusion of identity and presence. The name itself asserts the continuity of presence as an 'after-image of lamps', while in the last sentence, those lamps appear to illuminate genii of the place – 'those mound dwellers' – a qualification which expels history, leaving only the timelessness of repeated, fundamental acts. Their movement unites the visible with the invisible, while the exceptional moment of fracturing is regained as a metaphor for access to the source and the prospect of renewed growth:

> With pails and barrows
>
> those mound-dwellers
> go waist-deep in mist
> to break the light ice
> at wells and dunghills.

What is dissembled in such writing is that the apparent innocence, the ahistoricity, of the subject's relation to place is in fact preceded by an act of appropriation or repossession. 'Anahorish' provides an image of the transcendental unity of the subject, and correspondingly of history, exactly in so far as it is represented – far from innocently – as a property of the subject. The lush and somewhat indulgent sentiment of the poems of place in *Wintering Out* ('Anahorish', 'Toome', 'Broagh', and 'A New Song') can be ascribed to that foreclosed surety of the subject's relation to place, mediated as it is by a language which seeks to naturalise its appropriative function.

'Erotic mouth-music': it is indeed the seduction of these poems to open what would in the terms of its aesthetic be a regressive path through orality beyond the institution of difference in history and in writing. Hence perception of difference, through the poet's sense of his own difference, which is in fact fundamental to their logic of identity, has finally to be suppressed. Difference is of course registered throughout Heaney's work, at all those points of division and dispossession previously observed. Those divisions are, furthermore, embraced within sexual difference, which comes to provide for political, national and cultural difference a matrix of the most elementary, dualistic kind: 'I suppose the feminine element for me involves the matter of Ireland, and the masculine strain is drawn from the involvement with English literature' (*Preoccupations*, p. 34). This difference, however, is posed as the context for a resolution beyond conflict, in the poem as in relation to the land, which is at once pre-existent and integrating:

> I have always listened for poems, they come sometimes like bodies come out of a bog, almost complete, seeming to have been laid down a long time ago, surfacing with a touch of mystery. They certainly involve craft and determination, but chance and instinct have a role in the thing too. I think the process is a kind of somnambulist en-

counter between masculine will and intelligence and feminine clusters of image and emotion. ...

It is this feeling, assenting, equable marriage between the geographical country and the country of the mind, whether that country of the mind takes its tone unconsciously from a shared oral inherited culture, or from a consciously savoured literary culture, or from both, it is this marriage that constitutes the sense of place in its richest possible manifestation.

(Preoccupations, pp. 34, 132)

For all their rigid, dualistic schematisation, which is only the more rigid for its pretension to be instinctual and unsystematic, and for all the inanity of the content of that dualism – oral, feminine, unconscious image and emotion versus cultured, masculine, conscious will and intelligence – such formulations acutely register the form of integration which is projected. Non-differentiation lies in the matter which precedes all difference and is regained in the product which is the end of difference, the aesthetic object, the poem. Culture repeats primary cultivation, its savour is oral, racy of the soil. Masculine and feminine marry likewise in the moment the poem is forged out of their difference, reproducing a unity of word and flesh always assumed to pre-exist that difference. In the insistent formalisation of this rigidly gendered representation of difference, Heaney elides the complex and often contradictory heterogeneity of Irish social formations and their histories, recapitulating his similar dualisation of the oral and literate elsewhere.[21]

Only when special and explanatory status is pleaded for this consolatory myth do contradiction and difference return, to use a Heaneyish notion, with a vengeance, as in the series of bog poems which commences with 'The Tollund Man' in *Wintering Out*, and is extended through *North*. The origin of these poems in P.V. Glob's *The Bog People* is doubtless familiar, but it is as well to reproduce Heaney's own account:

It [Glob's book] was chiefly concerned with preserved bodies of men and women found in the bogs of Jutland, naked, strangled or with their throats cut, disposed under the peat since early Iron Age times. The author, P.V. Glob, argues convincingly that a number of these, and in particular the Tollund Man, whose head is now preserved near Aarhus in the museum at Silkeburg, were ritual sacrifices to the Mother Goddess, the goddess of the ground who needed new bridegrooms each winter to bed with her in her sacred place, in the bog, to ensure the renewal and fertility of the territory in the spring. Taken in relation to the tradition of Irish political martyrdom for that cause whose icon is Kathleen Ní Houlihán, this is more than an archaic barbarous rite: it is an archetypal pattern. And the unforgettable photographs of these victims blended in my mind with photographs of atrocities, past and present, in the long rites of Irish political and religious struggles.

(Preoccupations, pp. 57–8)

Heaney here posits a psychic continuity between the sacrificial practices of an Iron Age people and the 'psychology of the Irishmen and Ulstermen who do the killing' (*Preoccupations*, p. 57). This is effectively to reduce history to myth, furnishing an aesthetic resolution to conflicts constituted in quite specific historical junctures by rendering disparate events as symbolic moments expressive of an underlying continuity of identity. Not surprisingly, it is the aesthetic politics of nationalism which finds its most intense symbolism in martyrdom.

As with the question of identity, so the question as to whether archetypes and archetypal patterns exist is less significant than the formal role their invocation plays. Something of that role emerges in 'The Tollund Man' (*Wintering Out*), apparently the first of the bog poems to have been written:

> Some day I will go to Aarhus
> To see his peat-brown head,
> The mild pods of his eye-lids,
> His pointed skin cap.
>
> In the flat country nearby
> Where they dug him out,
> His last gruel of winter seeds
> Caked in his stomach,
>
> Naked except for
> The cap, noose and girdle,
> I will stand a long time.
> Bridegroom to the goddess,
>
> She tightened her torc on him
> And opened her fen,
> Those dark juices working
> Him to a saint's kept body ...

The distance of the historical observer rapidly contracts in this first section into an imaginary immediate relation to the corpse, and ultimately to the putative goddess as, in a singularly deft piece of composition, the appositions 'Naked except for/The cap, noose and girdle,' and 'Bridegroom to the goddess' slip between the poet and the victim. The immediacy of that relation, brought thus to the very brink of identification, facilitates the elimination of human agency, which is distilled to thematically equivalent operations of sacrifice (by which the corpse is worked 'to a saint's kept body') and poetic rememoration which reverses, by analogy with exhumation, the direction of sacrifice without invalidating it. The subordination of human agency to aesthetic form is reinforced in the second section as the two atrocities there described are contained within the faintly redeeming notion of their possible germination, their flesh scattered like seed:

> I could risk blasphemy,
> Consecrate the cauldron bog
> Our holy ground and pray
> Him to make germinate
>
> The scattered, ambushed
> Flesh of labourers,
> Stockinged corpses
> Laid out in the farmyards,
>
> Tell-tale skin and teeth
> Flecking the sleepers
> Of four young brothers, trailed
> For miles along the lines.

The matter of the form in which they will germinate, as Cadmus's warriors, perhaps, or as 'The Right Rose Tree', is carefully hedged.[22] In so purely aesthetic a performance, which evades the logic even of its own mythologies, the 'risk' of 'blasphemy' is easily carried. In the third section, the poet is confirmed as the stable centre of this tableau of identifications:

> Something of his sad freedom
> As he rode the tumbril
> Should come to me, driving,
> Saving the names
>
> Tollund, Grabaulle, Nebelgard,
> Watching the pointing hands
> Of country people,
> Not knowing their tongue.
>
> Out there in Jutland
> In the old man-killing parishes

> I will feel lost,
> Unhappy and at home.

What is the 'sad freedom' that the poet as tourist or pilgrim in Jutland will take over from the Tollund man other than that derived from the aesthetic rehearsal of rites whose continuity with the present is preassured by the unquestioned metaphoric frame of the writing, a writing whose dangers have been defused into pathos by their subordination to that same metaphoric function? Thus the repetition of place-names ('Tollund, Grabaulle, Nebelgard'), abstracted from context and serving a cultural purpose as synecdoches of continuity, overrides the actual alienation of one 'Not knowing their tongue', only to issue in the 'at home-ness' always available to those whose culture is a question of reterritorialisation. The bodies of Jutland are, one recalls, 'disposed under the peat' for the poet-archaeologist's appropriation.

Metaphorical foreclosure of issues, by which the proposed matter of the poem acts simultaneously as the metaphor justifying the mode of its treatment, has been a constant feature of Heaney's writing since such early poems as 'Digging', perfectly sustaining its drive towards cultural reterritorialisation and the suturing of identity, because the concepts of culture and individuation thus appear as the formal repetition of the primary ground to which they are thereby returned. The racial and psychological archetype, like the reified human nature of bourgeois ideology from which it stems, subserves this circularity. The archetype allows the process of individuation and the specific forms taken on by any given culture to be envisaged as retaining a continuity with an homogeneous, undifferentiated ground, such as indeed the symbol is supposed to retain with that which it represents and, crucially, of which it partakes. The regressive nature of this model is significant less in the evident psychoanalytical sense, which doubles Heaney's own temporal schema, than in the neatness with which the location of that archetypal or indifferent ground can be pushed back as far as required – from oral culture and territory to the abstract form of the land, for example. This regression, nevertheless, does not affect the essential structure by which the immediacy of a primary relation to origins and ground can be replaced by a cultural medium, though in sublimated form and with the gain of pathos, as in Heaney's myth of Antaeus:

a blue prong graiping him
out of his element
into a dream of loss

and origins – the cradling dark,
the river-veins, the secret gullies
of his strength,
the hatching grounds

of cave and souterrain,
he has bequeathed it all
to elegists.

(*North*)

That which is foregone is the most efficient myth of integration, supplying the lost object by which the work of mourning is transformed into the work of identification, specially, here, identification with an inheritance.

Contradiction returns where the myth that has most effectively furthered the goal of integration by obviating the state's need for overt coercion clashes with those 'civilised values' that it underwrites. For both unionists and nationalists in Ireland, in ways which agree in form but differ in specific content, concepts of racial identity asserted since the nineteenth century have performed such an integrative function in the service of domination, at the cost of institutionalising certain differences. That the interests promoted by these myths should have come into conflict at various periods, of which the current 'troubles' are only the latest instance, does not affect the correspondence that subsists between those ideologies. Even insurgent or anti-colonial violence, generally speaking directed against the state apparatus, can become in the strict sense 'terrorist' where it seeks by symbolic rather than tactical acts to forge integration or identity within the discursive boundaries already established and maintained by dominant hegemony. A socialist or feminist critique of such tendencies has to be located not in a generalised criticism of 'men of violence', but in the analysis of the totalising effect of an identity thinking that discretely links terrorism to the state in whose name it is condemned. For what is at stake is not so much the practice of violence – which has long been institutionalised in the bourgeois state – as its aestheticisation in the name of a freedom expressed in terms of national or racial integration. This aesthetic frame deflects attention from the interests of domination which the national state expresses both as idea and as entity.

The aestheticisation of violence is underwritten in Heaney's re-course to racial archetypes as a means 'to grant the religious inten-sity of the violence its deplorable authenticity and complexity' (*Preoccupations*, pp. 56–7). In locating the source of violence beyond even sectarian division, Heaney renders it symbolic of a fundamental identity of the Irish race, as 'authentic'. Interrogation of the nature and function of acts of violence in the specific context of the current 'troubles' is thus foreclosed, and history foreshortened into the eternal resurgence of the same Celtic genius. The conflict of this thinking with 'the perspectives of a humane reason' (*Preoccupations*, p. 56) is, within the poetry that results, only an apparent contradiction, in so far as the function of reason is given over to the establishment of myths. The unpleas-antness of such poetry lies in the manner in which the contradic-tions between the ethical and aesthetic elements in the writing are easily resolved by the subjugation of the former to the latter in order to produce the 'well-made poem'. Contempt for 'connivance in civilised outrage' is unexamined in the frequently cited 'Punishment' (*North*) where the 'artful voyeurism' of the poem is supposedly criticised as the safe stance of the remote and lustful 'civilised' observer, yet is smuggled back in as the unspoken and unacknowledged condition for the understanding of the 'exact-ness' of 'tribal, intimate revenge':

> I can feel the tug
> of the halter at the nape
> of her neck, the wind
> on her naked front.
>
> It blows her nipples
> to amber beads,
> it shakes the frail rigging
> of her ribs.
>
> I can see her drowned
> body in the bog,
> the weighing stone,
> the floating rods and boughs.
>
> Under which at first
> she was a barked sapling
> that is dug up
> oak-bone, brain-firkin ...
>
> My poor scapegoat,

I almost love you
but would have cast, I know,
the stones of silence.
I am the artful voyeur

of your brain's exposed
and darkened combs,
your muscles' webbing
and all your numbered bones:

I who have stood dumb
when your betraying sisters,
cauled in tar,
wept by the railings,

who would connive
in civilised outrage
yet understand the exact
and tribal, intimate revenge.

The epithet 'tribal' cannot, in this context, be immanently ques-
tioned, since it at once is sustained by and reinforces the metaphor
of tribal rites which organises the whole poem, and which is at once
its pretext and its subject-matter. Neither the justness of the
identification of the metaphor – the execution of an adulteress by
Glob's Iron Age people – with the actual violence which it supposedly illuminates – the tarring and feathering of two Catholic 'betraying sisters' – nor the immediacy of the observer's access to
knowledge of his object ('I can feel ... I can see') is ever subjected to
a scrutiny which would imperil the quasi-syllogistic structure of the
poem. Voyeurism is criticised merely as a pose, never for its function in purveying the intimate knowledge of violence by which it is
judged. As so often in Heaney's work, the sexual drive of knowing
is challenged, acknowledged, and let pass without further interrogation, the stance condemned but the material it purveys nevertheless
exploited. Thus a pose of ethical self-query allows the condemna-
tion of enlightened response – reduced in any case to paralytic
'civilised outrage', as if this were the only available alternative –
while the supposedly irrational is endowed as if by default with the
features of enlightenment – exactitude, intimacy of knowledge – in
order to compact an understanding already presupposed in the selection and elaboration of the metaphor. The terms of the dilemma
are entirely false, but the poem rehearses with striking fidelity the
propensity of bourgeois thought to use 'reason' to represent

irrationality as the emotional substratum of identifications which, given as at once natural and logical, are in fact themselves thoroughly 'irrational'.[23]

III

> So much in Ireland still needs to be done ... the definition of the culture, and the redefinition of it. If you could open students into trust in their own personality, into some kind of freedom and cultivation, you could do a hell of a lot.[24]

In its play with atavisms, with the irrational substrata of its identifications, aesthetic ideology effectively excludes both violence and difference from the ideal image of its own internal structure. The irrational – all which eludes the governing principle of identity – is reduced to the originating matter which is repeatedly to be cultivated into unity. While it supplies the ground for culture, it is debarred from either real agency or representation, and figures thenceforth when 'active' as a 'disruption' of the supposedly natural ordering of cultivation. Thus its return merely bolsters up the rationale of an essentially exclusive culture, supplying at once the pretext and the matter upon which that culture's work is performed. The discourse of culture itself originates in the moment that the division of intellectual and physical labour has become such that 'culture' as a specialisation is privileged yet entirely marginalised in relation to productive forces, and seeks to disguise, or convert, both privilege and marginalisation in a sublimation which places it beyond division and into a position whence it can appear to perform the work of unification. Hence the importance not only of the image of the man of culture as a non-productive worker, but also the idea of a method which brings to an epistemology already analogous to industrial processes the privilege of unity retained even in transition, that of the 'science of origins' which reconciles where it first dissolves and finds differences.[25] The discourse of culture consistently seeks, by representing itself as withdrawn from implication in social divisions, as indifferent, to forge a domain in which divisions are overcome or made whole. The realisation of human freedom is deferred into this transcendent domain, with the consequence that an ethical invocation is superadded to the exhortations of culture.

It is a cultural resolution of this order that Heaney proposes in *Field Work*, a generally acclaimed volume.[26] The sonnets composed in the 'hedge-school of Glanmore' pose as an apt centre-piece to the book, thematising at once the notion of withdrawal and the agricultural root of the culture which is its goal: 'Vowels ploughed into other, opened ground,/Each verse returning like the plough turned round' (Glanmore Sonnets, II). Though this withdrawal is envisaged as a return and a grounding, it is still a ground whose otherness is carefully contained as a metaphor for the locus and source of poetic activity, and as such is resolutely cultivable. Secure in its protected, pastoral domain, the writing is full of unrealised resolve, governed primarily by a conditional mood which mimes the celebration of conditions for writing, yet is in actuality reduced to the almost contentless formal reiteration of the paradigms which sustain its complacencies. The small reminders that might threaten the benediction of that 'haven', the word with which Heaney obliquely encapsulates his relief at being harboured in a poetic which allows him the shelter of the English tradition and voice (Glanmore Sonnets, VII), are either framed carefully on the outside – 'Outside the kitchen window a black rat/Sways on the briar like infected fruit' (Glanmore Sonnets, IX) – or smothered in a rhetoric so portentous that it merely accentuates the bathos of its referents:

> This morning when a magpie with jerky steps
> Inspected a horse asleep beside the wood
> I thought of dew on armour and carrion.
> What would I meet, blood-boltered, on the road?
> How deep into the woodpile sat the toad?
> What welters through this dark hush on the crops?
> (Glanmore Sonnets, VIII)

It is difficult to credit the solemnly voiced pursuit of an 'apology for poetry' (Glanmore Sonnets, IX) in these sonnets with any real intellectual strenuousness, reduced as they are to such highly strung aestheticism. Whatever slight resonances they evoke are gained from political and ethical concerns which the knowledge of matters beyond their refined scope must supply.

The sonnets' implicit thesis that the preciousness of art – and the pathos of human being – may lie in the vulnerability of its fragile pieties to the 'ungovernable and dangerous' ('Elegy') is elsewhere delivered over to the test of more exacting conditions. The elegy 'Casualty' – which, of the three in the volume, most nearly confronts the supposed saving power of art with 'danger' – labours uneasily with the realisation of the remoteness of this art from the pathos of the everyday which it celebrates elsewhere, and, as if in abreaction, asserts the more strongly the difference of art as the image of freedom posed against conformity to putative 'tribal' values. The assertion nevertheless regrounds itself through finding its paradigm in labour, in a labour, however, which is crucially predetermined as gratuitous, 'natural' and free, that of 'A dole-kept breadwinner/But a natural for work'. This image of the fisherman's labour as essentially free underwrites the concluding lines, which render fishing as a paradigm for art in its transcendence:

> I tasted freedom with him.
> To get out early, haul
> Steadily off the bottom,
> Dispraise the catch, and smile
> As you find a rhythm
> Working you, slow mile by mile,
> Into your proper haunt
> Somewhere, well out, beyond ...

At once natural and transcendent, freedom finds its image in gratuitous creative work, in a 'taste' which is shared beyond the divisions established by the 'incomprehensibility' of the poet's 'other life'. That such 'condescension' is always one-sided is debarred from consideration, as is the wider context of unfreedom which sustains that aesthetic once the idea of constraint has been reduced to the myth of the tribe.

The cautious limits which Heaney's poetry sets round any potential for disruptive, immanent questioning may be the reason for the extraordinary inflation of his current reputation. If Heaney is held to be 'the most trusted poet of our [*sic*] islands',[27] by the same token he is the most institutionalised of recent poets. At the functional level of school and college teaching and examination, much of the prominence given to Heaney's writing may be attributed to its aptness for the still dominant discipline of practical criticism. Almost without exception, the poems respond compliantly to analysis based on assumptions about the nature of the well-made lyric poem: that it will crystallise specific emotions out of an experience; that the metaphorical structure in which the emotion is to be communicated will be internally coherent; that the sum of its ambiguities will be an integer, expressing eventually a unity of tone and feeling even where mediated by irony; that the unity will finally be the expression of a certain identity, a poetic 'voice' (*Preoccupations*, pp. 43–4). On the side of the writer, writing is envisaged as at once constitutive and expressive of an identity liberated from the incoherent unity of its ground. That act of self-production gives the writer his representativeness as human despite the specialisation of his labour. For the reader, the act of reading appears also as a liberating act. To read, to criticise, is to exercise the right of private judgement and thereby to develop one's best self. The illusion of a free-market economy, where taste pretends to be an expression of the consumer's uncoerced judgement, thrives in the pedagogical method that furnishes the core of those literary institutions which in fact arbitrate cultural values.

In this period where the illusion of a free-market economy is disintegrating in crisis, it is appropriate that, within the increasingly marginalised domain of high culture, a pedagogy locating the autonomy of the individual subject in the private arbitration of value should become increasingly retrenched and all the more earnestly defended. It is perhaps only a small irony that the product of this pedagogy turns out to be such an unprecedented homogeneity of 'taste' that a reviewer can state, 'Everyone knows by now that Heaney is a major poet', and be confirmed not only by the accord of his peers, but by the remarkably high sales of the volumes concerned.[28] But that small irony – scarcely to be attributed to the benevolent dissemination of the sweetness and light of culture – is nonetheless symptomatic of a contradiction implicit in cultural discourse, and in some sense even recognised there, as if the terms of the discourse already resolved it. The contradiction, formally congruent with that produced by bourgeois ideology's attempts to 'reconcile individual liberty with association', lies in the fact that the cultivation of the individual's best self is to be conducted under the arbitration of an authority whose end is the constitution of a more integrated whole beyond divisions.[29] If that authority has tended to shift from the individual critic-teacher to institutions in which the existence of single tone-setting figures is much less apparent, this tendency belongs with a general shift from the concentration of power in the entrepreneur to its disposition through larger structures.[30] So much is implicit in common parlance when one speaks of one or other 'critical industry'.

The democratisation of education that has stemmed in large part from nineteenth-century cultural discourse has followed the track of industrialisation, and with similar effects in view. Where the net effect of increased technological efficiency has been to override the perception of difference with the homogenising image of general prosperity, the end of literary education has been to override class and individual difference with the image of a common culture, both as something inherited and as something currently produced. The concept of a common culture can be seen to double that of the common land (whence, indeed, the concept of 'culture' has always derived its specific etymological and metaphorical resonances), and this conveniently underwrites the nominal decentralisation of literary production. Pre-programmed as this development is, the resulting notion of the revitalisation of the centres of culture through the influence of less deracinated, less cultivated regional sensibilities, continues to subserve the linked fictions of indigenous and subjective identity. Just as rhetoric about enterprise and the free market exploits the image of individualism while masking the actual diffusion of power through larger heterogeneous structures, so the celebration of regionalism dulls perception of the institutional and homogenising culture which has sustained its apparent efflorescence at the very moment when the concept of locality, enclosed and self-nurturing, has become effectively archaic, and, indeed, functions as such. The pathos which the defenders of high culture and regional identity win from a stance offering to protect the vulnerable and vanishing against imponderable forces of technology and progress is gained in spite of the contradiction that the higher integration, which culture was to maintain beyond the class society, coincides perfectly with that being produced by technological development. The thematising and defusing of these elements within Heaney's poetry provides the basis of the trust with which it is currently accepted, at every point confirming – as only such poetry can – the aesthetic and cultural expectations whence it stemmed and to which it promises an apparently authentic renovation. The seeming coherence between this scenario of the elevation of a minor Irish poet to a touchstone of contemporary taste and a discourse whose most canonical proponent argued for the Celtic literature as a means to the integration of Ireland with Anglo-Saxon industrial civilisation is appropriate and pre-programmed.[31] It is, for all that, profoundly symptomatic of the continuing meshing of Irish cultural nationalism with the imperial ideology which frames it.

From David Lloyd, *Anomalous States: Irish Writing and the Post-Colonial Moment* (Dublin, 1993), pp. 13–40. (First published in *Boundary*, 2:13, 2–3 [1985].)

NOTES

[David Lloyd is like Thomas Docherty (essay 10) in privileging 'difference', 'the dialectical contrary to the concept of identity' (n. 15 below). In the main line of poststructuralist thought he sees the latter concept as governed by the Western intellectual tendency to postulate a humane centre for all discursive activity. 'Difference' for Lloyd is 'that which cannot be assimilated to the unity of identitarian thinking' (n. 15 below). Lloyd's own thought is systematically Marxist, following Adorno (nn. 15 and 23) and Gramsci (n. 11). He insists that social and political existence implies 'divisions' impervious to the ideology of identity: first between the non-productive and the productive worker (p. 176 above) and then between the developing postcolonial polity and neo-imperialism (pp. 161 and 180 above). According to Lloyd, the concern with identity manifested by Heaney's poetry (and the tradition in which it stands) ignores and conceals these divisions. His introduction to *Anomalous States* in which the essay was republished (Dublin [1993], pp. 1–12) makes explicit the relationship of his approach to that of other 'postcolonial theorists' like Franz Fanon, Homi K. Bhabha and Gayatri C. Spivak. (On all three see Selden and Widdowson, *A Reader's Guide to Contemporary Literary Theory* [Hemel Hempstead, 1993], pp. 188–97, 200–2.) Ed.]

1. Seamus Heaney, 'Hercules and Antaeus', *North* (London, 1975), p. 53.

2. Seamus Heaney, *Field Work* (London, 1979). The citation is from John Carey, 'Poetry for the World We Live In', review of Seamus Heaney, *Field Work*, and Craig Raine, *A Martian Sends a Postcard Home* (Oxford, 1979), in the *Sunday Times*, 18 November 1979, p. 40.

3. Mark Patrick Hederman, '"The Crane Bag" and the North of Ireland', *The Crane Bag* (Dublin), 4:2 (1980–1), 102, and Blake Morrison, *Seamus Heaney* (London, 1982), p. 69.

4. Denis Florence MacCarthy (ed.), *The Book of Irish Ballads*, new edn (Dublin, n.d.), pp. 15, 25–6.

5. 'Recent English Poets, No. 1 – Alfred Tennyson and E.B. Browning', *Nation*, 15 February 1845, 314.

6. Anonymous, 15 February 1845, 'Union Against the Union', *Nation*, 11 March 1848, 168. See also E. Kamenka (ed.), *Nationalism: The Nature and Evolution of an Idea* (London, 1973), pp. 9–10. Marx's 'Critique of Hegel's Doctrine of the State' in *Early Writings*, trans. Rodney Livingstone and Gregor Benton (New York, 1975), pp. 57–197, comprises an extensive critique of the state in terms of the split between the civil state of individualism and the political state of 'association'.

7. Elie Kedourie's *Nationalism* (London, 1961) supplies the wider European context of nationalism, and emphasises the ethical nature of its demands.

8. See the anonymous article, 'The Individuality of a Native Literature', *Nation*, 21 August 1847, 731.

9. In this particular context, I use the term 'reterritorialisation' in a more literal sense than do Gilles Deleuze and Felix Guattari, from whose *Anti-Oedipus* (New York, 1977) and *Kafka: pour une littérature mineure* (Paris, 1975) it is derived. This, and related terms, are well analysed in Vincent Descombes, *Le Même et l'Autre: quarante-cinq ans de philosophie française, 1933–1978* (Paris, 1979), pp. 205–6. Davis's essay was published in the *Nation*, 1 April 1843, 394.

10. Sigmund Freud, 'Some Psychical Consequences of the Anatomical Distinction between the Sexes', *The Complete Psychological Works* (London, 1958–68), XIX, p. 257.

11. I understand ideology, briefly, in relation to Gramsci's concept of hegemony, as consisting of the general shared structure of disseminating institutions and a set of discourses of analogous structure which operate not through coercion but through the 'naturalisation' of certain forms of thought. See, for example, Antonio Gramsci, *Selections from the Prison Notebooks*, ed. and trans. Quintin Hoare and Geoffrey Nowell Smith (New York, 1971), pp. 240–6. I have used the verb 'to double' throughout this essay to describe – by analogy with the word's musical sense – the way in which the structure of one discourse may appear congruent with that of another, giving rise to the 'knotting together' (see Gramsci, p. 240) of disparate hegemonic discourses into an apparently self-reinforcing, limiting structure of thought.

12. This is the general argument of John Breuily's persuasive study, *Nationalism and the State* (New York, 1982), see especially chs 2 and 3.

13. See George Boyce, *Nationalism in Ireland* (London, 1982), p. 239, where he remarks that 'one of the most important unifying themes of southern politics after the 1920s was *Hibernia Irredenta*'.

14. See Boyce, *Nationalism in Ireland*, pp. 364–5.

15. 'Difference' is employed throughout less in the Derridean sense than as the dialectical contrary to the concept of identity, i.e. that which cannot be assimilated to the unity of identitarian thinking. Theodor Adorno argues this to be an inescapable contradiction within such thinking; see *Negative Dialectics*, trans. E.B. Ashton (New York, 1973), pp. 5–6.

16. Seamus Heaney, *Death of a Naturalist* (London, 1966), pp. 13–14, and *Door into the Dark* (London, 1969), pp. 25–6.

17. Harold Bloom, 'The Voice of Kinship', *TLS*, 8 (February 1980), pp. 137–8.

18. Seamus Heaney, 'Feeling into Words', *Preoccupations* (London, 1980), p. 41.

19. Frank Kinahan, 'Artists on Art: An Interview with Seamus Heaney', *Critical Inquiry*, 8:3 (Spring 1982), 406; see also Seamus Heaney's lines in 'The Ministry of Fear', *North* (London, 1975), p. 65: 'Ulster was British, but with no rights on/The English lyric.'

20. See *Preoccupations*, pp. 36–7. I allude to the COED definition of 'vocable'.

21. For further discussion of gender issues in Heaney's writings that have appeared since this essay was first published, see Elizabeth Butler Cullingford, '"Thinking of Her ... as ... Ireland": Yeats, Pearse and Heaney', *Textual Practice*, 4:1 (Spring 1990), 1–21, and Patricia Coughlan, '"Bog Queens": The Representation of Women in the Poetry of John Montague and Seamus Heaney' in Toni O'Brien Johnson and David Cairns (eds), *Gender in Irish Writing* (Milton Keynes, 1991), pp. 88–111.

22. See Richard Kearney's comments on the intertwining of both aspects of this mythology in 'The IRA's Strategy of Failure', *The Crane Bag*, 4:2 (1980–1), 62.

23. See Theodor Adorno's remarks on this subject, specifically in relation to the mobilising of 'additional regressive memories of its archaic root' in the bourgeois nation state, in *Negative Dialectics*, p. 339.

24. See the interview with Seamus Heaney in John Haffenden, *Viewpoints* (London, 1981), pp. 59–60.

25. See Coleridge, 'Essays on Method', *The Friend*, ed. Barbara Rooke (Princeton, NJ, 1969), p. 476; Matthew Arnold, 'On the Study of Celtic Literature' in R.H. Super (ed.), *Lectures and Essays in Criticism*, vol. III of *The Complete Prose Works* (Ann Arbor, MI, 1962), p. 330. Adorno comments on the duplication of the mechanical reproductive process in Kant's *Critique of Pure Reason*. See *Negative Dialectics*, p. 387.

26. Reviews acclaiming *Field Work* range from Harold Bloom's in the *TLS* to one by Gerard Smyth in the *Irish Times* ('Change of Idiom', *IT*, 20 October 1979, p. 11). Reviewers are almost unanimous in regarding the volume as a steady advance on the previous body of work.

27. Christopher Ricks, 'The Mouth, the Meal, and the Book', review of *Field Work* in *The London Review of Books*, 8 November 1979, p. 4.

28. Neither Faber and Faber, nor Farrar, Straus and Giroux have been willing to divulge detailed figures concerning sales of Heaney's works.

I am, however, obliged to Craig Raine of Faber and Faber for the following 'approximate figures', whose 'general lesson is sound and obvious enough': 'We would probably have printed 2000–3000 copies of his first book, whereas now we would print somewhere in the region of 20,000 copies' (letter, 12 October 1983).

29. See Matthew Arnold, 'The Function of Criticism in the Present Time', *Lectures and Essays*, pp. 265–6: '*Force till right is ready*; and till right is ready force, the existing order of things, is justified, is the legitimate ruler' (original emphasis).

30. John Kenneth Galbraith, *The New Industrial State*, 2nd edn (Harmondsworth, 1974), especially ch. 5, 'Capital and Power'. The analysis, if not the conclusion, of this study is valuable, and challenging to any materialist view of the current economy.

31. Arnold, 'On the Study of Celtic Literature', pp. 296–7.

12

'Bog Queens': The Representation of Women in the poetry of John Montague and Seamus Heaney

PATRICIA COUGHLAN

I

This essay investigates the construction of feminine figures, and the vocabulary of roles allotted to them by two prominent contemporary Irish poets, John Montague and Seamus Heaney. Feminine figures and more or less abstract ideas of femininity play a major role in the work of both: how should this centrality of the feminine be interpreted? Is it, as it most usually announces itself, to be taken as a celebration? Or does it flatter to deceive, as has been remarked about Matthew Arnold's perhaps analogous celebration of the alleged Celtic virtues of passion, sensuousness, non-rational insight (see Cairns and Richards, 'Woman'[1])? I have chosen to discuss the work of male poets, believing strongly that both 'gynocritics' – the 'naming', recovery and revaluing of women's writing – and the persistent demystifying of representations of women in men's work must continue in tandem. The social and cultural construction of gender is a continuously occurring process, in which it is certainly not yet time to stop intervening. I shall argue that even able and

185

serious contemporary work is deeply and dismayingly reliant upon old, familiar and familiarly oppressive allocations of gender positions. Our celebration of this work must therefore be inflected by this question as to its effect: can poetry's implicit claim to universality of utterance and to utopian insight be upheld in the face of a reader's awareness of its gendered and therefore (perhaps unconsciously) partial perspective?

The representation of femininity which occurs most insistently in this material takes the form of dualistically opposed aspects: beloved or spouse figures versus mother figures, which are in turn benign and fertile or awe-inspiring and terrible. Very much as in the actual social construction of femininity, the various feminine functions are sometimes made to coalesce bewilderingly, sometimes set in opposition to one another. In Heaney, for example, the nature-goddess is simultaneously spouse, death-bringer and nurturer. This invocation of a *magna mater* figure is celebrated by some readers as an empowerment of women, but it is only dubiously so if the agency described is a death-bringing one; such representations of feminine power ultimately arise from a masculine psychological difficulty in acknowledging woman's subjectivity as a force *in itself*, and not merely as a relation to man's (see Dinnerstein).[2]

My discussion will attend particularly to the invocation of such allegedly immemorial archetypes of femininity and the various strategies by which that invocation is sustained. Especially important among these strategies are the attempt to reinvest with imaginative energy figures such as the sovereignty goddess from early Irish literature and myth as well as *magna mater* figures from other European contexts, and the projected conjunction in such figures of a neo-Jungian 'feminine principle' with the physical territory of Ireland. This combined representation is also merged with the imagery of woman-as-land-and-national-spirit from the tradition of Irish nationalist political rhetoric. In this poetry, such mythic representations are often projected, with varying degrees of explicitness, upon a repertoire of female figures presented by a lyric speaker as autobiographically given.

One must question in general the elision of history which is involved in this smooth passage from memory to myth – an elision which precludes the possibility of understanding history as the product of human actions and not merely as a fated, cyclical natural process. It is also necessary in particular to interrogate the notions of essential femininity and immemorially assigned female functions as the vehicles of this myth-memory passage, and to notice that it requires an implicit assumption of the inescapability of a gendered allocation of subject-positions, by means of which rationality, speech and naming are the prerogatives of the autobiographically validated male poet, and the various female figures dwell in oracular silence, always objects, whether of terror, veneration, desire, admiration or vituperation, never the coherent subjects of their own actions. This reification of traditional modes of perceiving feminine identity is also supported by tactics such as recalling the Irish *aisling* form, which invests a potentially amorous encounter with allegorical political content.[3]

A particular contradiction is discernible in Montague and Heaney between the project of speaking for a politically oppressed and therefore hitherto unspoken group, Northern Catholics – a project important both intrinsically and to the reception of these poets – and their failure, in general, to perceive their own reliance upon and tacit approval of the absence of women as speaking subjects and of female disempowerment. Their female figures function as crucially important forms of validation-by-opposition of the individual poet's identity, in a (sometimes almost comically blatant) neo-Oedipal struggle. In Heaney, this wresting of a speaking ego from the *magna mater* which is also the land is interestingly complicated by specifically political Irish/English stereotyping: the (necessarily, if self-expressing) male poet (phallically) digging and ploughing like his ancestors becomes the culturally female voice of the subjugated Irish, about to inundate the 'masculine' hardness of the planters' boundaries with 'feminine' vowel-floods (see 'A New Song', *Wintering Out* [London, 1972], p. 33; and 'Undine', *Door into the Dark* [London, 1969], p. 26).

Irish ideology tends to an idealisation of rural life. This is often centred on female icons of ideal domesticity, especially mother-figures, who are associated with unmediated naturalness. The feminist critique of this ruralist ideology must investigate the designation of spheres and human subjects as natural or cultural and their respective valuation. It is also necessary to bear in mind the way ideology has effectively denied women the freedom to develop a fully self-conscious ego and therefore to participate in civil society by allocating them a fixed position within the domestic sphere, and by the celebration of domestic virtues as constitutive of femininity. Feminist psychoanalytic demonstrations of the construction of human subjectivity as male and Oedipal also afford a perspective on which I have drawn.[4]

In the poetry I discuss, as in the culture which produces it, women are typically associated with that which is material, and defined in opposition to mind. They are nevertheless seen as possessors of a form of knowledge hidden from the masculine speaker; but this they mutely embody and cannot themselves expound. In Montague's and Heaney's lyrics each masculine speaker characteristically celebrates the domestic as immemorial and relishes it as sensually and emotionally satisfying, but defines himself in the performance of his most characteristic activity, poetry, in contradistinction from it. Woman, the primary inhabitor and constituent of the domestic realm, is admiringly observed, centre stage but silent. She is thus constructed by a scopic gaze, her imputed mental inaction and blankness being required to foreground the speaker's naming and placing of her.[5] What ostensibly offers itself as a celebration may rather be read, then, as a form of limiting definition, in which certain traditional qualities of the feminine are required to persist for a fit wife, mother or Muse to come into being. The constant naming of autobiographical 'originals' for these figures effectively masks this nearly ubiquitous blotting out of the individual qualities of *actual* women by the dominant – and stereotyped – *ideal*.

The reader may feel a general resistance as such to the mythicising mentality this examplifies: that is, to the dehistoricising effect of discerning, in some notional way as a truth *beneath* the actualities, an immemorial status quo which is represented as implicitly superior to modernity; and further, to the accompanying aestheticisation by the observer of the actual deprivation, suffering and hard work of others in the name of celebration. This objection applies whether it is farming life, Irish political violence or gender roles which are in question, and indeed in Montague and Heaney all three of these are, in fact, intimately bound together. Such mythicising moves are discerned as false ones by Montague himself in a moment of the 'Epilogue' of *The Rough Field* in the lines 'Only a sentimentalist would wish/To see such degradation again ...', and Heaney's work is perhaps more open to this charge than Montague's own. Yet Montague falls back upon just such sentiment later in the poem, when agricultural labour is once again interpreted as part 'of a world where action had been wrung/through painstaking years to ritual' in apparent nostalgia for the imputed absoluteness of such humble lives. The poem's ending stresses the poet's 'failure to return' for all his 'circling' round his rural origin (*The Rough Field* [Dublin, 1972], pp. 82–3). The point is the necessary exclusion of the speaker *as* poet from this rural scene – even if it had not been 'going'. The very practice of cosmopolitan literary expression marks off the poet-figure from his material throughout Montague's – and indeed Heaney's – work, however much rural *pietas* it shows. This self-exclusion from the whole rural world as it might be understood on its own terms is particularly focused in the female figures this poetry constructs, who cannot even be manipulated, as the men can, into role-models for the apprentice to poetry-making, divided, as they are, by gender and its assigned functions from the son-figures who construct them. Heaney's digging and ploughing ancestors can be, however transiently and superficially, nominated as ur-makers, but baking, praying, home-making women – icons of domesticity whether vibrant (mothers) or ruined (spinsters living by wells) are set apart from and by the poet who is concerned with conscious self-definition: an activity which must be pursued in explicit opposition to the encompassing space of a home.[6]

Heaney's attempt, in 'The Seed Cutters', to sink the sense of self into the immemorial betrays its own static quality, its relinquishing of the possibility of any significant action or change in its freezing into a final pose:

> O calendar customs! Under the broom
> Yellowing over them, compose the frieze
> With all of us there, our anonymities.
> (*North*, p. 10)

The formal qualities of this poetry require particular analytic strategies from the critic. It is very largely autobiographical and takes its claim to authenticity from that familiar covenant between reader and poet which tacitly agrees the immediacy and authority of such experience.[7] This fiction of autobiography is perhaps a necessary and enabling one for lyric poets not always exactly choosing to take up the challenge to the notion of a unitary self offered by the 'high' Modernists. But where the fictionality of the poetic speaker is routinely concealed, a responsible criticism must seek to recover the moment of his construction (it almost always is 'his'). If this work were to be read primarily as unmediated transcription of the experience of historical individuals, it would

become impertinent to question the constitution of the emotionally pivotal female figures – beloveds, wives, mothers, grand-
mothers – in it. My comments about these female figures, then, as
about the central male ones, concern fictive beings whose status is
virtual, not actual.

II

Turning to the representation of gender roles in Heaney's work in
particular, we find that he tends towards two opposing and possibly
complementary representations of gender interaction. One constructs an unequivocally dominant masculine figure, who explores,
describes, brings to pleasure and compassionates a passive feminine
one. The other proposes a woman who dooms, destroys, puzzles
and encompasses the man, but also assists him to his self-discovery:
the mother stereotype, but merged intriguingly with the spouse.
Members of the first group, representing masculine domination, are
'Undine' and 'Rite of Spring', in which the man's victory is achieved
in agricultural terms; 'Punishment' and 'Bog Queen', which
combine an erotic disrobing narrative (as in Renaissance and other
love poetry) and a tone of compassionate tenderness, with a very
equivocal result; and the political group including 'Ocean's Love to
Ireland', 'Act of Union' and 'The Betrothal of Cavehill', which
usually rehearse narratives of rape and sexual violation. The second
group contains 'The Tollund Man', 'The Grauballe Man' and the
intense and intriguing 'Kinship', which merges mother and spouse
as well as active and passive and, I shall argue, functions primarily
as a masculine-identity myth, despite its political ending and the
political criticism it has chiefly attracted.

  In Heaney's first two collections, the most prominent form of attention to gender roles is what may be termed vocational: an allocation of special domains to the masculine and feminine, of a
triumphantly traditional kind. Masculine actors find the greater
space: in *Death of Naturalist*, the very first poem 'Digging' fore-
shadows later, explicitly sexual, bog poems, with its all too relevant succession of phallic surrogates – pen, 'snug as a gun', spade –
and its sensuously rich material which waits passively to be 'dug'
('He … buried the bright edge deep', in the 'squelch and slap / Of
soggy peat' [p. 12]). The active prowess of the speaker's male ancestors is stressed, and he is concerned to present his own displace-

ment to intellectual performance as not interrupting his place in that succession.[8] Parallel to this insistence of inheritance, however, these early poems also rehearse the construction of an individuated masculine self: in the title poem 'Death of a Naturalist', the croaking bullfrogs – 'croaked on sods' – may be perceived as an invasion of maleness into the child's pre-pubertal feminised world, governed by 'Miss Walls' the teacher, whereas two poems later in 'An Advancement of Learning' the boy successfully faces down the slimy, 'nimbling' rat in a test of courage which confirms his own masculinity (pp. 15, 18).[9]

With increasing definiteness in the successive collections, the memory of an essentially unchanging rural world is rehearsed, with its traditional crafts and trades; and as a central part of that dispensation, male and female subject-positions are also construed as immemorially fixed. Once natural threats such as those represented by the rat, or by the eel-nits in 'Vision' (*Door into the Dark*, p. 45) have been overcome, the speakers of the poems identify admiringly with active natural creatures such as the bull 'Outlaw' (p. 16), and the trout which is rendered in strikingly phallic terms – 'Gunbarrel', 'torpedo', 'ramrodding' ('Trout', *Death of a Naturalist* p. 39). The trout's ballistic activity is contrasted with the neighbouring 'Cow in Calf', where bulk, slowness and recurrence of the same are stressed: 'Her cud and her milk, her heats and her calves/keeping coming and going' (p. 38).

There are human versions of such continuities: 'The Wife's Tale' with its rare female speaker is typical in celebrating, without obvious intentional irony, the separate spheres of farm and home labour: 'I'd come and he had shown me/So I belonged no further to the work.'[10] But Heaney's imagination is already dwelling more intensely on metaphors of *nature* as feminine than on the human version. Other strongly conventionalised female figures do also appear, especially mother figures signifying domesticity, intermittently from the earliest poems. But the centre of imaginative intensity is undoubtedly his curious and compelling construct of the land-cum-spouse-cum-deathbringer, with its active and passive aspects.

The hags and goddesses, classical and Celtic,[11] of Montague's poems are replaced in Heaney's by this figure. Its more politicised version, as it appears tentatively in *Wintering Out* and assertively in *North*, represents a merging of the north European fertility goddess, whom Heaney found described in P.V. Glob's study of Iron Age bog burials, with the rather vaguely realised notion of the land of Ireland as seeker of sacrifices, from nationalist political tradition.[12] In his bog poems Heaney sexualises the religious conceptions of Celtic and north European prehistory.[13] Gender in Celtic and other early mythologies was a metaphysical concept, one of several dyadic means of cosmic organisation (male:female lining up with black:white, left:right, north:south, and so forth); a proper service to male and female divinities of earth and air was connected with successful cultivation.[14] This is, of course, markedly different from the predominantly *sexual* interpretation of gender in our culture, which sees it as inextricably bound up with individual personal identity and affective fulfilment, an understanding deriving from Christian theology, the European tradition of courtly love, and the insights of psychoanalysis, among other sources. Heaney's archaising projection of specifically sexual feeling on to agricultural practices ('Rite of Spring', 'Undine') (*Door into the Dark*, pp. 25, 26) and human sacrifices to a fertility goddess (the bog poems) seems to be a bid to reach past urban and intellectual social forms and their accompanying thought-world, which are implicitly judged as wanting, to a notional state of physical naturalness and 'anonymities' whether folk or prehistoric. An obvious casualty of this attempt, were it to succeed, would be the impulse to individual self-determination and reflexivity. This is an impulse noticeably present in the self-construction of poets, but it is its assumed absence as a defining figure in the lives of Irish rural people and Iron Age Danes which seems to be being celebrated. Thus a disjunction appears between the speaking subjects of these writings and their unspoken objects. In particular the female figures in this conjured world are the epitome of a general silence, at the opposite pole from the describing, celebrating, expressing poet. Whether active or passive, these figures are spoken for, and this division is a highly problematic one.

The two successive poems, 'Rite of Spring' and 'Undine' are perhaps the first examples of an attempt to project sexual feelings into a landscape (*Door into the Dark*, pp. 25, 26). They are therefore ancestors of the more famous bog poems, but differ from them in using the second model I have outlined at the outset, one of male activity and female passivity. They project onto a water-pump and a stream respectively the figure of a sexually willing woman, who waits to be coaxed into satisfaction by farming skill: 'It cooled, we lifted her latch,/Her entrance was wet, and she came' (p. 25). This masculine narcissism is even more apparent in 'Undine', which ventriloquises the water-nymph's voice:

> ... And I ran quick for him, cleaned out my rust.
> He halted, saw me finally disrobed ...
> Then he walked by me. I rippled and I churned ...
>
> He explored me so completely, each limb
> Lost its cold freedom. Human, warmed to him.
>
> (p. 26)

It is difficult to read these pieces as other than classic fantasies of male sexual irresistibility: the moist pump-entrance, the flowing irrigation drain ('he dug a spade deep into my flank/And took me to him') seem almost like a parody of the narrative of erotic wish-fulfilment, in which the frigid female gladly warms to an expert and forceful man.[15] In one sense, the guise of a representation of rural life scarcely survives this sexual excitement, though in another it is being mobilised to legitimise the work, as eternal fact. One might read this conjunction of rural and sexual utopianism, foregrounding pleasure and promising a notional return to an earlier less repressed state; but the obliviousness of most sexual revolutionaries of the period to their own masculinist understanding of pleasure also marks Heaney's version, and hinders such an interpretation.[16] The pump and the stream are (preposterously, when one puts it like that) each imagined as 'fulfilled in spite of herself', which is to say disempowered; hence the real resemblance to pornographic fantasy. They cannot choose but be played upon, like the 'Victorian Guitar' which like its gentlewoman owner needs to be 'fingered' into pleasure (*Door into the Dark*, p. 33).

There is a further recurring feature of Heaney's work which connects with this nexus of ideas. This is the conceit of language as erotically enabling, joined in the following passage from 'Bone Dreams' with the female-body-as-landscape in a political conceit. The Irish poet 'colonises' with his charm – or force of language – the 'escarpments' of a female England. He projects himself as the phallic 'chalk giant':

> Carved on her downs.
> Soon my hands, on the sunken
> fosse of her spine
> move towards the passes.
>
> (*North*, p. 29)

The lover-speaker 'estimate(s) for pleasure/her knuckles' paving', and begins 'to pace' her shoulder: all usual amorous activities in which, however, the explorer's, 'estimator's', evaluator's position is the man's. Other instances of the association of speech with eros and energy or force in Heaney help to elucidate the topic. In 'Midnight' the eradication of wolves in Ireland is made the sign both of the seventeenth-century conquest and of emasculation. The poem ends:

> Nothing is panting, lolling,
> Vapouring. The tongue's
> Leashed in my throat
>   (*Wintering Out*, p. 46)

making a symptomatic equation of phallus, speech, predation and national strength almost too obvious to mention. 'Come To the Bower', which echoes the title of a favourite Irish parlour patriotic song, combines the traditional topos of disrobing with the richly sensuous apprehension of the landscape which is one of Heaney's most characteristic features:

> My hands come ...
>
> To where the dark-bowered queen,
> Whom I unpin,
> Is waiting ...

This land-spouse is herself rendered as a bog body, wearing the necklet or torc which stood for the goddess:

> A mark of a gorget in the flesh
> Of her throat. And spring water
> Starts to rise around her.
>   (*North*, p. 31)

The welling water indicates her fertility. The unpinning and marking encode her female disempowerment (precisely as pornographic texts do, since social life and the aesthetic utterances it produces form a symbolic continuum) and thus fix her role as an erotic object. At the end of the poem, she is further named, as wealth: 'I reach ... to the bullion/Of her Venus bone'. Here the reality of the ritual murders Heaney found recorded in Glob is metaphorised and explicitly eroticised, in a striking and disturbing mental transformation.

'Punishment', the poem describing Glob's 'Windeby girl' – the drowned body of a young woman with a halter round her neck – has attracted much commentary, chiefly about the analogy it makes with tarring and feathering in Northern Ireland. The speaker of it does to a certain degree interrogate his own position, discerning it as that of 'the artful voyeur', but the words' overt application here is to his sense of his political ambiguity: he would 'connive/in civilised outrage', but understand the 'tribal, intimate revenge' being exacted (*North*, p. 38).

The publicly expressible 'civilised outrage' belongs to a language which the persona of all these poems feels is denied him and his ethnic group; he constructs Northern Irish Catholics, as, like Celts to the ancient Romans, a race mysterious, barbarous, inarticulate, lacking in civility.[17] But, one might argue, the result of this expressed sense of marginalisation by the speaker is to make the girl seem doubly displaced: the *object* of equivocal compassion by a *subject* himself forced to be covert, himself the *object* in turn of others' dominant and therefore oppressive civility. Thus the fascinated details of the description which composes the girl as passive and observed object have the effect, whatever the intention, of outweighing the initial assertion of a shared subjectivity ('I can feel the tug/of the halter at the nape/of her neck ...'). The compassion is equivocal not just because of the half-sympathy with the punishers, but because of the speaker's excitement (can we not identify it as specifically sexual?) at the scopic spectacle of the girl's utter disempowerment ('It blows her nipples/to amber beads ...'). Hence the usual sense of the work 'voyeur' must suggest itself strongly.

Turning to the active feminine, Heaney's engagement with a female destructive principle is particularly intense, as an examination of his Ireland-spouse poems 'The Tollund Man' (*Wintering Out*, p. 47) and 'Kinship' (*North*, p. 40) shows.[18] In the 'Tollund Man', the sacrificed corpse is described as 'bridegroom to the goddess', who is credited with a murky amalgam of lethal and sexual acts:

> She tightened her torc on him
> And opened her fen,
> Those dark juices working
> Him to a saint's kept body ...
>   (*Wintering Out*, p. 47)

This, like 'Punishment', aestheticises the horror of a murdered corpse and presents it as a natural phenomenon ('The mild pods of his eye-lids,/His pointed skin cap'). But here it is also made an effect of erotic absorption and incorporation by a female energy conceived as both inert and devouring.[19] If one turns the motif this way round, for the moment understanding it primarily as a way of thinking about woman rather than about Irish political murder, it reveals an intense alienation from the female. Eros–Thanatos pairings generally do seem to rely on a perception of woman as channel for masculine fear and desire, and this is no exception.[20] When one readmits into one's mind the poem's parallel between Stone Age sacrifices to the fertility goddess and Irish political murders in the 1970s, one's increased awareness of the erotic-aesthetic frisson in the first section makes the analogy seem all the more shaky and difficult to assent to. Can this sexual thrill really have anything other than mischief to bring to our thought about the actual perpetration of torture and murder?[21]

'Kinship' at the dead centre of the collection *North*, also represents a centre of Heaney's project. Developing a hint at the end of the earlier 'Bogland' ('The wet centre is bottomless', *Door into the Dark*, p. 56) it presents Ireland's bogland as above all an encompasser – ruminant, storer, embalmer, 'insatiable bride', swallower, mideen, floe. At the end of the passage is a disrobing moment: the ground 'will strip/its dark side' as if undressing. As the poem's hero pulls out, then replaces, a turf-spade in the bog, 'the soft lips of the growth/muttered and split', leaving the spade-shaft 'wettish/as I sank it upright ...' (*North*, p. 42). Following this moment of phallic discovery (evidently granted with some reluctance by the bog) and reinsertion, recalling Heaney's many earlier digging and ploughing passages, there is an explicit merging of birth and death – 'a bag of waters/and a melting grave' – in this personified ground, a 'centre' which, unlike Yeats's, 'holds' (*North*, p. 43). The poet identifies himself as having grown out of this bog 'like a weeping willow/inclined to/the appetites of gravity'. In a turn to the overtly political at the end of this poem, he addresses Tacitus, Roman describer of Celtic Europe, wryly acknowledging the practice of 'slaughter for the common good' (which presumably represents both the ritual human sacrifices described in the *Germania* and Northern Ireland's deaths):

> Our mother ground
> is sour with the blood
> of her faithful,
>
> ...

Report us fairly,
...
How the goddess swallows
our love and terror.
(*North*, p. 45)

First, taking this passage politically, one might argue that the evident irony in the expression 'slaughter for the common good' does not solve the more general problem of a projection of the mythic and ritual onto history and the resulting blockage of rational understanding and possible action. The poet compulsively predicates his claim to intuitive identification with his landscape on personifying it as feminine and equating it with death ('The goddess swallows/our love and terror'). As others have suggested, this further entangles the gloomy facts of Irish political history with the heady rhetoric of nationalist ideology instead of interrogating them.[22] My second point concerns the poem's real priorities. It privatises and sexualises the political. Its early sections show much greater intensity than the later (which has probably contributed unnoticed to critics' questioning of the ending): the charged personal ode to the bog as mother and partner – giver and receiver of the spade-phallus – is no more than tenuously related to political references at the end, which risk seeming merely dutiful. I think the real focus is on the speaker's private myth of identity formation, on wresting a self from 'feminine' unbounded indeterminacy of the bog. This poem attempts a synthesis of the stereotypes of femininity: the bog-goddess is imagined as both mother and spouse, and as destroyer and provider, but it is still persistently (and in both senses) the *ground* on which the speaker's self and his very identity is predicated. The feminine is thus once again an Other but not really envisaged as an alternative subject or self: a relation of complementarity, certainly, but not of equality, and one which enshrines difference in the oppressive sense of that word.

Following the privatised and sexualised bog-Ireland poems, there is also a series of poems in *North* which mount a specifically political gender-historical narrative of English conquest and colonisation in Ireland. This series includes 'Ocean's Love to Ireland' and 'Act of Union'. Both these poems employ the conceit representing political conquest by acts of sexual possession, and 'Act of Union' makes the male/English violator its speaker; and/or: it is a love poem to a pregnant spouse. There is a crucial ambiguity about the sexual act

in both poems: rape (indicated by a reference to Elizabethan mas-
sacres) or seduction by a male force whose energy is attractively ir-
resistible? The language of 'Act of Union' strongly recalls that of
the exploring lover in 'Bone Dreams':

> ... I caress
> The heaving province where our past has grown.
> I am the tall kingdom over your shoulder
> That you would neither cajole nor ignore.
> Conquest is a lie ...
>
> *(North*, p. 49)

Her mutuality is said by the male speaker (England) to have supplanted violation of an unwilling woman (Ireland). How ironically
is that speech to be read? Does not the tone strongly recall the
gender triumphalism of 'Rite of Spring', which, after all, enthusias-
tically celebrated the farmer's sexualised thawing of the pump? The
speaker in 'Act of Union' regrets the pain of his partner's imminent
childbirth ('the rending process in the colony,/The battering ram')
but also reads it as the promise of a forth-coming Oedipal struggle:
'His parasitical and ignorant little fist already ... cocked/At me
across the water'. One can credit Heaney with a vivid rendering of
the complications, the tangled intimacy, of Anglo-Irish political relations. But one might also feel that to rehearse the narrative of
these relations in these terms is to re-mystify rather than to attempt
an understanding of the phenomena. What is especially questionable is the apparently unconscious equivocation in Heaney's de-
ployment of gender. The application of force in the agricultural
handling of nature, imagined as male sexual domination, is felt as
deeply right. But the occurrence of the same structure in political relations is (presumably, in the work of a poet of Catholic nationalist
origins) to be taken as reprehensible and grievous. Further, in the
structure of *North* the death-bringing goddess's claiming helpless
victims (female force) in the bog poems is matched with the rape-
narratives in the pendent colonisation series (male force). The sym-
metry of this deepens the sense of inevitability generated by the
whole project of the mythicisation of history. The social, economic
and constitutional conditions of modern Ireland are elided in this
reductive narrative which merges the chthonic personifications of
the Iron Age with a presentation of gender roles as immemorial.

The brief lyric 'The Betrothal of Cavehill' closes the series with a
quizzical moment:

Gunfire barks its questions off Cavehill
And the profiled basalt maintains its stare
South: proud, protestant and northern, and male.
Adam untouched, before the shock of gender.

They still shoot here for luck over a bridegroom.
The morning I drove out to bed me down
Among my love's hideouts, her pods and broom,
They fired above my car the ritual gun.
                                        (*North*, p. 51)

In the second stanza, the familiar moment when the land is taken
as spouse ('... to bed me down/Among my love's hideouts, her pods
and broom') allows us to identify the 'bridegroom' equivocally in
three possible ways: either as an autobiographical splinter of the
poet, or as an IRA man on the run and living rough in the countryside, or as the rock itself 'marrying' the prone land it surveys so
dominantly. So the familiar reprise of nationalist attachment to the
land as a betrothal to death is complicated by the ethnically double
male presence in the poem: the 'Adam untouched' figure of
Cavehill, which is made to represent the culturally masculine in-
transigence of northern Protestantism, disdaining converse with the
land-as-Eve; and the presumably Catholic 'bridegroom', who 'beds
down' in the land. Even the *culturally* feminine Catholic/nationalist
figure is *biologically* male: may we read this as a discreet Utopian
moment in which all (males) may merge their differences in a
general bedding down in the (female) land? As to politics, this may
be an improvement; but as to gender, it is the status quo as in all
the other poems: politics is seen in terms of sexuality, but not the
reverse. The mildly humorous characterisation of the rock as phallic
stops short of demythicising Genesis, however wry it is about
northern Protestant no-surrendering: the gender there was *before*
gender was already male.

It may seem that I am ignoring one of the prominent developments of Heaney's later work, namely his 'marriage poems', particularly in *Field Work*, and indeed the sprinkling of earlier personal
love poems. I believe, however, that these poems are mostly also
recuperable to this broadly dualistic active-passive pattern I have
outlined.[23] Poem VI in the sequence 'Station Island', for example
('Freckle-face, fox-head, pod of the broom'), is motivated by an
autobiographical 'plot', but centres on the constitutively masculine
gestures of watching and actively desiring an uncommunicative and

mysterious female figure, who is associated with bags of grain, like the sheela-na-gig in *Station Island*:

> Her hands holding herself
> are like hands in an old barn
> holding a bag open
>   (p. 49)

and what one might term a genial voyeurism is typical of the love poems in general: 'The Skunk' is a classic example (*Field Work*, p. 48).[24] 'Polder' (*Field Work*, p. 51), one of the 'marriage poems', is a kind of psychologised reprise of 'Kinship', shorn of political extrapolation. It retains the land-woman metaphoric equation: in the combined metaphor of possession and origination re-employed from 'Kinship', the woman is the territory where the man, 'old willow', has his 'creel of roots', and 'I have reclaimed my polder,/all its salty grass and mud-slick banks'. One might read the sequence *Field Work* itself, and its stress on the erotic excitement of retracing physical marks and stains on the spouse's limbs, as working to fetishise woman's body in much the same way as Montague's *The Great Cloak* does.[25]

So must we not conclude that the poetry of Montague and Heaney as a whole is insistently and damagingly gendered? Its masculine personae, whether in the narrative of personal identity, or that of nationality, must, it seems, possess or be possessed by a counter-force personified as feminine: an encounter of the genders as of aliens – dog eat dog, possess or be swallowed up – is forever occurring, even within and beneath politics. On this evidence, it remains very difficult for men, when they imagine self-formation as a struggle, to escape conceiving that struggle, however metaphorically or virtually, as *against* the feminine. The integral self counted as so precious to the capacity for expression of these poets is won against a necessarily subordinated ground of merely potential, never actual feminine selves. In Lacanian terms, they seem to be stuck in the self/not-self dualism of the mirror stage, failing to arrive at an acknowledgement of the existence of an autonomous subjectivity in others: a structure common to sexism and racism.[26] Just as 'every document of civilisation is a document of barbarism',[27] in Benjamin's phrase, so one is tempted to conclude that every feat of self-discovery by these masculine poets entails the defeat of a feminine ego. Or as Irigaray puts it:

the/a woman fulfils a twofold function – as the mute outside that sustains all systematicity; as a maternal and still silent ground that nourishes all foundations – ...[28]

From *Gender in Irish Writing*, ed. T. O'Brien Johnson and D. Cairns (Milton Keynes, 1991), pp. 88–92, 99–111.

NOTES

Patricia Coughlan identifies her own practice in terms of the second of two modes prescribed for feminist criticism by Elaine Showalter. The first, 'gynocritics' was to be concerned with the woman as writer. The second, 'the feminist critique', was to demonstrate how 'the hypothesis of a female reader changes our apprehension of a given text, awakening us to the significance of its sexual codes' ('Towards a Feminist Poetics', *Women Writing and Writing about Women*, ed. Mary Jacobus (London, 1979, pp. 25–6). The essay's wide range of reference to anthropology, psychology and the history of mythology and to critics like Walter Benjamin, Homi K. Bhabha and Luce Irigaray carefully subserves this purpose. I have, with the author's permission, excised from the original text of her essay a section devoted exclusively to John Montague's work. Montague remains, however, a comparative foil to Heaney in the development of her argument and the reader may wish to refer to his *New Selected Poems* (Newcastle, 1990) which contains all the poems discussed. Ed.]

1. David Cairns and Shaun Richards, 'Tropes and Traps: Aspects of Woman and Nationality in Twentieth-Century Irish Drama', *Gender in Irish Writing*, ed. Toni O'Brien Johnson and David Cairns (Milton Keynes, 1991), pp. 128–37.

2. Dorothy Dinnerstein, *The Mermaid and the Minotaur: Sexual Arrangements and Human Malaise* (New York, 1976).

3. Paul Muldoon's 'Aisling' which parodically refuses its due of reverence to this icon, substituting 'Anorexia' for Aurora and Flora, merely replaces a falsely idealised feminine figure with a self-destructive one arousing masculine distaste – inadequate as demystification (see *Quoof* [London, 1983], p. 39). See also Edna Longley, *Poetry in the Wars* (Newcastle, 1986), p. 207, for an approving view.

4. For the debate in feminist anthropology on the applicability of the nature–culture opposition to gender see: Sherry Ortner, 'Is Female to Male as Nature is to Culture?' in M. Rosaldo and L. Lamphere (eds), *Woman, Culture and Society* (Stanford, CA, 1974), pp. 67–88; Penelope Brown and Lydia Jordanova, 'Oppressive Dichotomies: the Nature–Culture Debate', Cambridge Women's Studies Group (eds),

Women in Society (London, 1981), pp. 224–41; Carol MacCormack and Marilyn Strathern (eds), *Nature, Culture and Gender* (Cambridge, 1980): and Shirley Ardener (ed.), *Perceiving Women* (London, 1975). On the limitation of women to domesticity, see Patricia J. Mills, *Women, Nature and Psyche* (New Haven, CT, and London, 1987); and on Freudian Oedipal dogmatism, Luce Irigaray, *Speculum of the Other Woman*, trans. Gillian C. Gill (Ithaca, NY, 1985). More specifically, I have been helped by John Goodby, whom I wish to thank for kindly showing me his research. Trevor Joyce's discussion with me on theoretical issues and his suggestions about drafts of this paper have been invaluable.

5. The phrase in Heaney's poem 'Punishment' (*North* [London, 1975], p. 38) describing the poet as 'artful voyeur' is only an explicit crystallising of a very general subject-position in his work, as I shall try to show. Laura Mulvey's classic discussion of the male gaze and the scopic is helpful here ('Visual Pleasure and Narrative Cinema', *Screen*, 16 [1987], 6–18).

6. For baking, see 'Mossbawn 1. Sunlight' (*North*, p. 8); the ploughing and digging fathers are enlisted in 'Digging' and 'Follower' (*Death of a Naturalist* [London, 1966], pp. 13, 34). [For spinsters living by wells, see Montague's 'The Music Box', in *The Dead Kingdom* (Dublin, 1984) and Heaney's 'A Drink of Water' in *Field Work* (London, 1979). Similar myth-based 'hag' figures occur in several poems by Montague like 'The Sean Bhean Bhocht', *Poisoned Lands* (Dublin, 1977) and 'The Wild Dog Rose' (*The Rough Field*, Dublin, 1972). In their dual aspect of horror and grace these realistically presented figures reflect the 'sovereignty goddess' met by the legendary hero as described in Alwyn and Brinley Rees, *Celtic Heritage* (London, 1961), pp. 73–4. Ed.]

7. Even the sequences of Montague and Heaney tend to be predicated as narrative on the personal experience of the poet.

8. See also 'Follower' (*Death of a Naturalist*, p. 24).

9. See Nicholas Roe's argument that this poem reveals what he calls Heaney's 'mythic wish' in an early form. Roe says that the female teacher who explains the natural history of frogs 'appears as external author of guilt – perhaps a sexual awakening' – and represents 'a sort of primary school Eve who bears responsibility for the ... child's lost innocence'. 'Wordsworth at the Flax Dam: an Early Poem by Seamus Heaney', Michael Allen and Angela Wilcox (eds), *Critical Approaches to Anglo-Irish Literature* (Gerrard's Cross, 1989), p. 169.

10. Though, of course, a feminist reader might not be able to avoid giving ironic *reading* to such a poem: 'I gathered cups .../And went. But they still kept their ease/Spread out, unbuttoned, grateful, under the trees'

(*Door into the Dark* [London, 1969], p. 27). I am grateful to Mary Breen for discussion of the issue of the masculinist representation of domesticity.

11. See note 6 above.

12. P.V. Glob, *The Bog People*, trans. Rupert Bruce-Mitford (London, 1971). See Heaney, *Preoccupations* (London, 1980), pp. 57–8, for his own account of his inspiration by Glob. The modern political half of the construct finds perhaps its most popular and familiar expression in the writings of Patrick Pearse.

13. The most sustained account of Heaney's whole bog complex is Jacqueline Genet's 'Heaney et l'homme des tourbières', J. Genet (ed.), *Studies on Seamus Heaney* (Caen, 1987) pp. 123–47, which crisply notices the poems' sexual emphasis and meanings, but forgoes interrogation of them.

14. See Alwyn and Brinley Rees, *Celtic Heritage*; Pamela Berger, *The Goddess Obscured: Transformation of the Grain Protectress from Goddess to Saint* (Boston, 1985). See also Proinsiais Mac Cana, *Celtic Mythology* (London, 1970), pp. 49–50, 85–94: 'the mythological role of love ... is of its nature functional or ritual rather than personal' (p. 85).

15. Neil Corcoran severely understates the case when he says 'the poem has, like "The Wife's Tale", its element of male presumption' (*Seamus Heaney* [London, 1986], p. 58).

16. See Patricia J. Mills, *Women, Nature and Psyche*, on the inadequacies of Marcuse's sexual libertarianism in *Eros and Civilization*, which greatly influenced thought in the 1960s. In the Irish context, Heaney is also revising the rural vision of Patrick Kavanagh, one of his primary enabling figures, to include sex, but sex neither as ideal romance nor as frustration, its two guises in Kavanagh. The crucial moment in earlier Kavanagh, of critique of the emotional and other deprivation attending Irish rural life, is, however, elided in Heaney.

17. See 'Freedman' (*North*, p. 60); 'The Toome Road' (*Field Work*, p. 15), with its British tank crews as 'charioteers', and also 'Kinship', discussed below.

18. It may be worth remarking that his sense of this identification seems quite different from that in early Irish mythology, in which several female war- and death-divinities appear; the hero or king must couple with them so as to ensure his victory or continued rule, but they – the Morrighan, the Badhbh, and Macha – are actively characterised as speaking figures. The territorial goddesses such as Anu dominated an area but were not especially thought of as murderous. Heaney's

version seems a modern and hybrid construct. See Mac Cana, *Celtic Mythology*, pp. 66, 86.

19. See Corcoran, *Seamus Heaney*, pp. 96ff., for an informed and intelligent commentary from a general point of view on these poems. Longley, *Poetry in the Wars*, pp. 140–69 gives a trenchant discussion which makes some good demystificatory points, but insists on a formalist and depoliticising understanding of poetry which is itself open to question ('Poetry and politics, like church and state, should be separated' [p. 185]). Elmer Andrews (*The Poetry of Seamus Heaney* [London, 1988]) is sensitive and painstaking, but his formalist approach tends to perpetuate the reification of gender-roles.

20. See Mills, *Women, Nature and Psyche*, pp. 157ff. on Freud, Marcuse and the notion of the 'primal horde': 'Because woman was Eros/Thanatos/Nirvana in "immediate" union she represented the threat of "mere nature" – "the regressive impulse for peace which stood in the way of progress – of Life itself"' (p. 157, quoting Marcuse's *Eros and Civilization* [1972]). One might add that Heaney's repeated meditations on the bog bodies are, of course, not at all concerned to open the enquiry anthropologically towards a rational investigation either of Stone Age religious and agricultural behaviour, or of Irish politics, but to make 'offerings or images that were emblems' (Heaney interview, 1977, quoted in Corcoran, *Seamus Heaney*, p. 96).

21. As Edna Longley has well said: 'Heaney does not distinguish between involuntary and voluntary "martyrdom", and the nature of his "archetype" is such as to subsume the latter within the former' (*Poetry in the Wars*, 151).

22. On the irony in the last section of 'Kinship', see Corcoran, *Seamus Heaney*, p. 119, against other commentators who accuse Heaney of a crude nationalism (Longley, *Poetry in the Wars*, pp. 185–210 and Morrison, *Seamus Heaney*, pp. 68, 81).

23. With the exception of the early 'Lovers on Aran', in which for once the stress is on a quality of mutuality and indistinguishableness in the lovers' relation: 'Did sea define the land or land the sea? ...' (*Death of a Naturalist*, p. 47), and occasional other poems such as no. X of the *Glanmore Sonnets* ('I dreamt we slept in a moss in Donegal ...') (*Field Work*, p. 42).

24. The engagingly self-mocking 'Sweeney's Returns' even discerns that voyeuristic structure as a comedy, but scarcely to the extent of dismantling it (*Station Island*, p. 114).

25. [John Montague, *The Great Cloak* (Dublin, 1978). See, for instance, poems like 'Snowfield' (p. 11) and 'Don Juan's Farewell' (p. 19). Ed.] It is fair to say, however, that Heaney's *The Haw Lantern* (London, 1988) marks a general turn away both from mythicising in the earlier

manner, and from sexual stereotyping in love poetry; but it is not yet clear whether this does signal a new politics in the most general sense.

26. As Homi K. Bhabha says, 'Colonial power produces the colonised as a fixed reality which is at once an "other" yet entirely knowable and visible' ('The Other Question: Difference, Discrimination and the Discourse of Colonialism', O. Francis Barker *et al.* [eds], *Literature, Politics and Theory* [London, 1986], p. 156). On the mirror stage and entry into the symbolic order as a passage beyond dualism, see J.P. Mueller and W.J. Richardson, *Lacan and Language; a Guide to Ecrits* (New York, 1982), p. 136. I thank Nick Daly for discussion of this point.

27. Walter Benjamin, 'Theses on the Philosophy of History', *Illuminations*, ed. Hannah Arendt, trans. Harry Zohn (London, 1992), p. 248. [Ed].

28. Luce Irigaray, *Speculum of the Other Woman*, p. 365.

13

Ana-; or Postmodernism, Landscape, Seamus Heaney

THOMAS DOCHERTY

'Back-up-again'; or, in Greek, 'ana-, ana-, ana-'. 'The Grauballe Man', ostensibly about a man who is 'back up again', is an exercise in what I shall call 'anagrammatology': it is a writing elaborated in various modes of this 'ana-': anamnesis, anagogy, anamorphosis and analysis. In the present essay, I will show the poem as a writing which occurs as an *event* in these four modes. This status of the writing, as an event and not a work, nor even a 'text' in the conventional sense, is important. 'Eventuality' opens writing to a postmodernism, as an anachronic or untimely meditation, countering the 'punctuality' of the Modern, which is concerned to map two points in time as if they were two stable points in space. Eventuality releases the interior historicity of those 'spots of time'. To think this writing as event enables an analysis which will be, literally, a setting free of its elements into a movement of emancipation. A philosophy of postmodernism will raise the stakes of the poem, disabling the conventional reading of it as a neo-Modernist exercise in myth-making and replacing the usual banal reading of its politics with something literally more compelling. Three elements construct the argument: the issue of historicity; an exploration of the poem's cinematism; and a consideration of the poem as an engagement with the issue of justice, judgement and criticism: a 'cutting' which attempts to *trancher la question*.

'THE BEARINGS OF HISTORY'

Once imagined, he cannot be seen
(Seamus Deane, 'A Killing')

On the face of it, Heaney's 'The Grauballe Man' seems an unlikely contender for the title of 'postmodernist poem'. In terms of obvious theme and style, it seems that most critics would think of it in terms of a 'late Modernist' text, Heaney as a late Modernist poet, the ephebe influenced by Yeats and by a Romantic tradition which was crucially concerned with landscape and a particular kind of eco-relation to the land.[1]

This 'economy', or law of space, however, is no longer available in the same way to Heaney as it was to the Romantics or even to the Modernists who were all so famously concerned with the issue of 'exile'. Contemporary space is what Virilio thinks as an 'espace critique', a space in which geometry is giving way to chronometry: our socio-political being is organised not primarily by spatial or geo-political mappings, but rather by temporal, chrono-political determinations.[2] Heaney lives in this different eco-consciousness of the aesthetic of space proposed by (for example) Beuys and Long, sculptors whose work is uncannily 'temporal' in that it is marked by its internal historicity and temporal mutability. A typical piece by Richard Long, say his 'A Line Made by Walking, England' is, in a certain sense, no longer 'there', except in the photographic record or image. Heaney's 'sense of place' is also – inevitably – now a sense of time. He writes:

> We are dwellers, we are namers, we are lovers, we make homes and search for our histories. And when we look for the history of our sensibilities I am convinced ... that it is to ... the stable element, the land itself, that we must look for continuity.[3]

This land is also a repository of history and continuity across time. It is the case that for Heaney, space has become critical in precisely another way close to this. Ireland itself is, of course, a 'critical space', a space built upon a 'critical difference' called 'the border' between North and South; it is built on that *stasis* or civil war which problematises any sense of its identity, specifically any sense of its historical identity. It is for this reason, of course, that the Field Day company, with whom Heaney works extremely closely, is crucially concerned to forge a history, to *remember*, as a therapeutic – and political – act which aims to 'suture' the wound to Ireland which is the border.

'The Grauballe Man' is, in a sense, a poem on poetry itself; its writing is precisely this kind of therapeutic anamnesis:

> I have always listened for poems, they come sometimes like bodies come out of a bog, almost complete, seeming to have been laid down a long time ago, surfacing with a touch of mystery.[4]

But it is a poetry which lies uncertainly between image (the photo-graph which prompted the poem) and memory (where 'now he lies/perfected'), between history and its representation. If anything, then, this is a poem which is about poetry as mediation or about a specific act of reading. Heaney is confronting the bog as 'the memory of a landscape', the palimpsest record of history which is now conceived as 'a manuscript which we have lost the skill to read'.[5] Most importantly, 'The Grauballe Man' is what we should think as a kind of 'interstitial' event, a writing half-way between image and text, figure and discourse.

For the neo-Romantic and Modernist traditions with which Heaney is conventionally aligned, 'imagination' forges a link between the Subject of consciousness and History as its Object. This enables the formulation of a transcendental Subject in Romanticism or – less gloriously – a Self capable of persistence in Modernism. This trans-historical or mythic Subject is, however, no longer easily available to Heaney, for the postmodern has prob-lematised the relation between the Subject and History, or between the 'real' and its 'representation'. If, in the 'society of the spectacle' or the 'hyperreal simulacrum', everything is now of the status of the image, then the 'real' has simply disappeared. The reality which is supposed to ground our representations, be it the presence of History as exterior fact or the presence-to-self of the supposed tran-scendental Subject, has itself become an image.[6]

This, in fact, is Heaney's problem, both a political and an aes-thetic problem. The 'ground' for his poetry, history itself in the Irish context, has disappeared, gone underground. As a result, a series of reversals takes place in 'The Grauballe Man': what seemed a tomb is a womb; what seemed a man gives a kind of birth while also being the baby itself; to dig is to discover not the past at all (history) but rather 'the presence of the past' (anamnesis). When Heaney wrote the poem, he was deeply aware of the presence of the past, not just in terms of his search for 'images and symbols adequate to our predicament',[7] but, rather, in terms of the very historicity of the present, his present as a moment in flux, his spatial present as a moment bifurcated, divided, a moment when space has gone critical, differential, historical rather than antiquarian. As Deane suggests, the mythologisation of history is more of a wound than a salve.[8]

The poem's crucial turn lies in a stanza which is itself an interstitial stanza:

> Who will say 'corpse'
> to his vivid cast?
> Who will say 'body'
> to his opaque repose?

This stanza asks: is history dead, a thing of the past; or is it alive, vivid, a presence of the past? It is the very posing of the question which opens the text to a postmodernism, to what I shall call its postmodern cinematism.

THE CINEMATISM OF THE POSTMODERN

'Postmodern' is frequently misunderstood: many follow a particular inflection of Fredric Jameson who, while theoretically aware of the complexity of the postmodern, takes it in his practice to mean a rag-bag of the art produced since 1945. But postmodernism, if it is to be taken seriously, is not to be understood as a simple periodising term like this. Rather, the postmodern calls into question this very manner of thinking history. Lyotard, for instance, asks:

> What, then, is the postmodern? What place does it or does it not occupy in the vertiginous work of the questions hurled at the rules of image and narration? It is undoubtedly a part of the modern. All that has been received, if only yesterday ... must be suspected. What space does Cézanne challenge? The Impressionists'. What objects do Picasso and Braque attack? Cézanne's. What presupposition does Duchamp break with in 1912? That which says one must make a painting, be it cubist. And Buren questions that other presupposition which he believes had survived untouched by the work of Duchamp: the place of presentation in the work. In an amazing acceleration, the generations precipitate themselves. A work can become modern only if it is first postmodern. Postmodernism thus understood is not

modernism at its end but in the nascent state, and this state is constant.[9]

Postmodernism is, as it were, the moment in the modern work when a critical difference becomes apparent; it is, for instance, the critical distance between Cézanne and Picasso when the latter paints in such a way as to call even the experimentalism of Cézanne into question; Picasso – postmodernist to Cézanne – becomes modern when a critical space is introduced by the works of Duchamp, and so on.

'Postmodern' does not describe a work, but, rather, an event; it is not a point in history, but an event in its historicity. The effect of this is to question a prevalent understanding of history itself. One view of history suggests that the past can be 'sliced into', and that certain nodal 'points' can be identified and epistemologically understood: thus, say, the 'history' of '1848'. Call this the 'Modernist' view, one shared by Jameson whose periodisations necessitate the location of some crucial 'points' in history. Another view suggests that this 'point' is merely an epistemological hypothesis: '1848' is not a point in time, but is itself internally historical, in the sense that within 1848 there is only a series of differing 'becomings' or events whose flux and mutability cannot be arrested. There is, as it were, an overlap between, say, January and February 1848, and it is this *overlap* or interstice which is history, not the points 'January' and 'February' between which the overlap eventuates. Call this the postmodern view: in this, epistemology becomes difficult; but the historicity of history is maintained. The Modernist view is, properly, the very contradiction of history.

This can be more easily explained in terms of a kind of cinematism which is extremely appropriate to Heaney's poem, which itself hovers undecidably between discourse and figure, between the photographic still and the properly cinematic moving image. Heaney's task in the text is not to discover an archaeological remnant of the past in its antiquarianism, but rather to write in the interstices of history itself, to be historical and to be aware of the flow and movement of history, history as 'becoming' even as he writes – or because he writes – the poem. It is an attempt to make movies out of the still image, which is, of course one of the reasons why most of the descriptions of the body describe it in fluid movement or flux.

Cinematism is precisely aligned with the postmodern. Bergson characterised 'old philosophy' as the belief that the flow of Being could be reduced to a series of '*coupes immobiles*' or 'stills'. Deleuze follows Bergson in the rejection of the still and its replacement with the '*coupe mobile*', a 'cut' which releases the temporality or cinematic heterogeneity (*l'espace critique*') held within the apparently still or homogeneous photographic image itself. For Bergson, according to Deleuze,

> le mouvement ne se confond pas avec l'espace parcouru, l'espace parcouru est passé, le mouvement est présent, c'est l'acte de parcourir ... les espaces parcourus appartiennent tous à un seul et même espace homogène, tandis que les mouvements sont héterogènes, irreductibles entre eux.[10]

> (movement is not mixed with space traversed, space traversed is past, movement is present, it is the act of traversing ... spaces traversed all pertain to a single, same and homogeneous space, whereas movements are heterogeneous, not reducible to each other.)

The reading of Heaney as a Modernist has to view this text as one in which there is an established homogeneity – a late symbolist 'correspondance' à la Baudelaire – between Jutland and Ireland which, as Deane has pointed out, can only be maintained by some 'forceful straining'.[11] Such a reading, further, has to ignore the literal movement of the text, which delineates not the past but the presence of the past as a living present and the mutability of that present, its fluidity or flux.

'The Grauballe Man' is an example of a kind of montage, which Eisenstein had described as a kind of dialectical process. Montage 'arises from the collision of independent shots',[12] as, for example, the collisions between Jutland and Ireland, the Iron Age and the IRA, the description of the man prior to the 'corpse/body' stanza and the child hinting at a Christian iconography, raising the issue of justice which dominates the latter half of the poem, and so on. Montage such as this gives what Deleuze calls

> l'image indirecte du temps, de la durée. Non pas un temps homogène ou une durée spatialisée, comme celle que Bergson dénonce, mais une durée et un temps effectifs qui découlent de l'articulation des images-mouvement.[13]

> (the indirect image of time, of duration. Not a homogeneous time or spatialised duration, like that which Bergson denounces, but a real duration and time proceeding from the articulation of the image-movement.)

It is a common misconception, deriving from much literary criticism, to suggest that Bergson had argued for the prioritisation of some kind of subjective time, a time which was to be measured within the Subject. Deleuze points out the fallaciousness of this. Far from time being within the Subject, the Subject is, that is, 'becomes', only through the agency of Time itself.[14] Virilio raises this to a sociological status:

> Au temps *qui passe* de la chronologie et de l'histoire, succède ainsi un temps *qui s'expose* instantanément. Sur l'écran du terminal, la durée devient 'support-surface' d'inscription, littéralement ou plutôt automatiquement: *le temps fait surface.*[15]
>
> (A time *which manifests itself* instantaneously thus takes the place of the time *which passes* of chronology and history. On the screen of the terminal, duration becomes 'support-surface' of inscription, literally, or, rather, automatically: *time becomes surface.*)

Time surfaces, a little like the body in the bog which is also, for Heaney, the poem itself in which time – or in my preferred term here, historicity – exposes itself.

This 'temps qui s'expose' is prefigured, as Virilio points out, in the techniques of photography and cinema.[16] Those techniques, of course, were precisely the techniques which Benjamin feared, on the grounds that they would make history less accessible, would derealise it in some way.[17] However, this derealisation is nothing more nor less than the denial of the availability of the *coupe immobile*, the denial of the still; and it bears repeating that the still itself is the very opposite of historicity as such; the still, or the *coupe immobile* which enables a stable knowledge of the past, the pastness of the past, is a kind of epistemological myth, however necessary. Heaney's text, however, is not about the pastness of the past but its presence. This is in accord with the living in a critical space of Ireland which Virilio would see as a paradigmatic postmodern condition. As a result of the movement away from perspectivism and its pieties towards cinematism, the inhabiting of time has supplanted the inhabiting of space itself. It is this issue which Heaney's poem is addressing: the anamnesis of history.

In anamnesis, according to Plato in *Meno*, we have something which Modernism articulated much later as a Proustian *souvenir involontaire*. In this, there is not so much a moment of knowledge of the past, but rather an actual recreation of the past, now present fully: it is, as it were, the actualisation of the virtual.[18] It is this process of 'actualisation' which is central to Heaney's poem. The body in the photograph starts off as a fluid being:

> As if he had been poured
> in tar, he lies
> on a pillow of turf
> and seems to weep
>
> the black river of himself

As the poem continues the description, we have what is in fact a process very like Robbe-Grillet's well-known description of a painting, 'La défaite de Reichenfels' in *Dans le labyrinthe* which, as it elaborates itself, becomes less static painting and more mobile scenario. A soldier, described fully as an image, begins to talk with a little boy, himself fully delineated within the frame of the painting; but as the description progresses the frame is transgressed and the boy and soldier leave 'La défaite de Reichenfels' (the title of the canvas: figure) and engage with each other in a fully narrative situation, *'dans le labyrinthe'* (the title of the novel: discourse).[19] This tendency towards the mobility and the mutability of narrative, the actualisation of the virtual, of that which seemed to be merely a representation – in short, the presentation of the unpresentable – occurs also in Heaney. The poet describes the corpse/body to the point where it is unclear whether it is alive or dead, on which side the grave it is; then recalls the photograph; and moves towards the perfection of the man in the memory of the poet, at which point the presence of the past becomes all the more telling in the issue of justice which the poem is addressing. It is 'the actual weight/of each hooded victim' which the poet feels. 'Actual' means 'current; present'; and the issue of justice is itself realised as now and present for the writing/reading of the poem. Through anamnesis, the virtual or hypothetical issue of justice which is proposed by the atrocity of the Northern Irish situation is made actual, current, an event. Its currency or fluency is also, of course, realised in the fluidity of bog man, who is seen not as a still but as a moving image: as a *coupe mobile*.

CURT CUTS

> the curt cuts of an edge
> Through living roots awaken in my head
> (Heaney, 'Digging')

In this cinematic poem, then, there is an arrangement around a crucial 'cut' or rupture. Within the text itself, that cut is the slashed throat of the bog man; and a slashed throat is also a throat which cannot speak. Heaney writes a poem about the difficulty of writing poetry within the problematic of injustice which determines the situation of the poet and his poem; both live in a terrain marked by a savage cut or crucial space which lodges them in history rather than in place. If people have no clearly demarcated terrain within which to identify themselves, they must turn to time and live in it. But the time is 'out of joint', in the sense that the history of Ireland is itself 'cut' or slashed, interrupted by a long colonial sojourn. These are Heaney's 'living roots' which quicken or come to life in his head. As Virilio indicates, 'le temps n'est un temps vécu ... que parce qu'il est interrompu' (time is a lived time only as and when it is interrupted).[20] The poem enacts this living time through its cut and montage organisation.

But this slashed throat raises another issue: that of justice and revenge. The text is clearly related to Heaney's 'Trial Pieces', poems exploring Viking culture in relation to his own:

> I am Hamlet the Dane,
> skull-handler, parabalist,
> smeller of rot
>
> in the state, infused
> with its poisons,
> pinioned by ghosts
> and affections,
>
> murders and pieties,
> coming to consciousness
> by jumping in graves,
> dithering, blathering.[21]

The Jacobean revenge motif in Heaney is closely related to the idea of 'finding a voice', with 'Feeling into Words', those 'words, words, words' which Hamlet reads/says when confronted with the not so wily spy, Polonius, who finds a 'pregnancy' in Hamlet's talk.[22]

Heaney's first prose collection, *Preoccupations*, opens with the word 'Omphalos' repeated three times ('words, words, words'), with which he 'would begin'. This is important to the Oedipal impetus in Heaney. In this poetry, the land frequently occupies the position of the maternal womb, a womanly space to be 'quickened by penetration' as Deane puts it.[23] Heaney 'speaks daggers' to this Gertrude earth, this 'Bog Queen'. Oedipalisation is, of course, a setting of time 'out of joint', for it enables the mythic attempt of the son to be at once both son and father of himself. In Heaney, this temporal *décalage* is made more evidently a 'presence of the past' in the ghostly apparition of Hamlet in 'The Grauballe Man' and his other 'Danish' poems.

This bog man is strangely androgynous. Firstly, we find that a 'ball' is like an 'egg'; there is a dark linguistic hint here that the testicle is like an ovary; and this linguistic slippage or ambivalence, this metaphor itself, merging ball and egg, produces that theme of pregnancy which dominates the latter half of the poem. Further, even his body takes on a female cast:

> His hips are the ridge
> and purse of a mussel ...

There is a kind of *anamorphosis* going on here, as the male character mutates into something female. A mussel typically is a container of sorts; and here it is as if the man's hips contain a 'currency', a pearly fluency. This fluency or fluidity in the cast of the body makes it an example of what Irigaray thinks as a *mécanique des fluides*,[24] a 'mechanics' which enables the poem to become mobile, a mutable *coupe mobile*. It is also a mechanics which enables the poem to articulate a 'becoming womanly'; and again, the drive towards becoming rather than being is a drive towards the historicity of eventuality rather than to the fixity of a punctuality. This engagement with gender places the text in the mode of anamorphosis.

The man is 'pregnant' in these lines: but what he is pregnant with is, of course, the presence of a future. The poem, then, is written in this peculiar future anterior tense which, according to Lyotard, describes the typically postmodern event. Further it again recalls Deleuze who cites Augustine's notion:

> il y a un présent du futur, un présent du présent, un présent du passé, tous impliqués dans l'événement, enroulés dans l'événement, donc simultanés, inexplicables. De l'affect au temps: on découvre un temps intérieur à l'événement ...[25]

> (there is a present of the future, a present of the present, a present of the past, all implicated in the event, rolled together in the event, and

thus simultaneous with each other and inexplicable. From affect to
time: one discovers a time which is interior to the event ...)

This slipperiness of the 'actual', the constant and fluid actualisation
of a virtual which organises the poem, is manifest in all the slipperiness which threatens to be arrested but which the text constantly
strives to release or to loosen. If the man is in a sense giving birth to
himself from the female bog in which there lies a 'Bog Queen', then
it follows that the poetry is in a sense also giving birth to itself,
originating itself or authorising itself in this peculiar act. The poet is
Hamlet giving birth to himself, the poet as ephebe delineating a
birth to himself through a violent act of self-wounding. For the
poem is itself paradigmatic of poetry for Heaney; it is a poem about
his own writing, which comes from the bog or from anamnesis, but
it is also thus a poem which delineates how the poetry must derive
from an act of self-wounding anamorphosis.

In my epigraph to this section, Heaney has described himself as
the man suffering from the cut or bruise to the living root which is
not in the Grauballe Man's head but in his own. The poem is his
epithalamium, in a sense, the wedding text which tries to wedge together the wounding, a suturing which is involved in the act of love.
It is the 'Wedding Day' on which:

> I am afraid.
> Sound has stopped in the day
> And the images reel over
> And over. ...[26]

It also brings to mind his dream of freedom:

> I had to read from Martin Luther King's famous 'I have a dream'
> speech. 'I have a dream that one day this nation will rise up and live
> out the full meaning of its creed' – and on that day all men would be
> able to realise fully the implications of the old spiritual, 'Free at last,
> free at last, Great God Almighty, we are free at last.' But, as against
> the natural hopeful rhythms of that vision, I remembered a dream
> that I'd had last year in California. I was shaving at the mirror of the
> bathroom when I glimpsed in the mirror a wounded man falling
> towards me with his bloodied hands lifted to tear at me or to
> implore.[27]

The Grauballe Man is, as it were, the image in Heaney's mirror:
it is his Imaginary, his dream of freedom. As an Imaginary, it fits

in with the idea of anamnesis in the poem. For what we have is a situation in which the world, that alien space, turns out, according to the logic of the poem, not to be an unknown alien realm at all, but rather simply what the poet always knew but had simply forgotten: it is as if the world is, as it were, a latent unconscious for the poet, his Imaginary; and the writing of the poem is the therapeutic act of recovering what had been re-pressed and facing it. In these terms, the atrocities of violence in Ireland are a return of the repressed pagan rites of sacrifice. Paganism, of course, is itself aligned by Lyotard with a certain postmodernism.[28]

But there is another image which fits this in the text as well. That image is an image of Robert Lowell, who ghosts this poem. Lowell ghosts the poem in the stanza which describes the head of the Grauballe Man:

> The head lifts,
> the chin is a visor
> raised above the vent
> of his slashed throat ...

What we have here is a situation again reminiscent of Hamlet, espe-cially that Hamlet who tests the veracity of Horatio when the latter is testifying to seeing Hamlet's dead father, returned from the grave rather like a proto-Grauballe Man. In that sense, Hamlet asks whether the ghost was armed:

> Hamlet: Armed, say you?
> All: Armed, my lord.
> Hamlet: From top to toe?
> All: My lord, from head to foot.
> Hamlet: Then saw you not his face.
> Horatio: O, yes, my lord. He wore his beaver up.[29]

This can be easily translated back into Heaney's text. Here, the idea of the chin as a visor which is raised above the throat suggests a literal 'disfiguration' in the sense that the face disappears in a par-ticular way. It implies a closeness of the eye and the mouth, or, as Lowell would have thought this, a closeness of 'Eye and Tooth'. In Lowell's poem of that name, we have an examination of a particu-lar kind of justice, the justice of a biblical mode (eye for eye, tooth for tooth, etc.) which is placed at the service of a political ideology,

that which is identified in Lowell's poem by the imperialist
American eagle:

> No ease from the eye
> of the sharp-shinned hawk in the birdbook there,
> with reddish brown buffalo hair
> on its shanks, one ascetic talon
>
> clasping the abstract imperial sky.
> It says:
> *an eye for an eye,*
> *a tooth for a tooth.*[30]

In a certain sense, then, Heaney's 'bog poems' become his version
of a text '*For the Union Dead*': a volume which is, of course, a validation of America's 'North'. Heaney's 'Act of Union' sees the relation of imperialism in precisely the same Oedipal terms which 'The
Grauballe Man' explores.

In the interstices of the poem, then, there comes a pressure
which breaks it from within. It is, in a sense, an allegory
of Ireland's situation. But whereas the Modernist reading would
see this in terms of a spatial allegory: in which the text would be
regarded as falling into two halves, marked by the interstitial
line of Lowell and/or Oedipus, and would thus think of this
breakage or interruption in spatial terms, what my own reading
shows is that this Irish situation, this 'curt cut', is itself a temporal cut, hence allegory as *anagogy*, one which involves history
and which sees the poem as itself a historical event. Heaney here
is not map-making, but history-making: one of the 'history
boys'.[31] When Lowell appears as the ghostly father figure in the
way I have described, we have 'the presence of the past', not its
pastness.

Lyotard suggests that the 'post' of postmodern be understood in
terms of 'ana-': it is a 'procès en ana-':

> Tu comprends qu'ainsi compris, le 'post-' de 'postmoderne' ne
> signifie pas un mouvement de *come back*, de *flash back*, de *feed back*,
> c'est-à-dire de répétition, mais un procès en 'ana-', un procès
> d'analyse, d'anamnèse, d'anagogie, et d'anamorphose, qui élabore un
> 'oubli initial'.[32]
>
> (You understand that understood in this way, the 'post-' of 'post-
> modern' does not signify movements of the type *come back, flash
> back, feed back*, that's to say of repetition, but rather a process in

'ana-', a process of analysis, of anamnesis, of anagogy, of anamorphosis, a process which elaborates an 'initial forgetting'.)

Heaney's poem is precisely such a process. It is analysis: literally a setting free and into mobility of elements which had seemed to be irreversibly conjoined. It is anamnesis, in its articulation of and actualisation of the presence of the past, even of disparate pasts. It is anagogical in its allegorical enactment of the historical split which is the *espace critique* of Ireland. It is anamorphic, a distorted drawing or representation with its abnormal transformations of Heaney into Oedipus, Oedipus into Lowell, Ireland into America, *North* into *For the Union Dead*, Jutland into Ireland, and so on: all those montage effects of this cinematic poem. It is in short the elaboration of an 'initial forgetting', a forgetting of the violence of origin itself.

From *Postmodernism: A Reader,* ed. T. Docherty (1991)

NOTES

[In his review of Heaney's *The Government of the Tongue* (essay 10 above) Thomas Docherty envisaged the poet beginning to hear 'the alterity, the incomprehensible otherness' as a preferable alternative to his 'imperialist thinking'. In this later essay Docherty finds this projected shift of awareness already accomplished in 'The Grauballe Man' which he diagnoses as a 'postmodernist poem'. One of his main aims is to provide an adequate definition of postmodernism and my own Introduction tries to summarise his conclusions. But another aim is to 'raise the stakes' of the poem (and possibly of other related poems) so that Heaney is seen as engaging experimentally with a wider range of contemporary issues than has yet been acknowledged in recent criticism of his work.

Docherty assumes knowledge of Plato's dialogue, *Meno*, of the writing of Robbe-Grillet, Lowell and Fredric Jameson, of the sculpture of Richard Long as well as the paintings of Cézanne and Picasso, but the main challenge to the reader is linguistic. Docherty's first sentence (p. 206 above), for instance, offers three meanings for the Greek prefix upon which his argument is hinged, but the OED definition (up, in place or time, back, again, anew) usefully complements what the 'play' of Docherty's critical text provides. The following short glossary is similarly intended to bring dictionary definitions fruitfully to bear on Docherty's sometimes cryptic vocabulary:

Anagogy. Mystical or spiritual understanding or interpretation.

Anagrammatology. Docherty has combined 'Anagram' (transposition of the letters of a word or, more loosely, the elements of an utterance, so that a new word or utterance is formed) with 'Grammatology' (the scientific study of writing systems).

Analysis. Resolving something complex into its simple elements (etymologically, loosing back and up).

Anamnesis. Recalling of things past.

Anamorphosis. Distorted projection of something which when seen from one particular point appears regular.

Cutting. The action of the verb 'cut' in various senses; an intersection; also a section; also used in film-making.

Décalage (Fr.). Shifting the zero of an instrument. (*Décalage horaire*: time shift).

Event. An incident or occurrence; also the outcome of a course of action.

Palimpsest. Parchment on which you can write and then erase what you have written.

Simulacrum. A mere image, a specious imitation or likeness.

Trancher (Fr.). To slice (bread); to cut; to settle (question) once and for all. Ed.]

1. See, for example, Seamus Deane, 'The Timorous and the Bold', in his *Celtic Revivals* (London, 1985); Elmer Andrews, *The Poetry of Seamus Heaney* (London, 1988); Neil Corcoran, *Seamus Heaney* (London, 1986). In their 'Introduction' to *The Penguin Book of Contemporary British Poetry* (Harmondsworth, 1982), Blake Morrison and Andrew Motion made a polemical claim for Heaney as '[t]he most important new poet of the last fifteen years', one in the forefront of a new 'departure' in poetry 'which may be said to exhibit something of the spirit of postmodernism'. The hesitancies in this final phrase reveal the fact that their notion of postmodernism was extremely underinformed and undertheorised. Antony Easthope trounces their suggestion in his piece, 'Why Most Contemporary Poetry Is So Bad', *PN Review*, 48 (1985), pp. 36–8, where he also argues that 'The Grauballe Man' is, in fact, 'resolutely *pre-modernist*'. Both views miss some essential points of what is at stake in the postmodern, as I'll argue here.

2. Paul Virilio, *L'espace critique* (Paris, 1984). At the simplest level, this corresponds to an organisation of life in terms of 'quality time' or 'labour time' rather than its organisation in terms of the 'metropolis' and the 'suburbs'. Cf. the work of Gilles Deleuze, especially with regard to the idea that social, political and psychological life are all organised around 'lines of flight', making territorialisations and deterritorialisations.

3. Seamus Heaney, *Preoccupations (London, 1980), pp. 148–9*. For a more detailed explication of this aesthetic in Long, see Thomas Docherty, *After Theory* (London, 1990), pp. 22–4.

4. Heaney, *Preoccupations,* p. 34.

5. Heaney, *Preoccupations,* pp. 54, 132; the latter phrase is attributed to John Montague.

6. See Guy Debord, *La Société du spectacle* (Geneva, 1967); Jean Baudrillard, *L'échange symbolique et la mort* (Paris, 1976); Baudrillard, *Amérique* (Paris, 1986). This tendency in poetry is perhaps most marked in the work of John Ashbery. But it has been there in a great deal of modernist writing, where there was a marked interest in the 'interstitial'. Modernist writers did not chart the 'death of the Self': they were interested in the self-in-time, and in the interstitial moments between those significant moments of assured selfhood or supposed self-presence. Hence Proust was interested not in the heartbeat itself but in the 'intermittences du coeur'; Woolf was interested not in actions but in what goes on 'between the acts'; Bergson was interested in the time 'between' marked instants; Eisenstein in the dialectical relation between the images which constituted montage in cinema; Saussure in the relations 'between' signs rather than in signs themselves; Einstein in 'relative' rather than absolute measure; and so on. It is this 'interstitial' area which determines Heaney's writing here.

7. Heaney, *Preoccupations,* p. 56. 'The Presence of the Past' was the title of the 1980 Venice Biennale which initiated the 'postmodern debate' in architecture.

8. Deane, *Celtic Revivals,* p. 179.

9. Jean-François Lyotard, *The Postmodern Condition* (Manchester, 1984), p. 79; cf. Fredric Jameson, 'Postmodernism; or, the Cultural Logic of Late Capitalism', *New Left Review,* 146 (1984), 53–92; and Jameson, 'The Politics of Theory', in his *The Ideologies of Theory,* II (London, 1988), pp. 103–13.

10. Gilles Deleuze, *Cinéma 1: L'image-movement* (Paris, 1983), p. 9.

11. Deane, *Celtic Revivals,* p. 179.

12. Sergei M. Eisenstein, *Film Form,* as quoted in Gerald Mast and Marshall Cohen (eds), *Film Theory and Criticism,* 2nd edn (New York, 1979), p. 104.

13. Deleuze, *Cinéma 1,* p. 47.

14. See Deleuze, *Différence et répétition* (Paris, 1968), p. 116, especially the passage on Kant and what Deleuze thinks as the 'je fêlé', which marks the becoming of the Subject, its existence in historicity or in the form of time.

15. Virilio, *Espace critique,* p. 15

16. Ibid., p. 77.

17. See 'The Work of Art in the Age of Mechanical Reproduction', *Illuminations*, ed. Hannah Arendt, trans. Harry Zohn (London, 1992), pp. 210–44. [Ed.]

18. See, for example, Georges Poulet, *Proustian Space* (Baltimore, MD, 1977).

19. Alain Robbe-Grillet, *Dans le labyrinthe* (Paris, 1959), pp. 24–31 *et seq*.

20. Virilio, *Espace critique*, p. 103; cf. Deleuze, *Kant's Critical Philosophy* (Minneapolis, 1984), pp. vii–viii.

21. Heaney, 'Viking Dublin: Trial Pieces', in *North* (London, 1975), pp. 21–4.

22. See Heaney, 'Feeling Into Words', in *Preoccupations*; the references here are to Shakespeare's *Hamlet*, II.ii.

23. Deane, *Celtic Revivals*, p. 177.

24. Luce Irigaray, *This Sex Which Is Not One* (Ithaca, NY, 1985).

25. Deleuze, *Cinéma 2: L'image-temps* (Paris, 1985), p. 132.

26. Heaney, 'Wedding Day', in *Wintering Out* (London, 1972), p. 57.

27. Heaney, *Preoccupations*, p. 33.

28. See Lyotard, *Rudiments paiens* (Paris, 1977) and *Instructions paiennes* (Paris, 1977), *Tombeau de l'intellectuel* (Paris, 1984), *Le postmoderne expliqué aux enfants* (Paris, 1986).

29. Shakespeare, *Hamlet*, I.ii.

30. Robert Lowell, 'Eye and Tooth', in *For the Union Dead* (London, 1965), pp. 18–19.

31. Seamus Deane, 'Send War in Our Time, O Lord', in *History Lessons* (Dublin, 1983), p. 12.

32. Lyotard, *Le postmoderne explique aux enfants*, p. 126.

14

The Distance Between: Seamus Heaney

STAN SMITH

A PLACE TO COME FROM

Perhaps Seamus Heaney's commonest critical mannerism is the teasing out of innuendoes and ambiguities in some ordinary locution, as for example in his comments in *The Government of the Tongue*[1] on Robert Lowell, whose poetic 'resources proved themselves capable of taking new strains, in both the musical and stressful sense of that word'. Heaney's device doesn't always take the strain, sometimes seeming more a tic of rhetorical routine than a necessary complication: 'that strain again, it had a dying fall'. As with his recurrent arguing from etymology, too much of the argument's strain can be taken up in a verbal play which substitutes for logic and demonstration. Most notorious perhaps is the schoolboy *double entendre* of that lecture given at the Royal Society of Literature in 1974, 'Feeling into Words', which effectively exposed Leavisite pieties by touching up their lower parts as a discourse of sexual displacement. But it is apparent even in such apparently innocuous items as his 1977 lecture at the Ulster Museum, 'The Sense of Place', a phrase which he glosses as 'our sense, or – better still – our *sensing* of place'.

Nevertheless, the linguistic strategy is deeply symptomatic. It effects a kind of destabilisation on the ground of language itself, unsettling what he calls the 'sovereign diction'[2] with alternative, subversive voices. This is apparent in the slant light cast on the 1977 lecture by a later one given at the Wordsworth Summer

Conference at Dove Cottage. 'Place and Displacement: Recent Poetry of Northern Ireland' makes it clear, in terms of a Saussurean binary, that place is impossible to define without displacement. Displacement, one might say, is the necessary ground upon which to find or found one's place.

> 'I hate how quick I was to know my place.
> I hate where I was born, hate everything
> That made me biddable and unforthcoming',

the poet mouths at his 'half-composed face/In the shaving mirror' (Joyce's 'cracked looking-glass of the servant') in a moment of confessional self-loathing in 'Station Island'. But really knowing your place means refusing to settle for being put in your place, whether it is your own people or an occupying presence (Joyce's Haines) which is doing the placing – means learning, in the ghostly ventriloquism of 'Station Island', 'that what I thought was chosen was convention'. The subtitle of this lecture significantly speaks of poetry *of* Northern Ireland, not *from* it, and a whole world of difference can hang on such a preposition. In *The Haw Lantern*, four parables give a precise twist to this topographic insistence: 'From the Frontier of Writing', 'From the Republic of Conscience', 'From the Land of the Unspoken', 'From the Canton of Expectation'. The preposition in one sense simply indicates the place of origin of the missive (as in 'A Postcard from Iceland'). But that 'from' carries more weight than this. In the first poem he *writes from* the frontier; but as the last three stanzas indicate he also experiences a sense of release at having *come away from*, escaped across it:

> And suddenly you're through, arraigned yet freed,
> as if you'd passed from behind a waterfall ...
>
> past armour-plated vehicles, out between
> the posted soldiers flowing and receding
> like tree shadows into the polished windscreen.

The prepositions do much here in effecting the sense of relief in passage, 'passed from behind... past... out between... receding... into'. That 'through', a preposition turned adverb and then colloquially a verb complement, takes on a heavy freight of meaning. If it 'concentrates an identity in a heave of renewal' it also 'disperses it in a blast of evacuation', a process which in *The Government of the Tongue*[3] Heaney finds 'morbid' in Sylvia Plath's 'Daddy' – where, though he does not remark on it, the word acquires a similar duplicity:

> So daddy, I'm finally through.
> The black telephone's off at the root,
> The voices just can't worm through ....
> Daddy, daddy, you bastard, I'm through.

Working it through, getting through, may mean saying you're through with it for ever. This poem Heaney disapproves of (though he nevertheless calls it a 'brilliant ... *tour de force*'), is highly apposite to the frontier of writing. Heaney too is not only through the roadblock. He is also through with that country: with its exposed positions, with having to justify himself, with perpetual interrogation. In the light of Plath's usage, 'through' picks up the resonance of that 'spent' applied to the self earlier – spent, that is, like a used cartridge, or a life 'spent' by an over-itchy trigger finger:

> the sergeant with his on-off mike repeating

> data about you, waiting for the squawk
> of clearance; the marksman training down
> out of the sun upon you like a hawk.

The prepositions themselves relentlessly train *down out of upon* the 'subjugated, yes, and obedient' self held in its place down the sights of 'cradled' guns.

That the preposition is a key resource in Heaney's poetic armoury is confirmed by his remarks, in 'The Sense of Place', on a line of Kavanagh's:

> And the same vigour comes out in another little word that is like a capillary root leading down into the whole sensibility of Kavanagh's place. In the first line, 'the bicycles go by in twos and threes'. They do not 'pass by' or 'go past', as they would in a more standard English voice or place, and in that little touch Kavanagh touches what I am circling. He is letting the very life blood of the place in that one minute incision.[4]

'Pass by' may be a sly dig at Yeats's horseman. Heaney, *at* the frontier, we note, is *suddenly through*, as if by magic without any apparent act of transit, only in a simile *passing from behind, passing out between*. The 'From' of the poem's title takes up but also takes on the title of W.H. Auden's play *On the Frontier*. In 'Sounding

Auden', the second lecture of *The Government of the Tongue*, Heaney remarks on the oddity of the preposition 'between' at another frontier of decision in Auden's verse:

> Who stands, the crux left of the watershed,
> On the wet road between the chafing grass
> Below him sees ...[5]

Similarly, in analysing the effect of 'chafing'[6] he tunes in, finely, on its inbetweenness: 'disturbed by a lurking middle voice' between active and passive, it 'occupies' (a loaded word before the Popean noun phrase) 'a middle state between being transitive and intransitive, and altogether functions like a pass made swiftly, a sleight of semantic hand which unnerves and suspends the reader above a valley of uncertainty'. When he writes of 'this deferral of a sense of syntactical direction' Heaney is indicating some of the preoccupations of his own poems in *Station Island* and *The Haw Lantern*, which also, like early Auden, turn upon 'the necessity of a break, of an escape from habit, an escape from the given...only to expose their ultimate illusory promise'.[7]

If Auden's poems 'sound back' to earlier ones, Heaney's own poem here resounds with this earlier source in Auden, coming out 'from behind a waterfall/on the black current of a tarmac road'. Auden's advice to the stranger, 'frustrate and vexed', is to 'Go home', or find himself equally emptied and subjugated by a land which 'cut off, will not communicate'. Heaney's poem inhabits an occupied 'middle state' and 'middle voice' full of spoken and unspoken communications (the 'intent' of the rifles, the atmosphere of 'pure interrogation'), of knowledges of the self withheld from it, and of the silent messages of fear, obedience and power that grow from the barrel of a gun. In 'The Mud Vision' this is identified as that state of Irish paralysis in which, once, 'We sleepwalked/The line between panic and formulae', unable to 'dive to a future'. 'Terminus', recalling his variously divided childhood, takes a more balanced position – between rural and urban, agrarian and industrial, active and passive, transitive and intransitive, weighing pros and cons. If 'Baronies, parishes met where I was born', so that he grew up 'Suffering the limit of each claim', these 'limits' are not only passively borne (suffered) as limitations on the self but also tolerated, in a learnt and active sufferance, as limited claims, which can be put in their place *because* they are limited. Coming to understand such limits can then offer insight:

> Two buckets were easier carried than one.
> I grew up in between.

'Second thoughts' thus become the first fruits of thinking itself, and the poem's second thoughts, moving out from between, end at a watery margin which is also a crossing point, a place of negotiation between opposing forces which figures the stance of one whose end is peace, 'in midstream/Still parleying, in earshot of his peers'.

Whereas the early Auden stands repeatedly transfixed 'Upon this line between adventure', caught 'Between attention and attention', ordered to 'Turn back' before he reaches any frontier by a man with a gun, because 'There is no change of place',[8] Heaney's prepositional space is a different one, not transfixed but moving 'with guarded unconcerned acceleration' from 'out between'. In 'Station Island' the ghost of William Carleton speaks of his own hardness in a hard time as maybe containing a lesson for the poet, '"whoever you are, wherever you come out of"'. Freedom may be found in displacing oneself. But, as Heaney observes in 'The Sense of Place', citing Carson McCullers, 'to know who you are, you have to have a place to come from'.

SOUNDING OUT THROUGH

For such 'an earnest of the power of place' this essay returns to the world of Heaney's own childhood:

> The landscape was sacramental, instinct with signs, implying a system of reality beyond the visible realities. Only thirty years ago, and thirty miles from Belfast, I think I experienced this kind of world vestigially and as a result may have retained some vestigial sense of place as it was experienced in the older dispensation.[9]

The Celtic Twilight, for all its naïveties, was 'the beginning of a discovery of confidence in our own ground, in our place, in our speech, English and Irish', a discourse 'that would bind the people of the Irish place to the body of their world'. This bodiliness of a world 'instinct with signs', I shall suggest, is important. Heaney's model here is Patrick Kavanagh's assertion that 'Parochialism is universal; it deals with fundamentals...now that I analyse myself I realise that throughout everything I write, there is this constantly recurring motif of the need to go back'. Kavanagh's 'sense of his place involves detachment', for it is only when one is fully *in* and *of* a place that one can feel fully Kavanagh's need to be 'detached, remote ... take part but ... not belong'. As with Wordsworth, these native places are 'influential in the strict sense of the word "influential" – things flowed in from them'. As Heaney elaborates the argument, the prepositions once again pre-position the preoccupied subject, in this 'middle state' where things *flow in from* and *flow out to*.

Etymology is summoned to explain this relation at the beginning of the Plath lecture, speaking of a Yeats

> less concerned in his criticism to speak about the actual tones and strains of poetic language than to evoke the impersonal, impersonating, mask-like utterance which he takes all poetry to be. We are reminded how *persona* derives from *personare*, meaning 'to sound out through', how the animation of the verb lives in the mask's noun-like impassiveness. For Yeats, the poet is somebody who is spoken through.[10]

'Sounding back' in the discussion of Auden has its corollary in this 'sounding out through'. 'Through', as we have seen, is 'another little word' fraught with ambivalence. 'Poetry makes nothing happen', Auden said famously, in what is clearly a direct response to Yeats's fretful questions about poetic responsibilities in 'The Man and the Echo'. But it is nevertheless, in a less frequently cited line, 'A way of happening, a mouth'. This is what Heaney argues in the opening, title lecture of *The Government of the Tongue*, quoting the Polish poet Anna Swir on the poet as 'an antenna capturing the voices of the world, a medium expressing his own subconscious and the collective subconscious':

> Poetry's special status among the literary arts derives from the audience's readiness to concede to it a similar efficacy and resource. The poet is credited with a power to open unexpected and unedited communications between our nature and the reality we inhabit.[11]

Heaney's habit of ringing all the possible changes on an equivocal word or phrase comes from a refusal to be pinned down prematurely in a fixed place, a wish to keep open those channels of communication which allow all the ambivalences of his Northern Irish provenance to sound through. As 'From the Republic of Conscience' indicates, dual citizenship as an Irishman and an Ulster Catholic has its poetic equivalents. To *come back from* is to carry no baggage of duty-free allowance; but, as the comic circumlocution makes clear, it does carry the duty to be oneself, and to speak conscientiously, and without relief, as an ambassador of this freedom:

> I came back from that frugal republic
> with my two arms the one length, the customs woman
> having insisted my allowance was myself

and the old man at immigration

> therefore desired me when I got home
> to consider myself a representative
> and to speak on their behalf in my own tongue.

In the Republic of Conscience, 'You carried your own burden and .../your symptoms of creeping privilege disappeared'. But if this is a place where the salt has not lost its savour, it is also a place where everything has to be taken with a pinch of salt. For speaking in your own tongue means avoiding the folly of 'the fork-tongued natives' of 'Parable Island', who 'keep repeating/prophecies they pretend not to believe', and who, in some perpetually deferred future, are going to start mining for truth beneath the mountain where, it is said, 'all the names converge', and the conflicting narratives are reconciled.

In 'Station Island', the ghost of Carleton laments being made by Ribbonmen and Orange bigots 'into the old fork-tongued turncoat/who mucked the byre of their politics'. In 'Whatever You Say Say Nothing' (*North*) it is difficult not to be 'fork-tongued on the border bit' in a world 'Where tongues lie coiled, as under flames lie wicks' and '"You know them by their eyes", and hold your tongue'. It is in the context of these locutions and locations that we must understand the title of *The Government of the Tongue*. It is a characteristically tricksy phrase, and its tricks lie in that multiple-choice preposition: government of the tongue, by the tongue, for the tongue? The book itself offers the first two possibilities:

> what I had in mind was this aspect of poetry as its own vindicating force. In this dispensation, the tongue (representing both a poet's

personal gift of utterance and the common resources of language itself) has been granted the rights to govern. The poetic art is credited with an authority of its own. As readers, we submit to the jurisdiction of achieved form, even though that form is achieved not by dint of the moral and ethical exercise of mind but by the self-validating operations of what we call inspiration.[12]

However, such a jurisdiction may be that of a poetic Diplock Court, and a poet who has inscribed in a poem's title the homespun political wisdom of the Irishism 'Whatever You Say Say Nothing' (almost a performative injunction, self-exemplifying, nullifying itself in a paradox in which nothing is said, twice), knows that utterance is never quite so undemanding. I am not myself sure whether Heaney picked up this phrase from an existing political slogan, or whether the Provisional IRA got it from Heaney. In either case, the poetry accrues legitimacy to the political slogan, putting the poem in the same compromised place as those writings Yeats fretted over in 'The Man and the Echo', opening up a whole new area in the relations between poetry and politics. The poem refers to 'The famous/Northern reticence, the tight gag of place'. If, in *The Government of the Tongue*, Heaney claims that 'I have, on the whole, been inclined to give the tongue its freedom',[13] the poem defines the constraints of a freedom which 'Still leaves us fork-tongued on the border bit'. The border may be the bit that is between the teeth, but the poem leaves us with the biter bit, and biting his own tongue. *The Government of the Tongue* likewise speaks with a forked tongue, immediately qualifying its grandiose reiteration of Romantic clichés with a word to the wise:

> All the same, as I warm to this theme, a voice from another part of me speaks in rebuke. 'Govern your tongue,' it says, compelling me to remember that my title can also imply a *denial* of the tongue's autonomy and permission. In this reading, 'the government of the tongue' is full of monastic and ascetic strictness. One remembers Hopkins's 'Habit of Perfection', with its command to the eyes to be 'shelled', the ears to attend to silence and the tongue to know its place.[14]

Its place here is firmly in the cheek. It's noticeable that Heaney nominates an equally Romantic, inspirational source for this countervailing instruction: 'a voice from another part of me ... compelling me'. Yet it is an impersonal 'one' who remembers, not from the poet's original place, but from a position where the voice assumes, not the vatic authority of the bard, but that of a well-placed member of the literary ascendancy, languidly calling up fellow members of the club. Just which place is it that Heaney is knowing about, here?

A moment in *The Haw Lantern* sneakily qualifies this authority, reminding us from what part of himself that voice may in fact have spoken, as well as *what* he may know better, in the fourth of his sonnet elegies for his mother:

> With more challenge than pride she'd tell me, 'You
> Know all them things.' So I governed my tongue
> In front of her, a genuinely well-
> Adjusted adequate betrayal
> Of what I knew better.

The maternal reproach arises from her own 'Fear of affectation', her mispronunciation of words 'beyond her' expressing – possibly – fear of betraying 'The hampered and inadequate by too/ Well-adjusted a vocabulary'. The already readjusted poet, condescendingly relapsing into 'the wrong/Grammar which kept us allied and at bay', only obliquely questions how this community's demotic is somehow ruled 'wrong' in the discourse of polite society. Although the poet is instructed to govern his tongue, it seems that it is the mother's tongue – the mother tongue – which is put in its place, and that place is *in the wrong*. However, the poem's tongue is subtle and diverse here, as I will argue later.

There is another moment in *The Haw Lantern* where the poet governs his tongue, self-consciously submitting, not to the voice of inspiration, but to a formal tradition of occasional verse which has 'English' written all over it. 'A Peacock's Feather' is a poem written for the christening of an 'English niece' (as the text designates her), and it squirms with polite embarrassment at so bridling its tongue as to utter something alien but in keeping with the pastoral 'mellowness' of a Gloucestershire landscape. Even here the poem still knows where it comes from:

> I come from scraggy farm and moss,
> Old patchworks that the pitch and toss
> Of history have left dishevelled.
> But here, for your sake, I have levelled
> My cart-track voice to garden tones,
> Cobbled the bog with Cotswold stones.

But it's not so sure of where it's going. Compelled by occasion, status, loyalty, to write a light celebratory poem, one thinks of Yeats, that earlier voice which spoke with Ascendancy accents in a good cause:

> While I, a guest in your green court,
> At a west window sat and wrote
> Self-consciously in gathering dark.
> I might as well be in Coole Park.

Slyly coiled in the 'in-law maze' of the tongue, in the poem's absolving 'touch of love', the voices wait to speak out through the mask: 'Couldn't you do the Yeats touch?' One thinks too, that is, of Joyce, deflating Yeats's flattery of Lady Gregory: 'The most beautiful book that has come out of our country in my time. One thinks of Homer.'[15]

The tone is very different from Yeats's, a 'billet-doux', a nursery rhyme, quiet, casual, governed, wishing no harm, its blushful whimsy calling up the de la Mare of *Peacock Pie*. But there is an altogether more strident resonance to the bird, recalling that peacock which screamed among a rich man's flowering lawns in Yeats's 'Ancestral Houses', betokening the end of a civilisation, adding a deeper darkness to the gathering dark. 'The future's not our own'. But neither is the past. This levelled landscape requires a prayer for its future precisely because of that past:

> May tilth and loam
> Darkened with Celts' and Saxons' blood
> Breastfeed your love of house and wood.

That 'blood/Breastfeed' is a dark enjambement, in which the mother's milk runs with blood.[16] The slate of the opening may not, after all, be wiped clean, for all our pious hopes. The poem sounds out through the persona it assumes against the place to which it is quite sincerely addressed – a place identified in an essay in *Preoccupations* as 'In the Country of Convention: English Pastoral Verse'. Pastoral is a conventionally innocent realm, certainly; but England is a country governed by the false naïveties, the feigned ingenuousness, of pastoral.

THINKING IN AND BACK INTO

Kavanagh's landscapes, Heaney says, are 'hallowed by associations that come from growing up and thinking oneself in and back into the place'.[17] Heaney's own most Kavanaghish poem is probably 'The Old Team' in *The Haw Lantern*, but even here the real places 'Have, in your absence, grown historical', part of a history which is a repertoire of antagonistic stories. The title of *Field Work* had pointed the way to these later developments, poised equivocally between the local – the real fields and hedges of this sequence, from which the particular poetic talent emerged – and the larger field of meanings within which that life now finds itself, which, as indicated in a poem such as 'A Postcard from North Antrim', is always *elsewhere*. 'A Postcard from Iceland' in *The Haw Lantern* reads like an ironic postscript to Auden's and MacNeice's *Letters from Iceland*. Auden may have had his Ulster travelling companion in mind when he wrote, in the opening poem to that volume, 'North means to all: reject!'. Certainly Heaney seemed to be recalling this when, in the title poem of his own *North*, he 'faced the unmagical/invitations of Iceland', foremost of which is the invitation to encompass by going beyond, rejecting his native culture as Auden did in casting from Iceland a cold anthropologist's eye on Englishness. Heaney's island parables (including 'Station Island' and 'Parable Island' itself), all test and transcend the limits of Irish insularity, the better to return to and interpret it – to rediscover, thinking in and back into the place, 'How usual that waft and pressure felt/When the inner palm of water found my palm.'

It is from outside the field that the pattern of forces can best be understood, rather than simply suffered. That identity is best found in displacement, in both the literal and the psychoanalytic sense, is the point of the important lecture on *Place and Displacement* Heaney delivered at Dove Cottage in 1984, seeing in the uprootedness of the returning native Wordsworth, a displaced person, *persona non grata* in his own country, a model for all subsequent poetic displacements:

> The good place where Wordsworth's nurture happened and to which his habitual feelings are most naturally attuned has become...the wrong place. He is displaced from his own affections by a vision of the good that is located elsewhere. His political, utopian aspirations deracinate him from the beloved actuality of his surroundings so that

his instinctive being and his appetitive intelligence are knocked out of alignment. He feels like a traitor among those he knows and loves.[18]

Recent Northern Irish poetry, he says, reveals the same double displacement. The way to cope with 'the strain of being in two places at once, of needing to accommodate two opposing conditions of truthfulness simultaneously'[19] is not despair, however, but Jung's strategy of finding a 'displaced perspective' in which the suffering individual can outgrow particularist allegiance while managing to 'keep faith with...origins', 'stretched between politics and transcendence...displaced from a confidence in a single position by his disposition to be affected by all positions, negatively rather than positively capable'.[20]

The echo of Keats's 'negative capability' as an answer to Wordsworth's 'egotistical sublime' indicates the way out Heaney was to find from the Northern Irish deadlock from *Field Work* onwards. It is in the 'lyric stance', in language as itself a site of displacement, 'the whispering gallery of absence', 'the voice from beyond',[21] that the writer can seek the hopeful imaginary resolution of real conflicts. Heaney's poetry has pursued language as political metaphor and metonymy through to its source, to a recognition of language as both place of necessary exile and site of a perpetual return home. *Station Island* is the product of such a recognition, a volume full of departures and returns. Displacement is here seen not as exile but as freedom, whether in the wide-blue-yonder of America or the poetically licensed otherworlds of Dante's *Divine Comedy*. The loving fidelity of the émigré who, like Wordsworth, is necessarily now just 'visiting' that which he's left behind provides the motive force for the volume, and a poem such as the ironically entitled 'Away from it All' catches some of the complexities of such a position. In *The Haw Lantern* Heaney goes a step further, beyond the margins altogether, to deconstruct those blarney-laden tales of nativity, decentring and redefining a self-regarding Irishness. In the words of the title poem, it is not enough to bask in 'a small light for small people'. The modest wish to 'keep/the wick of self-respect from dying out,/not having to blind them with illumination' is too limited, too easy an ambition. Now 'it takes the roaming shape of Diogenes/with his lantern, seeking one just man' to be the true measure of this field, scrutinising with a gaze which makes 'you flinch.../its blood-prick that you wish would test and clear you'. The terror of being tested, assessed, and the

anxious yearning for clearance, run through most of the poems in
the volume. The gaze that 'scans you, then moves on' here brings to
bear both a moral and a poetic measure. 'Parable Island' tells us
that there are no authenticating origins, only a plethora of story-
tellings which push the origin further back into an original emptiness, scrawled over with too much meaning. It is in this area of
dense secondary signification, where script dissembles an original
emptiness, that Ireland 'begins'.

DRAWING A LINE THROUGH

'Whatever You Say Say Nothing' speaks of the ends of art:

> To lure the tribal shoals
> To epigram and order. I believe any of us
> Could draw the line through bigotry and sham
> Given the right line, *aere perennius*.

The word 'order' crosses its customary frontiers here, negotiating
familiar transactions between political and literary structures, as
that pun on 'line' as boundary demarcation, poetic line and, possibly, ideological narrative indicates. The further, suppressed
meaning of 'line' (taking up 'gaff and bait') adds a rather more
dubious resonance, for the fisher of men may lure the tribal shoals
into those Joycean nets which ensnare the soul, though purification,
in the echo of Mallarmé mediated by Eliot, is clearly the poet's aim.
In 'The Sense of Place', Heaney writes *en passant* of Synge 'whom
Yeats sent west to express the life of Aran, in the language of the
tribe', thereby creating 'a new country of the mind'[22] and, although
he sees this here as positive, in 'A Tale of Two Islands: reflections
on the Irish Literary Revival' he speaks rather more warily of
Synge's enterprise, invoking in support not only Kavanagh but,
most potently, Stephen Dedalus's intense and satiric rejection, at
the end of *Portrait*, of the old man of the west whose mountain
cabin is 'hung with the nets of nationality, religion, family, the ar-
resting abstractions'. But, Heaney adds, though Stephen fears, he
will not destroy him:

> The old man is as much a victim as the writer. His illiterate fidelities
> are the object of Stephen's scepticism, the substance of what Stephen
> rejects; and yet they are a part of Stephen himself. Stephen is angry

> that all his culture can offer him for veneration is this peasant oracle,
> yet understanding the ruination that he and the old man share, he is
> not prepared to struggle to the death.[23]

There is a poetic course to be charted here between the demands of
'native' orality and 'universal' writing. But if the siren voices of an
illiterate oracle are not to run the project aground on populist mud-
banks it must take on board those instructions to 'purify the dialect
of the tribe' from 'Little Gidding' which resonate in Heaney's own
ghostly Dantean sequence, 'Station Island'. And indeed, Eliot,
Dante and Jung rub shoulders in the last displacing moments of the
essay. However, the fullest account of Dante as role-model in this
later poetry is given in Heaney's 1985 article, 'Envies and
Identifications: Dante and the Modern Poet':

> The way in which Dante could place himself in an historical world
> yet submit that world to scrutiny from a perspective beyond history,
> the way he could accommodate the political and the transcendent,
> this too encouraged my attempt at a sequence of poems which would
> explore the typical strains which the consciousness labours under in
> this country. The main tension is between two often contradictory
> commands: to be faithful to the collective historical experience and
> to be true to the recognitions of the emerging self.[24]

Heaney's use of the phrase 'the language of the tribe' in 'The
Sense of Place' is suggestive, for it reproduces the mis-citation of
Eliot Donald Davie deploys throughout *Purity of Diction in English
Verse*[25] a book not unrelated in theme and argument to Heaney's
recurrent concerns. (Davie speaks of '"Mr Eliot's phrase, to purify
the language of the tribe"'[26] and uses this formula for the title of his
crucial chapter.) Davie's book, written while he was a lecturer in
Dublin, also deploys Synge as an example of a suspect linguistic
populism which exploits the 'bathetic' and 'brutal'; while in an important chapter he sets up Dante as an antithetical model of how
poetry should relate to 'the vulgar tongue'. Davie's introduction
raises questions of diction as political and moral touchstones in
terms which are strikingly consonant with Heaney's:

> [T]he poet who uses a diction must be very sure of the audience
> which he addresses. He dare not be merely spokesman of their senti-
> ments and habits, for he must purify the one and correct the other.
> Yet he dare not be quite at odds with his age, but must share with his
> readers certain assumptions... At this point, discussion of diction

becomes discussion of the poet's place in the national community, or, under modern conditions (where true community exists only in pockets), his place in the state. This aspect of the matter will become clearer when we ask how the poet, in his choice of language, should be governed, if at all, by principles of taste. And this is inseparable from the question of what Goldsmith and others understood by chastity and propriety in language.[27]

Dante's treatise *De Vulgari Eloquentia* is a key item in Davie's argument,[28] and the terms in which Dante negotiates the relation between the vernacular ('The Vulgar Tongue') and 'Grammar' (Latin) are cast in a language suggestively similar to that Heaney deploys in *The Haw Lantern*. This is specifically a question of the relations between 'the language of the tribe' and its many dialects, and the distinction, in many ways corresponding to the Saussurean one between *langue* and *parole*, explains why both Davie and Heaney misquote Eliot's formula.

Davie observes: 'Dante remarks that no one of the dialects can be considered the most illustrious, since the best poets have always departed from their own dialect for the purposes of their poetry.' What Dante calls the 'Illustrious Vulgar Tongue' is 'the perfection of a common language', 'intelligible to all ... but peculiar to none'. And, in words which recall the figure of the lantern-bearing Diogenes in the title poem of *The Haw Lantern*, 'our Illustrious Language wanders about like a wayfarer and is welcomed in humble shelters' and 'shines forth illuminating and illuminated'. It recognises no local princely court or court of justice, because it is itself 'courtly' and 'curial', carrying within itself 'the justly balanced rule of things which have to be done', itself the final court of linguistic appeal, 'though, as a body, it is scattered'.[29] This is, in fact, language as that 'frugal republic' with 'embassies ... everywhere' of which the poet is required to be 'a representative/and to speak on their behalf in my own tongue', in 'From the Republic of Conscience'.

Dante's discourse on the 'Illustrious Language', and Davie's commentary on it, call up many of the preoccupations of *Station Island* and *The Haw Lantern*. In particular, they go some way to explaining that complex, multiply punning play on 'clear' and 'clearance' in the latter volume, linking the 'blood-prick' of the haw lantern 'that you wish would test and clear you', 'the squawk of clearance' of 'From the Frontier' to the running motif of the elegiac sequence

'Clearances', where his mother's death effects a clarification of meanings and clears a space which is momentarily common:

> And we all knew one thing by being there.
> The space we stood around had been emptied
> Into us to keep, it penetrated
> Clearances that suddenly stood open.
> High cries were felled and a pure change happened.

The inconspicuous metaphor 'felled' then leads on to the final clearance of the sequence, and the poet's sense of his own mortality in the image of the chestnut tree, coeval with him, now long gone from the hedge where it was planted, no more than 'a space/Utterly empty, utterly a source', having 'lost its place', 'become a bright nowhere,/A soul ramifying and forever/Silent, beyond silence listened for'. The motif here is not finally personal life and death, but the sources and ends of poetry, calling up both that line quoted in *The Government of the Tongue* as evidence of Larkin's unlikely affinity with Dante, 'Such attics cleared of me, such absences',[30] and Auden's elegy for Yeats, who 'became his admirers', 'scattered among a hundred cities/And wholly given over to unfamiliar affections'.

Heaney's prose gloss of this anecdote in 'The Placeless Heaven: Another Look at Kavanagh' makes it clear that it is a parable about the relation between the poet's actual and his verbal universe. As a child, he says, he identified with the tree; now he identifies with the 'luminous emptiness' its absence creates:

> Except that this time it was not so much a matter of attaching oneself to a living symbol of being rooted in the native ground; it was more a matter of preparing to be unrooted, to be spirited away into some transparent, yet indigenous afterlife. The new place was all idea, if you like; it was generated out of my experience of the old place but it was not a topographical location. It was and remains an imagined realm, even if it can be located at an earthly spot, a placeless heaven rather than a heavenly place.[31]

Dante offers an authority for effecting such a clearance of the linguistic ground, asking, of the 'Illustrious Vulgar Tongue' in a metaphor Heaney seems to pick up, 'Does it not daily root out the thorny bushes from the Italian wood? Does it not daily insert cuttings or plant young trees? What else have its foresters to do but to bring in and take away as has been said?' with the result that writing is 'brought to such a degree of excellence, clearness, completeness, and polish'. Heaney, however, in a poem such as 'The Mud Vision', knows how easy it is to forfeit such clarification (a poem 'ends in a clarification of life', says *The Government of the Tongue*, echoing Frost), to let the truly vulgar overwhelm the possible 'new place', 'transparent, yet indigenous', of the illustrious language:

> Just like that, we forgot that the vision was ours,
> Our one chance to know the incomparable
> And dive to a future. What might have been origin
> We dissipated in news. The clarified place
> Had retrieved neither us nor itself.

For this project of clarifying and clearance Davie's polemic offers ample precedents. His exposition of Owen Barfield's analogy between 'metaphor: language: meaning:: legal fiction: law: civil life' runs parallel with Heaney's own recurrent analogy between poetic form and political jurisdiction:

> For just as law is consistent, inflexible and determinate, yet must, to keep pace with social changes, have recourse to fictions; so language is fixed and determinate, to satisfy needs of logic, yet must, to keep pace with changes in thought and life, evolve new meanings by way of metaphor.[32]

But of singular application to this volume is Davie's account of how diction can be purified when 'the dead metaphors of poetry are brought to life by the tang of common usage; and vice versa'. This revivification of dead metaphors has itself a social and political implication: 'For if the poet who coins new metaphors *enlarges* the language the poet who enlivens dead metaphors can be said to *purify* the language.' Heaney exposes the artifice of language throughout *The Haw Lantern* by showing both these processes at work. He foregrounds language, not by thickening it into the opacities of his earlier work, reinforcing that 'sensation of opaque fidelity' which is the history of 'a dispersed people' in 'From the Land of the Unspoken', but by insisting instead on a classical austerity and bareness of diction. The more transparent it is, 'a bare wire' after all that 'textured stuff'[33] the more, paradoxically, it manifests its status as language, a medium.

Heaney in fact does a remarkable thing in this volume. He inverts the traditional critical argument that language is inflected either towards its signifieds or to its signifiers, either self-effacingly presents its meanings or self-importantly calls attention to itself as a medium. In the empiricist ideology, language should ideally efface itself, act as a clear window through which its meanings are immediately and unmediatedly visible. In the radical, Modernist assault on this, language is distrusted as a suborner of meanings, and has to be fractured, dislocated, foregrounded in order to expose its ideological predisposings. Baring the device alerts us to the fact that language is not innocent but complicit, distorting or transforming that which it communicates. Heaney in these later poems demonstrates the opposite. The clearer, the more transparent the language, the more we become aware of its artifice. For in this apparent bareness it becomes clear that *no* language is free of metaphor, every word may double its meaning, and all discourse can turn back on itself in coy or brazen self-consciousness. If the clogged, sedimented streams of his earlier poetry here run clear, free of mud visions, they are still (in the words of 'The Summer of Lost Rachel') 'thick-webbed currents', and, in an image from 'Grotus and Coventina' which recalls analogies in Mandelstam and Pasternak, this clear flowing can bring

> Jubilation at the tap's full force, the sheer
> Given fact of water, how you felt you'd never
> Waste one drop but know its worth better always.

Moving towards an eighteenth-century clarity of utterance, Heaney in such parables as 'From the Land of the Unspoken' and 'From the Canton of Expectation' is able to write of his condition in cool, generalising narratives which imply a view of relation and order in the universe, and in Davie's words, 'turn their back upon sense-experience and appeal beyond it, logically, to known truths deduced from it'.[34] Personified concepts like 'Conscience', Davie says, 'specify only to the extent that they place a thing in its appropriate class, or assign it its appropriate function',[35] in a system of classification like that of Linnaeus. This verse, as Heaney says of Elizabeth Bishop, 'establishes reliable, unassertive relations with the world by steady attention to detail, by equable classification and level-toned enumeration'.[36] Of personification Davie observes, 'an abstraction is personified to some extent as soon as it can govern an active verb'. Heaney turns this to good effect when in 'Alphabets', he depicts language taking precedence over the subjects who utter and are uttered by it: 'Declensions sang on air like a *hosanna*', rising up like columns of cherubim and seraphim in the young boy. 'The Song of the Bullets' is even more explicitly classical in its personifications ('As justice stands aghast and stares') though it marries these with a Hardyesque bitter whimsy. Such techniques combine with periphrasis and circumlocution to make us see things in a new way, draw new lines through experience, in parables about the dangers of confusing story-telling with reality such as 'Parable Island' and 'From the Canton of Expectation', or fables about fable-making like 'A Daylight Art'.

STANDING IN AND STANDING FOR

The Haw Lantern shows a remarkable retreat from the linguistic density of metaphor which characterised Heaney's earlier volumes. Metaphor overrides all the differences between tenor and vehicle, concentrating them into some fused and compacted unity of meaning. Instead, these poems demonstrate language's incessantly metaphoric power by foregrounding it in the cooler, more explicit procedures of simile, where likeness is established between two items which nevertheless remain discrete, unfused. These poems abound in the quasi-prepositional connective 'like', from the very first analogical moment in 'Alphabets', where the child is initiated into the human world of comparisons, shadows and reflections that become substances, similes that overwhelm their referents, as the father's hands make on the wall a shadow 'like a rabbit's head'. Throughout the poem, the child grows up by learning to recognise and make analogies for himself, acquiring that simile-making process which maps a world of general categories, constructing more and more elaborate systems out of comparisons between the discrete phenomena of the world, learning to seek out 'the figure of the universe/And "not just single things"'. 'The Spoonbait' reveals the secret of this analogical habit at the heart of language. Inflected into archaism by its preposition, the process takes on an odd and artificial character. We cannot slide unselfconsciously from tenor to vehicle as if this were the most natural thing in the world:

> So a new similitude is given us
> And we say: The soul may be compared
>
> Unto a spoonbait that a child discovers ...

As the analogy is developed, metaphor crowds out the original similitude until the narrative generates its own new simile ('Like the single drop that Dives implored'). But the poem then disrupts this naturalising of simile into metaphor by offering two equally unexpected alternative endings, foregrounding the fact that we are dealing here with analogies, not literal acts. One is a fanciful metaphor achieved simply by omitting the 'like'; the other stresses its 'alternative' status, and insists once again on the gratuitousness of the simile, 'spooling out of nowhere' and 'snagging on nothing'.

By calling our attention to the process of analogy-making, these poems emphasise that meaning is a linguistic act, subject to choice and capriciousness, and not a natural event. 'Parable Island' is the clearest exploration of such a process. Stressing in the idea of parable the gratuitous and deliberate drawing of analogies between one narrative and another, it offers a metanarrative in the parable-making act itself. Even Heaney's own recurrent argument from etymology is here satirised, in deriving 'Island' from 'eye' and 'land', in this parable of visions and revisions. The dilemma of 'Parable Island' is that the competing narratives that dominate this terrain, so close and so far from 'Ire-land', do not know they are metaphoric, and so condemn themselves to beating their heads against stone. As so often, Heaney's precedent here is Joyce. Not, this time, the much-quoted encounter between Dedalus and the old English Dean but that earlier episode in which the infant Stephen naïvely tries to resolve the political and religious squabbles of the Christmas dinner by dissolving them into problems of metaphor and metonymy: 'Tower of Ivory', 'House of Gold'. Purifying the dialect of the tribe is then not just an act of linguistic reclamation. It also clarifies moral and political confusions generated by the opacities of language itself, melting down and reforging in the smithy of the soul those clanking narratives 'From the Canton of Expectation' calls 'songs they had learned by rote in the old language'.

The poems in *The Haw Lantern* illustrate the ways in which the dead political and religious metaphors of everyday language can come alive in unexpected clarifications of meaning. There is 'The Wishing Tree', for example, 'lifted, root and branch, to heaven'. In the sequence 'Clearances', 'Cold comforts *set* between us' sees the ordinary past participle of place turn into a verb which sets (seals and solidifies) a covenant of comfort between mother and son. The dead metaphor of 'bring us to our senses' in the same poem is renewed by being taken literally, just as the priest going 'hammer

and tongs at the prayers for the dying' comes alive in the echo back
to the coal hammer of the opening, the household implements of
the previous poem and the soldering iron, bucket and 'fluent
dipping knives' of this. In another poem in the sequence the simple
chore of folding sheets 'hand to hand' and 'touch and go' opens up
these dead metaphors by figuring them forth in real space as
enacted moments in a complicated relation:

> So we'd stretch and fold and end up hand to hand
> For a split second ...
> Beforehand, day by day, just touch and go,
> Coming close again by holding back.

An implied pun in 'Parable Island' says it all, speaking of archaeolo-
gists who variously interpret stone circles as 'pure symbol' or 'as-
sembly spots or hut foundations':

> One school thinks a post-hole in an ancient floor
> stands first of all for a pupil in an iris.
> The other thinks a post-hole is a post-hole.

The exasperation of that last bald statement restores the dead
metaphor of 'stands for' back to an original literalness, in which a
post-hole *stands* for the post which *stood in* it. A change of preposition converts literal into metaphoric and back again. By insisting on
such clarifications of experience in language the poet can, in the
words of 'The Sense of Place', define 'where he stands and he can
also watch himself taking his stand.'

It is perhaps in the Latinate pun that Heaney most clearly fulfils
Davie's prescription for purity of diction. 'The clarified place' of
'The Mud Vision' refers to both a physical and an intellectual
process. The soul 'ramifying' in 'Clearances' extends the analogy
with the chestnut tree. 'Clearances' is particularly rich in the device.
Religious and everyday meanings of 'incensation' are brought out
by juxtaposition with 'the psalmist's outcry taken up with pride'. A
scarcely noticed series of these in the fourth sonnet plays on a range
of etymologies to suggest the complex negotiations of mother and
son. The mutual jostlings of 'affectation' and 'affect' (to put to,
aspire to something beyond, put on), 'adequate' (made level with,
equal to) and 'adjusted' (put next to) open up the central ambiguity
of the clause 'whenever it came to/Pronouncing words "beyond
her"'. The relation of the here and now ('came to') to a 'beyond' is

in fact the subtext of the whole sequence, even at the level of its prepositions. 'Adjusted' (actually from *adjuxtare*) according to the *OED* was early confused with the idea of an equalising 'justice' (*ad justus*) which put things in their proper place, thus establishing a kind of punning relation with 'adequate'; and the poet enacts this adequation by juxtaposing them in his own 'genuinely well-/ adjusted adequate betrayal'. 'Pronouncing words "beyond her"' thus overlays the simple speech act with the pronouncement of an edict of expulsion by and from the tongue's seat of government. This in turn opens up the politic adjustments of 'manage': in 'affecting' incompetence (all she could manage) she adroitly manoeuvres the son to fall fittingly back into his place ('decently relapse').

The Latinate pun is most brilliantly affected, however, in the conclusion of the poem:

> I'd *naw* and *aye*
> And decently relapse into the wrong
> Grammar which kept us allied and at bay.

'Allied' (from *alligare*) can mean bound together either by kinship or treaty, and so keeps open the nature of the truce negotiated between them. 'At bay', however, is a dead metaphor which ramifies into remarkable life when its etymology is considered. According to the *OED* (p. 712):

> Two different words seem to be here inextricably confused. Originally the phrase *to hold at bay* seems ad. OF *tenir a bay* (Godefroy) It. *tenere a bada*, where *bay, bada*, means the state of suspense, expectation, or unfulfilled desire, indicated by the open mouth (late L. *badare* to open the mouth); but *to stand at bay, be brought to bay*, correspond to mod. Fr. *être aux abois*, meaning to be at close quarters with the barking dogs, and *bay* is here aphetically formed from ABAY, a. OF *abai* barking.

'Allied and at bay' is itself a state of suspension between decency and lapse, wrong grammar and right place. The poem's openmouthed closure, a fork-tongued moment of unfulfilled desire in the government of the tongue, speaks from the central reticences of Heaney's verse. What 'Grammar' (Greek *gramma*, a written mark) and 'at bay' (open-mouthed) set up at either end of this line is the same antithesis uttered in the Latinate pun of the prefatory poem of the sequence, which speaks of a 'co-opted and obliterated echo' struck off the real world, which may 'teach me now to listen/To strike it rich behind the linear black' of a written text. 'Obliterated', literally, means *erased from writing*: in a Derridean sense, the voice's echo or trace erased and yet co-opted in the lines of writing. It is by making such clearings in the undergrowth of language that the bewildered self can find a place to stand, a place to make a stand.

THE DISTANCE BETWEEN

The relation between mother and son, 'allied and at bay', is also a relation between two moments of language – between writing and speech, and between *langue*, 'Grammar', and *parole*, voice. It is a relation of kinship and treaty, not hostility. It reproduces, there-fore, a more condign version of that stand-off Stephen Dedalus effects in relation to the 'illiterate fidelities' of a 'peasant oracle'. An alternative relation in *Portrait* is figured in a passage to which Heaney has adverted more than once, Stephen's encounter with the old English Dean. 'Stephen, in that famous passage', Heaney says in the lecture 'Among Schoolchildren', 'feels inadequate when he hears the English Jesuit speaking English.' The differences between them, differences according to Heaney of 'cultural and geographic placing', are the oral register, 'on his lips and mine', of a *différance* within a shared 'language, so familiar and so foreign' ('allied and at bay'). Heaney first drew on this passage for the epigraph to 'The Wool Trade' (*Wintering Out*), where the words are finally left to 'hang/Fading, in the gallery of the tongue'. In the lecture, however, he moves on, calling our attention to Stephen's less frequently re-marked comeback, in which, brooding on his linguistic displace-ment, he looks up the world 'tundish' in the dictionary only to 'find it English and good old blunt English too'. Heaney's comment is significant:

> What had seemed disabling and provincial is suddenly found to be corroborating and fundamental and potentially universal. To belong to Ireland, to speak its dialect, is not necessarily to be cut off from the world's banquet because that banquet is eaten at the table of one's own life, savoured by the tongue one speaks. Stephen now trusts what he calls 'our own language' and in that trust he will go to encounter what he calls 'the reality of experience'. But it will be his own specific Dublin experience, with all its religious and historical freight, so different from the English experience to which he had heretofore stood in a subservient relationship.[37]

In his encounter with the ghost of Joyce at the end of 'Station Island', the poet returns to this episode, referring to it jokily as 'The Feast of the Holy Tundish', canonising it among his stars as Stephen had turned it into a governing myth in his diary.

I take these three writing events to be crucial for Heaney. Stephen recuperates the event by writing it up, and he turns to the higher authority of the dictionary to find the true lineage of the word restored in the authentic history on the printed page, rather than in the unreliable local narratives of the oral order. He thus delivers the rationale for Heaney's own compulsive resort to etymology, not as a search for lost origins, but so as to restore language to a living, changing history, to underwrite (I use the metaphor deliberately) the written synchronic *langue* and the diachronic spoken *parole* with the print that establishes authentic historic relation between them. Joyce refuses to be displaced by linguistic nationalism, English or Irish, because, as Heaney notes in a Latinate pun, he 'is against all such alibis'. In refusing to claim he was somewhere else, 'he is also intent on deconstructing the prescriptive myth of Irishness which was burgeoning in his youth and which survives in various sympathetic and unsympathetic forms to this day.'

Rewriting this episode in 'Station Island', Heaney attempts a similar deconstruction, putting words into the mouth itself into a highly material simile of *writing*:

> His voice eddying with the vowels of all rivers
> came back to me, though he did not speak yet,
> a voice like a prosecutor's or a singer's,
>
> cunning, narcotic, mimic, definite
> as a steel nib's downstroke, quick and clean.

Joyce's peroration likewise homes in on writing as a physical act, something effected by that hand which grasps the ash plant, which grips that of the younger writer, and which Joyce once joked noone would ever want to kiss who knew what other things it had done besides writing *Ulysses*:

> ... The main thing is to write
> for the joy of it. Cultivate a work-lust
> that imagines its haven like your hands at night
>
> dreaming the sun in the sunspot of a breast.

A final ironic transformation turns the broadcast voice into a metaphor of that writing which most intimately defines the unique, autonomous self:

> swim
> out on your own and fill the element
> with signatures on your own frequency.

Heaney here gives a subtle, original twist to the cliché of the poet finding his own voice. It is no accident, then, that the poem which follows this and opens the next sequence, 'The First Gloss', should instruct the poet to hold his pen like a spade ('Take hold of the shaft of the pen'), in an intensely physical act of writing which recalls the resolution in the first poem of his first collection:

> Between my finger and my thumb
> The squat pen rests.
> I'll dig with it.

'Subscription', in 'The First Gloss', means paying one's dues, accepting a lineage and an authority, even as the first step is 'taken/from a justified line/into the margin'. 'Alphabets', the opening poem of *The Haw Lantern*, spells out this subscription in the most literal of terms, exploring the child's conscription to his culture through the succession of writings he acquires. Writing here is a manual labour, acquired with difficulty: 'there is a right/Way to hold the pen and a wrong way'. We are reminded that words themselves, no matter how seamlessly interwoven in utterance, are really made up of more primary units, represented by written signs (*gramma*) which arbitrarily and artificially stand in for consonants and vowels. The poem plays games with its own origin, starting with the alphabetic Greek of the Harvard 'Phi Beta Kappa' poem, to reconstruct a whole series of other signs the child has lived through, from his father's shadow-drawing, through modes of writing pictographically only a step away from this – the letter Y seen as a forked stick, 2 as a swan's neck and back, A as 'Two rafters and a cross-tie on the slate', O a schoolroom globe, the teacher's tick 'a little leaning hoe' – through the joined-up writing of 'new calligraphy that felt like home', the Ogham whose letters were trees, 'The lines of script like briars', the bare Merovingian style, the Latin capitals of the sky-writing IN HOC SIGNO which converted Constantine, until it returns abstract signs to material reality in the balers dropping bales 'like printouts where stooked sheaves/Made lambdas', the potato pit with a 'delta face', and omega as the shape of a horseshoe over the door.

Such analogies between arbitrary signs and the referents they invoke are not just accidental but, as this aetiology of writing suggests, grow out of an incorrigible tendency to see correspondences in the world itself, to draw similitudes, deploying that little word 'like' which runs through the poem to construct 'the figure of the universe/And "not just single things"'. The astronaut is the first human whose O is not a figure of the world but the great globe itself, seen unprecedentedly not as an emblem but as

> all he has sprung from,
> The risen, aqueous, singular, lucent O
> Like a magnified and buoyant ovum.

Going back to the origins, this poem proposes, means rediscovering in one's own prehistory (before writing) the origin of the species as a sign-making, tool-making animal; means recovering a state where writing is seen to be as material as that 'buoyant ovum', and as manual a labour as plastering a wall:

> Or like my own wide pre-reflective stare
> All agog at the plasterer on his ladder
> Skimming our gable and writing our name there
> With his trowel point, letter by strange letter.

This estrangement is simultaneously a homecoming – not a return to origins but to a new '*sensing* of place' in a landscape 'instinct with signs'. In his interview with Rand Brandes published in *Salmagundi* Heaney explained the origin of the poem as a commission:

> I had a real problem: Write a poem for the Phi Beta Kappa at Harvard that had to be spoken aloud, and be concerned with learning. And that poem is precisely about the distance that intervenes between the person standing up in Sanders' Theatre, being the donnish orator, and the child, pre-reflective and in its pre-writing odd state.[38]

That 'pre-writing odd state' is not in any sense *innocent*, prior to discourse, the poem makes clear, since the child is already captured in the nets of language, and the whole poem explores the succession of discourses, as of alphabets, through which he learns to construct, not just a writing, but a self. And it is in some Popean 'middle state' that both poem and speaker find themselves, in that intercalated 'distance ... between' of which Heaney speaks in the interview:

> there is a bemused, abstracted distance intervening between the sweetening energy of the original place and the consciousness that's getting back to it, looking for sweetness.

Contemplating a prehistoric 'dried-up source' in the last poem of *Station Island*, Heaney speaks of keeping a stone-faced vigil 'For my book of changes',

> until the long dumbfounded
> spirit broke cover
> to raise a dust
> in the font of exhaustion.

Neil Corcoran[39] sees this as a holy water font, and so it is. But it is also the font of print itself, which is where all new texts find their origins. Here, in the punning metaphoric overlaying of particular life and printed page, Heaney figures forth that relation between place and displacement which is the very ground of his writing.

From *The Chosen Ground: Essays on the Contemporary Poetry of Northern Ireland*, ed. Neil Corcoran (Bridgend, 1992), pp. 35–61.

NOTES

[Stan Smith is particularly concerned to justify the Heaney of *The Haw Lantern* (a book in which some reviewers found a diminution of imaginative power). He examines Heaney's later poetic language, its combination of bareness of diction with syntactic vigour, and particularly its prepositional manoevres. His approach combines an interest in the grammar and syntax of poetry prompted by the English critic Donald Davie with a post-structuralist awareness of the shifts and contradictions of textual structures.

Smith's essay shows not only the influence of key theoretical works like Derrida's *On Grammatology* (see my Introduction, p. 15 above) but a more pervasive resort to the general assumptions which have followed in the wake of Saussure. The 'binary' way 'place' and 'displacement' define each other (p. 224) offers Smith a way of acknowledging Saussure's major premiss that meaning is determined by the difference of one arbitrary signifier from another. Smith accepts Saussure's assumption that language can be seen either *synchronically* (as a simultaneous system) or *diachronically* (in its historical development) (p. 246); he also uses Derrida's coinage *différance* (p. 245) which involves not only the 'difference' through which language functions but also the constant 'deferral' of conclusive meaning within the play of signification (*Writing and Difference* [London, 1978]).

Smith's approach shows a recognition (in Peter Widdowson's words) that 'theory' may be tactical and strategic rather than seemingly philosophically absolute ... and that it is to be *put to use*' (*A Reader's Guide to Contemporary Literary Theory* [Hemel Hempstead, 1993], p. 7). As with Christopher Ricks (See my introduction, p. 7 above), Smith shows a sense of 'play' governed by a creative relationship between poet and critic. He responds for instance, to Heaney's praise (on p. 120 of *the Government of the Tongue*) of his own specialist work on Auden by providing some specific illustrations for Heaney's general account of that poet (p. 226 above). Other literary references are to Kavanagh's 'Iniskeen Road, July Evening' (p. 225) and to his 'The Parish and the Universe' (*Collected Pruse* [London, 1973], p. 283); to Mallarmé's 'Le Tombeau d'Edgar Poe' (p. 235) and to Larkin's 'Absences' (p. 238). 'Diplock Courts' (p. 230): the juryless courts instituted in Northern Ireland in 1973 to deal with terrorist offences. Ed.]

1. Seamus Heaney, *The Government of the Tongue* (London, 1988), p. 132.

2. Ibid., p. 137.

3. Ibid., p. 168.

4. Seamus Heaney, *Preoccupations* (London, 1980), p. 138.

5. 'Sounding Auden', *The Government of the Tongue*, p. 118.

6. Ibid., p. 123.

7. Ibid., p. 110.

8. Ibid.

9. *Preoccupations*, pp. 131–49.

10. *The Government of the Tongue*, p. 149.

11. Ibid., p. 93.

12. Ibid., p. 92.

13. Ibid., p. 166.

14. Ibid., p. 96.

15. James Joyce, *Ulysses* (1937 text), pp. 204–5.

16. W.B. Yeats, 'Ancestral Houses', in *The Tower*, 1928.

17. *Preoccupations*, p. 145.

18. Seamus Heaney, *Place and Displacement* (Grasmere, 1984), p. 3.

19. Ibid., p. 4.

20. Ibid., p. 8.

21. Seamus Heaney, *Field Work* (London, 1979), pp. 7, 9, 10.

22. *Preoccupations*, p. 135.

23. Seamus Heaney, 'A Tale of Two Islands', *Irish Studies 1*, ed. P.J. Drudy (Cambridge, 1980), 1–20.

24. Seamus Heaney, 'Envies and Identifications: Dante and the Modern Poet', *Irish University Review* (Spring 1985), 15–19.

25. Donald Davie, *Purity of Diction in English Verse* (London, 1952).

26. Ibid., p. 31.

27. Ibid., pp. 16–17.

28. Ibid., pp. 82–90.

29. Ibid., pp. 86–9.

30. *The Government of the Tongue*, p. 22.

31. Ibid., pp. 3–4.

32. Ibid., pp. 29ff.

33. Neil Corcoran, *Seamus Heaney* (London, 1986), p. 153.

34. *Purity of Diction in English Verse*, p. 48.

35. Ibid., p. 52.

36. *The Government of the Tongue*, p. 102.

37. Seamus Heaney, '*Among Schoolchildren*' (Belfast, 1983). pp. 10–11.

38. *Salmagundi*, no. 80 (1988), 20.

39. *Seamus Heaney*, p. 179.

15

Paradigms of Possibility:
Seamus Heaney

RICHARD KIRKLAND

> The tightness and the nilness round that space
> when the car stops in the road, the troops inspect
> its make and number and, as one bends his face
>
> towards your window, you catch sight of more
> on a hill beyond, eyeing with intent
> down cradled guns that hold you under cover
>
> and everything is pure interrogation
> until a rifle motions and you move
> with guarded unconcerned acceleration –
>
> a little emptier, a little spent
> as always by that quiver in the self,
> subjugated, yes, and obedient.
>
> So you drive on to the frontier of writing
> where it happens again. The guns on tripods;
> the sergeant with his off-on mike repeating
>
> data about you, waiting for the squawk
> of clearance; the marksman training down
> out of the sun upon you like a hawk. ...[1]

Seamus Heaney's journey through two frontier check points presents a readily identifiable parable of the literary self-conscious; a parable which poetry from Northern Ireland has had recourse to many times. In 'From the Frontier of Writing', the journey from doubt, through confrontation, to a visionary state of artistic confidence is one which offers a paradigm of poetic development which Heaney has located in the work of Patrick Kavanagh[2] and which also, microcosmically, images Heaney's own poetic career from *North*, through *Station Island*, and into the future tense with *Seeing Things*.[3] The final state of achievement is one dependent on the 'squawk of clearance' granted by literary criticism, an examination which leaves him 'a little emptier' ('as always') but to which he is equal. While such a reading may seem to portray Heaney's poetic manoeuvres as slightly pat, I would rather emphasise the liberation through cynicism that 'From the Frontier of Writing' proffers; an interpretation which allows the poem a prefigurative quality beyond the ineffable world of the transcendent or prophetic. Central to this is the intersection of the British military presence in Heaney's known landscape and the preponderance of literary critical terminology ('Frontier of Writing', 'nilness round that space', 'pure interrogation') which describes their operations within the parameters of the poetic artefact. I have previously demonstrated how British empirical paradigms of criticism were imported into Ireland and how these paradigms not only have had a prolonged existence in Ireland beyond British criticism but, in some instances, have been used to protect partition itself. 'From the Frontier of Writing' carries a similar awareness and, as such, is analogous to the dissection of British literary critical colonialism Heaney undertakes in his Field Day pamphlet 'An Open Letter'.[4] It is not that the forces of coercion and cultural interpretation are seen as equally oppressive or equally undesirable but rather that both require Heaney to submit to their strictures in order to gain poetic subjecthood. Significantly, the result of this process is to render the subject as typical in all aspects. To acknowledge the poem's ultimate status of being 'arraigned yet freed' is to allow the poet the status of the visionary or the prophet but only once that status has been valorised by the process of examination which renders the individual as exemplary. David Lloyd, in an astute essay on Heaney, has codified this trope as one in which 'the identity of the individual, his integrity, is expressed by the degree to which that individual identifies himself with and integrates his difference in a national consciousness'.[5] This goes some way towards depicting the central dilemma to which Heaney's poetry has continually addressed itself. While the binary oppositional nature of Northern Irish society makes such an integration unavoidable – as do, in a sense, the binary comparative methods of literary criticism (gestured by the 'on-off mike' of the sergeant) – Heaney's fundamentally bourgeois poetic has chosen to represent that integration as a constant crisis of interest between the urge to a full individuation and the desire for assimilation. As existing within the genre of the journey poem then, 'From the Frontier of Writing' is swept along 'the black current of a tarmac road' to a destination which is always in view and which is not to be evaded. It culminates with Heaney's knowledge of his assured canonical status, a status posthumously conferred on both Kavanagh and Yeats before him, and, in another sense, can be said to mark the transition from writing to poetry.

It is interesting to test this progression against the critical reception accorded to Heaney since the publication of his latest collection of poetry, *Seeing Things*, a title which, if ironically, suggests the kind of visionary state which looks beyond the critical judgement in itself and on towards posterity. For John Carey writing in the *Sunday Times*,[6] the experience was transcendent: 'Reading these and several other poems, you feel what the first readers of, say, Keats's odes or Milton's 1654 (*sic*) collection must have felt – the peculiar excitement of watching a new masterwork emerge and take its permanent place in our literature.' As an English critic (and one perhaps sensitive to Heaney's previous statements of dissent from British traditions), Carey can only adumbrate his praise in terms of the sensation of reading not criticism. This allows a form of appropriation to take place but only within the liberal framework of 'our literature'; an absolute inversion of Roland Barthes' famous statement that, 'to go from reading to criticism is to change desires; it is no longer to desire the work itself but to desire one's own language'.[7] Secure in his language, Carey desires *Seeing Things* as a readerly pleasure; it is presented as literally *beyond* criticism. Certainly, as Declan Kiberd pointed out in his own review of the collection, 'Greater love no English critic hath than to write such lines of an Irish poet'[8] yet this only begins to tell part of the astonishing story of Heaney's rise. As now undoubtedly the most famous Irish poet since Yeats, Heaney is the physical embodiment of George Moore's belief that art 'must be parochial in the beginning to become cosmopolitan in the end'.[9] To witness the unfolding of each stage of his deep design is to become aware of the slightly anomalous position he now holds in relation to other contemporary Irish poets. While the rapid rise to pre-eminence of Irish poetry in general and Northern Irish poetry in particular over the last twenty-five years has been echoed by a concomitant interest in Irish literary and cultural criticism (of which *Field Day* is the clearest example), Heaney's work now places him fundamentally beyond the parameters of such interpretation.[10] Instead, his work often occupies a landscape of absolutes, a location in which language becomes only an unwarranted intrusion in the on-going drive to present unity and reconciliation within the transcendent experience:

> I am trying to name and describe magic, the magic of a poetry deft, accurate and pure, but I might as well try to spear satellites with a pitchfork. There is a Sufi term, *baraka*, which connotes, among other things, blessedness, as in the unmediated blessedness of being. This is a book steeped in *baraka*, a pure poetry of what almost escapes us in this extraordinary world.[11]

Having invoked an absolute as a definitive term, Dorgan is left with no other option but to invoke another. The book itself becomes an icon, a receptacle for all that is left perfect in a fallen world, and a text which forms its own community – beyond social fracture – of pure believers. With this awareness *Seeing Things* becomes the Koran of modern poetry, while Heaney, appropriately, figures as the prophet raised up from the people. Sharing their difficulties yet simultaneously removed from them he is rendered exotic, displaced, within the quotidian actualities of everyday life:

> The problem with a conversation with Seamus Heaney is its range is so wide, its levels so various and its diversions so many that, unintentionally – he is the most courteous of men – questions become redundant. They assume an emaciated, tentative tone, as one becomes aware of the resonances of his talk, the mastery of his language and the searching restlessness of his mind.
>
> Not that he is ungenerous with his time, his ideas, and, above all, discussion of his craft. Sustained by coffee, digestive biscuits and the offer of malt whisky, I was gripped by the diversity of his phrases, the intricacy of his word relationships and the luminosity of his thought. He used no word that wouldn't be at home on his Derry farm or in a Belfast or Dublin pub. But the words and phrases were formed by a rare golden vision.
>
> I had asked him to talk about the difference between a playwright and a poet, and I was reminded of another poet as he answered. A poet is a human being speaking to others – albeit one endowed with more lively sensibility, more enthusiasm and tenderness, with greater knowledge of human nature and a more

> comprehensive soul than are supposed to be common among humankind.
>
> Wordsworth's words are not, I imagine, those that would be chosen by Heaney for himself. But they echoed in my mind as he spoke.[12]

It is in the reconciliation of the division between 'digestive biscuits and the offer of malt whisky' and the 'rare golden vision' that, for John Keyes, Heaney's success becomes explicit. His example forges a unity between the present and the canonical ghosts of the past which transcend not only historical fracture, but the division between the quotidian, fallible individual and the great work of art. A recent study of Heaney by Michael Parker[13] extended this perception into a full poetic biography and was revealingly sub-titled *The Making of the Poet*. Through the course of the book the narrative portrays Heaney as simultaneously typical of the south Derry community from which he comes while emphasising the paradigmatic nature of his lifework in the production of a universal poetry. With this, as with the Keyes article, the overall emphasis falls on the role of the poet as mediator of experience: a central aspect of Romantic ideology as Keyes's quotation from the 'Preface to *Lyrical Ballads*',[14] wittingly or not, demonstrates.[15] Perhaps in this instance, Heaney is only the most successful embodiment of an idea of the poet in Northern Ireland present since the 1960s. Centrally placed within this ideal is a notional ideology of poetics predicated on the belief in an achievable perfection of the matured voice; a tendency first located in Heaney by Clive James in 1972:

> With Seamus Heaney, an already achieved, uniquely precocious maturity is being deepened into a tragic voice. He has already left the point at which his contemporaries are now arriving. Soon people are going to start comparing him with Yeats.[16]

James's early awareness of the analogous nature of Heaney's poetic persona (although, it should be noted, this is an awareness carefully expressed) is one which has become increasingly popular and further allows the tentative codification of a number of assumptions about the Northern Irish poet which can be organised for the sake of this chapter as a general paradigm. I am here following Antony Easthope's definition of the term in *Literary Into Cultural Studies*,[17] as one amenable to my own methods in that it 'signals the dependence of understanding on discourse while including the idea of knowledge, and so, crucially, an epistemology involving a subject/object relation'. Moreover, while a paradigm does not expect nor desire to find any particular subject existing in perfect relation to the objective paradigm itself, it can, in Easthope's terms, bring 'object and subject into a *relation* of knowledge'. The particular paradigm of Northern Irish poetics I am attempting to outline necessarily involves a consideration of the subject as both the poem as text and the poet as creator and embodiment of those texts. This need not be contradictory or overtly problematic if the poet is approached textually within the framework of the object. There are then six features which constitute this paradigm as I have identified it. These are:

1. a reading of the poet as rooted to a physical location and community;
2. a sense of the poet as exemplifying the values of that community;
3. an insistence that the poet can mediate the truths already inherent in the community to the community;
4. a field of interpretation in which the poem does not so much represent truth as embody it in its actuality;
5. the assumption that within the poet is the possibility of teleological perfection;
6. a literary critical practice which recognises both the primacy of the poem and the limits of its own discursive empirical practices in relation to it.

It should be recognised that these features are not necessarily restricted to Northern Irish poetry. As Easthope points out (after Kuhn), 'paradigms are inter-paradigmatic, internalising for themselves features shared by other paradigms'. However in this is the possibility of making explicit naturalised or traditional forms as well as a method of identifying the inevitable declensions from the paradigm as they are present in each particular example. Naturally, as such codification can tend towards the stereotypical there are other ways of presenting this subject/object distinction. In 1974, *Fortnight*, aware of the growing interest in Northern Irish poetry as a recognisably distinct entity, carried a feature on 'The Ulster Poets' by Harry Chambers.[18] To illustrate this article on the front cover of the magazine was a cartoon by Martyn Turner[19] – perhaps the most incisive of Irish political caricaturists – which presented the stereotypical Ulster poet (with 'Ulster' probably taking a wry look back at Kavanagh) and his environment. Perhaps the intention was to play this stereotyped image against the specific differences Chambers encountered in his consideration of particular poets: an aim frustrated by Chambers' own reluctance to dispense with that homogeneous model. However, Turner's cartoon provides a visual representation of most of the features of the paradigm I have previously outlined. In the foreground is the figure of the poet sporting clipped goatee beard, checked shirt and ill-fitting jacket. His right hand clutches a loose leafed manuscript, his left is upraised in a gesture of enunciation. In the background is a divided landscape sundered (or linked) by the figure of the poet. To the left is an image of a rural agrarian location, to the right, the barbed wire, burning houses and broken glass of a riot-torn Belfast, Derry, Portadown, or wherever. The foregrounded figure of the poet mediates our reading of the background. Northern Ireland is not encountered through the poetry in his hand but through the values embodied in the stance he adopts. Moreover it is only the poet figure who can link the two disparate landscapes in continuity. The urban/rural divide signals one form of fracture while gesturing both to a temporal discontinuity (past/present) and a conflict, understood empirically, between reality and image. It is only possible to quantify these juxtapositions by recourse to the central figure who can embody, reconcile, and represent the oppositions within his own example. A critical practice which destabilises this centre cannot, therefore, hope to access the privileged continuities it offers.

This paradigm was most fully tested by the publication, one year later, of Heaney's *North*, a collection which relied heavily on the mediating figure of the poet to reconcile the mythological elements of the work to the political actuality which became its insistent function. While there is a danger of overstressing Heaney's reliance on this model within a reductive argument ill-equipped to analyse its complications, it is fair comment to note that Heaney's painful agonisings through *North* about the role of the poet within society are best understood as a series of abdications and reaffirmations from and to the paradigm as I have previously outlined it. Moreover, in interview, Heaney could comment:

> The Tollund Man seemed to me like an ancestor almost, one of my old uncles, one of those moustached archaic faces you used to meet all over the Irish countryside. I felt very close to this. And the

sacrificial element, the territorial religious element, the whole mythological field surrounding these images was very potent. So I tried, not
explicitly, to make a connection between the sacrificial, ritual, religious element in the violence of contemporary Ireland and this terrible sacrificial religious thing in *The Bog People*. This wasn't thought
out. It began with a genuinely magnetic, almost entranced relationship with those heads. ... And when I wrote that poem ('The Tollund
Man') I had a sense of crossing a line really, that my whole being was
involved in the sense of – the root sense – of religion, being bonded
to something, being bound to do something. I felt it a vow; I felt my
whole being caught in this. ... I'm very angry with a couple of snotty
remarks by people who don't know what they are talking about and
speak as if the bog images were picked up for convenience instead of
being a deeply felt part of my own life.[20]

The necessary emphasis on intuition stresses a framework of interpretation absolutely beholden to the figure of the poet as a mediating presence. With this the possibility of theorising the relationship
between present day violence and ritual sacrifice, even if it were
possible, is significant only in that it would challenge the position of
Heaney as the central function of the myth; it has to be accepted on
his terms or cannot be understood at all. Read in this way, the
'snotty remarks by people who don't know what they are talking
about' can be seen as the frustrated aspiration of certain aspects of
literary criticism to overthrow the primacy of poetry as a privileged
discourse within Irish culture. Heaney's connections to the original
myth, both familial ('like an ancestor almost') and ineffable,
prevent any sympathetic consideration of the effectiveness of his
parallels which do not first acknowledge an implicit trust in
Heaney's instinctive judgement. Edna Longley, not usually the sort
of critic inclined to trust the opinion of the poet over the content of
the poem, recognises this in her own consideration of *North* and
begins her analysis with the admission that, 'His reaction to the
Man's photograph deserves the much abused term "epiphany",
with its full Joycean connotations: a revelation of personal and
artistic destiny expressed in religious language'.[21] As further on in
the essay Longley can comment that 'Heaney may have mistaken
his initial epiphany for a literal signpost, when it was really a destination', this becomes a mode of criticism aware of the fact that to
challenge the initial validity of Heaney's vision would be to render
the complete volume as synthetic and open to theoretical procedure.
Its primary structural principle being one which revolves around

the mysteries of Heaney himself. Similarly, Conor Cruise O'Brien, in an influential review of *North*,[22] commented:

> I had the uncanny feeling, reading these poems, of listening to the thing itself, the actual substance of historical agony and dissolution, the tragedy of people in a place: the Catholics of Northern Ireland. Yes, the Catholics: there is no equivalent Protestant voice. Poetry is as unfair as history, though in a different way. Seamus Heaney takes his distances – archaeology, Berkeley, love-hate of the English language, Spain, County Wicklow (not the least distant) – but his Derry is always with him, the ash somehow, now standing out even more on the forehead.

Again it is in the realm of the mysterious, 'the uncanny', that Heaney's work transubstantiates into 'the thing itself'. Beyond representation, the poetry becomes an embodiment of the real angst of the community and its place, while Heaney is absolutely assimilated into its people. As always, the more Heaney's achievement becomes remarkable, the more typical he is rendered. Inevitably the result of such procedures deeply underplays the complex relationship of the contemporary political situation in Northern Ireland to the ongoing violence. As Lloyd has noted, by basing his poetic in the concept of identity Heaney is 'unable ever to address the relation between politics and writing more than superficially, in terms of thematic concerns, or superstitiously in terms of a vision of the poet as a diviner of the hypothetical pre-political consciousness of his race'.[23] Ciarán Carson, in a perceptive review of *North*,[24] was one of the first critics to identify this tendency. Observing that Edward McGuire's recent portrait of Heaney allowed the poet the 'status of myth, of institution' while 'forestall[ing] criticism', he comments:

> One can hardly resist the suspicion that *North* itself, as a work of art, has succumbed to this notion; Heaney seems to have moved – unwillingly perhaps – from being a writer with the gift of percision (*sic*), to become the laureate of violence – a mythmaker, an anthropologist of ritual killing, an apologist for 'the situation', in the last resort, a mystifier. It make (*sic*) *North* a curiously uneven book. ... No-one really escapes from the massacre, of course – the only way you can really do that is by falsifying issues, by applying wrong notions of history instead of seeing what's before your eyes.

Ultimately Carson's most vivid comment on the difficulties of this aesthetic was not found in prose but in the relentless probing of identity which constituted his collection *The Irish For No*,[25] yet his preliminary accusations were well aimed. Unwilling or unable to reconcile liberal individuation to social assimilation, much of Heaney's poetry can only find resolution of the contradiction within the notional closure offered by the well-made poem. A technique informed by practical criticism, Heaney's predominantly lyrical style allows a notional poetic voice to achieve a reconciliation of issues – a perfection of form – which addresses the contradictions inherent in his commitment to the paradigm. Such an interpretation, ironically if one considers 'From the Frontier of Writing', takes its methodology and example from within the institution and conforms to what Easthope (after Jane Tompkins) refers to as 'the Modernist reading'.[26] Within this, the text is intransitive, is presumed to be significant in the interaction of all possible meanings, yet simultaneously is restrictive of those meanings in the overall unity of the text. This often contradictory process is reliant on the transformative power of the ineffable statement; an absence which Barthes identified in *Writing Degree Zero* as one located within the poetic word itself which: 'shines with an infinite freedom and prepares to radiate towards innumerable uncertain and possible connections'.[27]

Able to reconcile all difference, the modernist reading's central emphasis on the poetic word not only encourages the play of meaning within the artefact but requires such play as a crucial factor in its overall efficacy. This has been necessarily important to the assimilation of Northern Irish poetry into an English interpretative framework. The specificities of difference, expressed as the strange or the dissenting ambiguity, can be welcomed in so far as they contribute to the overall richness of the poem's textual fabric – a progression which places the textual manifestation of the paradigm of Northern Irish poetics as I have previously outlined it within an institutional context. Heaney has written of his induction into this process with mixed feelings.[28] At one level he maintains his insistence on the connection between 'the core of a poet's speaking voice and the core of his poetic voice', on another he recognises the benefits which can accrue through the modernist reading:

> I couldn't say, of course, that I had found a voice but I had found a game. I knew the thing was only word-play, and I hadn't even the guts to put my name to it. I called myself *Incertus*, uncertain, a shy soul fretting and all that. I was in love with words themselves, but had no sense of a poem as a whole structure and no experience of how the successful achievement of a poem could be a stepping stone in your life. Those verses were what we might call 'trial-pieces', little

stiff inept designs in imitation of the master's fluent interlacing patterns, heavy-handed clues to the whole craft.

It is difficult to assess the significance of this apprenticeship to Heaney's later work if only because his sense of the process as 'a game' – an artificial impediment to his primary and natural love of words – conflicts with his later awareness of the transformative possibilities of the lyric form to the lifework. As with the critical thought militia of 'From the Frontier of Writing', Heaney's poetic undergoes an examination which leaves him 'arraigned yet freed'. He is granted a certain liberty yet remains absolutely implicated in the machinations of the literary critical institution. Indeed this conflict is reinforced by the Foreword to *Preoccupations*[29] which deems it necessary to highlight those prose pieces which bear the hallmark of 'the slightly constricted utterance of somebody who underwent his academic rite of passage when practical criticism held great sway in the academy'. Heaney's 'slightly constricted utterance' has been well documented and criticised[30] but its root cause has rarely been located as part of a specific critical practice. However, if this argument is accepted it can be seen that it is solely within the modernist reading that Heaney's expression of dissent has its being; an awareness which gives credence to Lloyd's contentious accusation that 'almost without exception, the poems respond compliantly to analysis based on assumptions about the nature of the well-made lyric poem'.[31] Desmond Fennell, coming from an entirely different tradition of criticism to Lloyd's, has similarly noted the welcome afforded to Heaney's work by academics (who he places in opposition to 'Ordinary Readers'),[32] while Heaney, in an interview with Randall, has commented that many of his poems are 'usually pulled tight at the end with little drawstrings in the last line or two'.[33] Perhaps this tendency is most clearly expressed by reference to the lyric poem 'Making Strange'. Part of the 1984 collection *Station Island* – a volume often considered as undertaking the sternest form of self-analysis within Heaney's canon – it subtends its nominal consideration of identity as expressed in relation to geography under a desire to achieve a satisfactory form of coherent closure within its own formal limits:

> I stood between them,
> the one with his travelled intelligence
> and tawny containment,
> his speech like the twang of a bowstring,

and another, unshorn and bewildered
in the tubs of his wellingtons,
smiling at me for help,
faced with this stranger I'd brought him.

Then a cunning middle voice
came out of the field across the road
saying, 'Be adept and be dialect,
tell of this wind coming past the zinc hut,

call me sweetbriar after the rain
or snowberries cooled in the fog.
But love the cut of this travelled one
and call me also the cornfield of Boaz.

Go beyond what's reliable
in all that keeps pleading and pleading,
these eyes and puddles and stones,
and recollect how bold you were

when I visited you first
with departures you cannot go back on.'

Michael Parker has helpfully noted that this poem has its genesis
in a guided tour of South Derry undertaken by Heaney for the
benefit of the Jamaican poet Louis Simpson.[34] Encountering a
childhood acquaintance, Heaney is cast as a mediator between the
two men, who concomitantly embody aspects of his own lyric
persona. It is in this mediation that a reconciliation of the
parochial with the universal is made possible. Heaney as the articulate expression of his community is asked 'for help' by its voice-
less, 'bewildered' aspects. Embodying the location through the
relationship of dialect to territory, Heaney's strategy is, at first,
'cunning'; a mode of evading the awkward confrontation. This is
eased by the shift the poem takes towards formal closure through
its emphasis on the poetic voice; a transformation which Parker
notes approvingly: 'As a result of the stranger's presence, and
because of the increased sophistication of his technique, he is able
to re-cover his country, rediscover its familiar features and figures
by means of metaphor and allusion that "make strange".' While
this reading of the process delimits the full range of *poetic* co-
herencies available it should be noted that it allows Heaney a
closure which would be unobtainable in any other form. Rather
than suggesting a rediscovery of the location, the pressure implicit
to the concept of 'making strange' formalises Heaney's initial

impressions of the country, rendering the absolute fracture between the community and the individual gestured by 'I stood between them' as little more than an ironic aftertouch by a poet securely in command of his craft. In this sense, while Heaney acknowledges the difference engendered by his induction into 'the game' he remains satisfied with the ultimate forms of closure it offers. 'Making Strange' can be seen as asking sterner questions of Heaney's relationship with his poetic than the longer title poem 'Station Island', yet those questions are not so much left unanswered as evaded through its insistence on being judged as a wellmade poem. In other words, the aspects of Heaney's work which conform to the paradigm can only remain unproblematic if approached via the intransitive self-contained modernist reading.

From Richard Kirkland, *Literature and Culture in Northern Ireland since 1968: Moments of Danger* (London, 1996), pp. 149–60.

NOTES

[Richard Kirkland is interested in poetry as a cultural 'product' and in whether Heaney's poetry contributes to the kind of cultural initiative required to push Northern Irish society forward and through its present social and political arrest. He sees Heaney's readiness to function within the parameters of New Criticism as a serious drawback in this connection. Like Jonathan Dollimore ('Culture and textuality', *Textual Practice*, 4 [1990], 91–100), whose 'cultural materialism' he to some extent shares, Kirkland is keen to divest literary studies of a 'lingering attachment to Englit.' and is deeply suspicious of critical modes with a compliant relationship to what he calls 'ineffable statement' (p. 261 above). He shares with David Lloyd (essay 11) a belief that the 'identitarian' thinking which lies behind New Criticism is allied to that which underpins the bourgeois status quo; and that the critic's 'theoretical procedure' (p. 259 above) should undermine both. He refers on p. 253 above to Chapter 4 of his book *Literature and Culture in Northern Ireland since 1965* entitled 'Unconscious Partitionism: Northern Criticism in the Nineteen-eighties'. Ed.]

1. Seamus Heaney, *The Haw Lantern* (London, 1987), p. 6.

2. Seamus Heaney, 'The Placeless Heaven: Another Look at Kavanagh', *The Government of the Tongue* (London, 1988), pp. 3–14.

3. Respectively published London (1975) (1984) (1991).

4. *Ireland's Field Day* (afterword by Denis Donoghue; London, 1985), pp. 23–30.

5. David Lloyd, '"Pap for the Dispossessed": Seamus Heaney and the Poetics of Identity', *Anomalous States: Irish Writing and the Post-Colonial Moment* (Dublin, 1993), p. 15.

6. John Carey, 2 June 1991, cited in Declan Kiberd's 'Heaney's Magic', the *Sunday Tribune* (9 June 1991), p. 21.

7. Roland Barthes, *Criticism and Truth*, trans. Katrine Pilcher Keuneman (London, 1987), p. 143.

8. Kiberd, 'Heaney's Magic', 21.

9. George Moore, *Hail and Farewell* (1911), ed. Richard Allen Cave (Gerrards Cross, 1985), p. 56.

10. It is an awareness of 'Heaney's quasi-institutional acceptance on both ideas of the Atlantic as a major poet' which led to Lloyd's 'Pap for the Dispossessed'. [See essay 11. Ed.]

11. Theo Dorgan, 'Heaney's Vision Throws Light on the Ordinary', *Sunday Tribune Books Supplement* (9 June 1991), p. 3.

12. John Keyes, 'A Dramatic Conversation', *Fortnight*, 288 (October 1990), 25. For a similar early example of this tendency see: John Haffenden, 'Meeting Seamus Heaney', *London Magazine* (June 1979), 5–28.

13. Michael Parker, *Seamus Heaney: The Making of the Poet* (Dublin, 1993).

14. *William Wordsworth*, 'The Oxford Authors', ed. Stephen Gill (Oxford, 1987), p. 603.

15. For a fuller, if contentious, reading of this phenomenon see Lloyd, 'Pap For the Dispossessed', pp. 14–18.

16. Clive James, Review of *Wintering Out*, *Observer* (26 November 1972), p. 25.

17. Antony Easthope, *Literary Into Cultural Studies* (London, 1991), pp. 9–10.

18. *Fortnight*, 81 (5 April, 1974), 12–13.

19. This cartoon was republished in *Troubled Times: Fortnight Magazine and the Troubles in Northern Ireland 1970–91*, ed. Robert Bell et al., (Belfast, 1991), p. 106. A later cartoon of Heaney by Peter Brookes used to illustrate Lachlan MacKinnon's review of *Seeing Things* ('A Responsibility to Self', *Times Literary Supplement*, 4601, 7 June 1991, p. 28) presented Heaney's head as the contours of Ireland itself. Although it is unlikely that Brookes knew of Turner's earlier cartoon, questions of mediation and embodiment, this time to an all-Ireland state, are similarly represented.

20. James Randall, 'An Interview with Seamus Heaney', *Ploughshares*, 5:3 (1979), 18–19.

21. Edna Longley, '"Inner Emigré" or "Artful Voyeur"? Seamus Heaney's *North'*, *Poetry in the Wars* (Newcastle, 1986), p. 140.

22. Conor Cruise O'Brien, 'A Slow North-east Wind', *The Listener* (25 September 1975), pp. 23–4.

23. Lloyd, 'Pap for the Dispossessed', p. 14.

24. Ciarán Carson, 'Escaped From the Massacre?', *The Honest Ulsterman*, 50 (Winter, 1975), 183–6.

25. Ciarán Carson, *The Irish For No* (Oldcastle, 1987).

26. Easthope, *Literary Into Cultural Studies*, pp. 16–17.

27. Roland Barthes, *Writing Degree Zero*, trans. Annette Lavers and Colin Smith, ed. Susan Sontag (New York, 1968), p. 47.

28. Seamus Heaney, 'Feeling Into Words', *Preoccupations: Selected Prose 1968–78* (London, 1980), p. 45.

29. Ibid., p. 13.

30. Most infamously in Desmond Fennell's pamphlet, '*Whatever You Say, Say Nothing*': *Why Seamus Heaney is No. 1* (Dublin, 1991). Fennell's work forms possibly the most sustained attack on Heaney's poetry, particularly from within Ireland itself.

31. Lloyd, 'Pap for the Dispossessed', p. 35.

32. Fennell, '*Whatever You Say, Say Nothing*', p. 21.

33. Randall, 'An Interview With Seamus Heaney', p. 18.

34. Parker, *The Making of the Poet*, p. 189.

Further Reading

I have grouped these suggestions for further reading into sections and, except in the final section, I have listed them chronologically. This is so that the reader can relate dates of publication, where appropriate, to the time-span covered in the Introduction.

INTERVIEWS

According to Rand Brandes, 'dozens of interviews' with Heaney have been published ('Secondary Sources: a Gloss on the Critical Reception of Seamus Heaney, 1965–1993' *Colby Quarterly* [Spring, 1994], pp. 63–77). The most influential are:

Randall, James, 'An Interview with Seamus Heaney' *Ploughshares*, 5:3 (1979), 7–22.
Haffenden, John (ed.), interview with Seamus Heaney, *Viewpoints: Poets in Conversation with John Haffenden* (London: Faber and Faber, 1981), pp. 57–75.
Kinahan, Frank, interview with Seamus Heaney, *Critical Inquiry* (Spring 1982), 405–14.
Deane, Seamus, 'Unhappy and at Home', interview with Seamus Heaney, *The Crane Bag Book of Irish Studies*, ed. Mark Patrick Hederman and Richard Kearney (Dublin: Blackwater Press, 1982), pp. 66–72.

AUTHORED BOOKS AND COLLECTIONS OF ESSAYS ON HEANEY

There were over twenty such titles when Brandes wrote his article. The number will probably have doubled before this New Casebook appears. The following seem to me the most helpful:

Curtis, Tony (ed.), *The Art of Seamus Heaney* (Dublin: Wolfhound, 1994 [first published 1982]).
Morrison, Blake, *Seamus Heaney* (London and New York: Routledge, 1993 [first published 1982]).
Corcoran, Neil, *Seamus Heaney* (London: Faber, 1986).
Bloom, Harold (ed.), *Seamus Heaney* (New Haven, CT: Chelsea House, 1986).

Burris, Sydney, *The Poetry of Resistance: Seamus Heaney and the Pastoral Tradition* (Athens, GA: Ohio University Press, 1990).

Andrews, Elmer (ed.), *Seamus Heaney: a Collection of Critical Essays* (Basingstoke and London: Macmillan, 1992).

Hart, Henry, *Seamus Heaney: Poet of Contrary Progressions* (Syracuse, NY: Syracuse University Press, 1992).

Parker, Michael, *Seamus Heaney: the Making of the Poet* (Dublin: Gill and Macmillan, 1993).

O'Donoghue, Bernard, *Seamus Heaney and the Language of Poetry* (Hemel Hempstead: Harvester Wheatsheaf, 1994).

Foster, J. Wilson, *The Achievement of Seamus Heaney* (Dublin: Lilliput, 1995).

Durkan, Michael J. and Rand Brandes, *Seamus Heaney: A Reference Guide* (New York: G.K. Hall, 1995).

Garratt, Robert F. (ed.), *Critical Essays on Seamus Heaney* (NY: G.K. Hall; London: Prentice-Hall, 1995).

CONTEXTS

List A assembles some books which help the reader to place Heaney among the Northern poets and in the Northern Irish context. List B is of books which assume a broader Irish, archipelagic or world context.

A

Brown, Terence, *Northern Voices: Poets from Ulster* (London: Gill and Macmillan, 1977).

Stewart, A.T.Q., *The Narrow Ground: the Roots of Conflict in Ulster* (London: Faber, 1977).

Ormsby, Frank (ed.), *Poets from the North of Ireland* (Belfast: Blackstaff Press, 1979; revd, enlarged edn, 1990).

Whyte, John, *Interpreting Northern Ireland* (Oxford: Clarendon Press, 1990).

Hughes, Eamonn (ed.), *Culture and Politics in Northern Ireland, 1960–1990* (Milton Keynes: Open University Press, 1991).

Ormsby, Frank (ed.), *A Rage for Order: Poetry of the Northern Ireland Troubles* (Belfast: Blackstaff Press, 1992).

Corcoran, Neil (ed.), *The Chosen Ground: Essays on the Contemporary Poetry of Northern Ireland* (Bridgend: Seren Books, 1992).

Wills, Clair, *Improprieties: Politics and Sexuality in Northern Irish Poetry* (Oxford: Clarendon Press, 1993).

B

Dunn, Douglas, *Two Decades of Irish Writing: A Critical Survey* (Cheadle: Carcanet, 1975).

Morrison, Blake and Motion, Andrew, *The Penguin Book of Contemporary British Poetry* (Harmondsworth: Penguin, 1982).

Paulin, Tom, *Ireland and the English Crisis* (Newcastle upon Tyne: Bloodaxe, 1984).

Deane, Seamus, *Celtic Revivals* (London: Faber, 1985).

Johnston, Dillon, *Irish Poetry After Joyce* (Indiana: Notre Dame, 1985).

Sekine, Masaru, *Irish Writers and Society at Large* (Gerrards Cross: Colin Smyth; Totowa, VJ: Barnes and Noble, 1985) (see George Watson, 'The Narrow Ground: Northern Poets and the Northern Ireland Crisis', pp. 207–24).

Garrett, Robert F., *Modern Irish Poets: Tradition and Continuity from Yeats to Heaney* (Berkeley and Los Angeles: University of California Press, 1989 [first published 1986]).

Longley, Edna, *Poetry in the Wars* (Newcastle upon Tyne: Bloodaxe, 1986).

Muldoon, Paul (ed.), *Faber Book of Contemporary Irish Poetry* (London: Faber, 1986).

Lyons, F.S.L., *Ireland since the Famine* (London: Fontana, 1987).

Brown, Terence, *Ireland's Literature: Selected Essays* (Gigginstown: Lilliput Press, 1988).

Cairns, David and Richards, Shaun, *Writing Ireland: Colonialism, Nationalism and Culture* (Manchester: Manchester University Press, 1988).

Foster, R.F., *Modern Ireland, 1600–1972* (Harmondsworth: Penguin, 1988).

Brown, Terence and Grene, Nicholas (eds), *Tradition and Influence in Anglo-Irish Poetry* (London: Macmillan, 1989).

Fallon, Peter and Mahon, Derek (eds), *The Penguin Book of Contemporary Irish Poetry* (London: Penguin, 1990).

Eagleton, Terry, Jameson, Fredric and Said, Edward W., *Nationalism, Colonialism and Literature* (introduction by Seamus Deane; Minneapolis: University of Minnesota Press, 1990).

Longley, Edna, *From Cathleen to Anorexia: the Breakdown of Irelands* (Dublin: Attic Press, LIP Pamphlet, 1990).

Foster, John Wilson, *Colonial Consequences: Essays in Irish Literature and Culture* (Dublin: Lilliput Press, 1991).

Johnson, Toni O'Brien and Cairns, David, *Gender in Irish Writing* (Milton Keynes and Philadelphia: Open University Press, 1991).

Andrews, Elmer (ed.), *Contemporary Irish Poetry: a Collection of Critical Essays* (Basingstoke and London: Macmillan, 1992).

Lloyd David, *Anomalous States: Irish Writing and the Post-Colonial Moment* (Dublin: Lilliput Press, 1993).

Longley, Edna, *The Living Stream: Literature and Revisionism in Ireland* (Newcastle upon Tyne: Bloodaxe, 1994).

Kibert, Declan, *Inventing Ireland* (London: Cape, 1995).

Kenneally, Michael (ed.), *Poetry in Contemporary Irish Literature* (Gerrard's Cross: Colin Smythe, 1994) (see, in particular, Peter Macdonald, 'Seamus Heaney as a Critic', pp. 174–89).

INTRODUCTORY APPROACHES TO LITERARY THEORY

As with the last section I have included anthologies here as well as discursive texts. Seldon and Widdowson's *Reader's Guide* provides excellent booklists for further theoretical study.

Eagleton, Terry, *Literary Theory: an Introduction* (Oxford: Blackwell, 1983).

Seldon, Raman and Widdowson, Peter, *A Reader's Guide to Contemporary Literary Theory* (Hemel Hempstead: Harvester Wheatsheaf, 1993) [first published with the late Raman Seldon as sole author, 1985].

Adams, Hazard and Searle, Leroy (eds), *Critical Theory Since 1965* (Tallahassu: Florida State University Press, 1986).

Lodge, David (ed.), *Modern Criticism and Theory: a Reader* (Harlow: Longman, 1988).

Culler, Jonathan, *Structuralist Poetics: Structuralism, Linguistics and the Study of Literature* (London: Routledge, 1975).

Culler, Jonathan, *On Deconstruction: Theory and Criticism after Structuralism* (London, Melbourne and Henley: Routledge and Kegan Paul, 1983).

Notes on Contributors

Neil Corcoran is Professor of English at the University of Wales, Swansea. In addition to his book on Heaney, his publications include *The Song of Deeds: A Study of 'The Anathemata' of David Jones* (Cardiff, 1982), *English Poetry since 1940* (London, 1993) and, as contributing editor, *The Chosen Ground: Essays on the Contemporary Poetry of Northern Ireland* (Bridgend, 1992).

Patricia Coughlan teaches at University College, Cork. She is contributing editor of *Spenser and Ireland: An Interdisciplinary Perspective* (Cork, 1989) and has also written on seventeenth-century English discourse about Ireland. She has published several essays and articles on later Anglo-Irish literature, including the work of Mangan, Maturin, Le Fanu, Kate O'Brien and Samuel Beckett. She is contributing co-editor with Alex Davis of *Irish Poets of the 1930s: a Revisionary Approach* (Cork, 1994) and is currently studying the representation of gender in contemporary Irish poetry by women.

Seamus Deane is Keough Professor of Irish Studies at Notre Dame University, Indiana. In addition to *Celtic Revivals* (London, 1985), his publications include *The French Revolution and Enlightenment in England, 1789–1832* (Cambridge, MA and London, 1988), *A Short History of Irish Literature* (London, 1986) and a number of volumes of poetry including *Gradual Wars* (Shannon, 1972), *Rumours* (Dublin, 1977), *History Lessons* (Dublin, 1983) and *Selected Poems* (Dublin, 1988). He was General Editor of *The Field Day Anthology of Irish Writing* (Derry, 1991) and the author of two of the most influential Field Day Pamphlets, *Civilians and Barbarians* (Derry, 1983) and *Heroic Styles: the Tradition of an Idea* (Derry, 1984).

Thomas Docherty is Professor of English at Trinity College Dublin. His publications include *Reading (Absent) Character* (Oxford, 1983), *John Donne, Undone* (London, 1986), *On Modern Authority* (Brighton, 1987), *After Theory: Postmodernism/ Postmarxism* (London, 1990) and, as editor, *Postmodernism: a Reader* (Hemel Hempstead and New York, 1992). His latest publication is *Alterities: Criticism, History, Representation* (Oxford, 1996).

Terry Eagleton is Thomas Warton Professor of English Literature at the University of Oxford. Among his publications are *Myths of Power: a Marxist Study of the Brontës* (London, 1975), *Marxism and Literary Criticism* (London, 1976), *The Rape of Clarissa* (Oxford, 1982), *Literary Theory: an Introduction* (Oxford, 1983), *The Ideology of the Aesthetic* (Oxford, 1990), *Ideology* (London, 1991) and *Heathcliff and the Great Hunger: Studies in Irish Culture* (London, 1995). He is author of two plays, *Saint Oscar* (1989) and *The White, the Gold and the Gangrene* (1993).

Seamus Heaney's most recent volume of poems is *The Spirit Level* (1996). He is Boylston Professor of Rhetoric at Harvard and was, until recently, Professor of Poetry at Oxford. His *Preoccupations* (London, 1980), *The Government of the Tongue* (London, 1988) and *The Redress of Poetry* (London, 1995) are important critical adjuncts to the poetry. In October 1995 he was awarded the Nobel Prize for Literature.

Eamonn Hughes is a lecturer in the School of English at Queen's University, Belfast. He has edited *Culture and Politics in Northern Ireland, 1960–1990* (Milton Keynes, 1991) and is currently completing a book on *Irish Writing, 1800–1990*. He is the author of a number of articles on Irish writing and is doing research on Irish Literary Autobiography.

Richard Kirkland lectures in English at Keele University. He is the author of *Literature and Culture in Northern Ireland since 1965: Moments of Danger* (London 1996) and essays on Irish poetry in various literary journals and is currently joint-editing a volume of essays: *The Mechanics of Authority: Ireland and Cultural Theory*.

David Lloyd teaches at the University of California at Berkeley. Among his publications are *Nationalism and Minor Literature: James Clarence Mangan and the Emergence of Irish Cultural Nationalism* (Berkeley and London, 1987) and *Anomalous States: Irish Writing and the Post-Colonial Moment* (Dublin, 1993).

Edna Longley is Professor of English at Queen's University, Belfast. Among her publications are *Poetry in the Wars* (Newcastle, 1986), *Louis MacNeice* (London, 1988), *From Cathleen to Anorexia: the Breakdown of Irelands* (Dublin, 1990), *The Living Stream: Literature and Revisionism in Ireland* (Newcastle, 1994) and editions of Edward Thomas's poetry (*Poems and Last Poems*, London and Glasgow, 1973) and prose (*A Language not to be Betrayed*, Manchester, 1981). She is an editor of the *Irish Review* and has written on poetry in many journals and collections of criticism.

Conor Cruise O'Brien, until recently Consultant Editor of the *Observer* and now a Contributing Editor of *The Atlantic*, entered the Department of External Affairs of Ireland in 1944 and was Head of the UN Section and Member of the Irish Delegation to the UN from 1956 to 1960; he then served as Representative of the UN Secretary-General in Katanga in 1961, when he resigned from the UN and Irish service. He has since been

Vice-Chancellor of the University of Ghana (1962–5); Albert Schweitzer Professor of Humanities, New York University (1965–9); Member of the Dublin parliament (1966–77); Minister for Posts and Telegraphs (1973–7); Member of the Irish Senate (1977–9): Pro-Chancellor of Dublin University since 1973; Visiting Fellow of Nuffield College, Oxford (1973–5); Fellow of St Catherine's College, Oxford (1978–81); and Editor-in-Chief of the *Observer* (1978–81). Among his many publications are *Parnell and his Party, 1880–90* (Oxford, 1957), *To Katanga and Back, a UN Case History* (London, 1962), *Camus* (London, 1970), *States of Ireland* (London, 1972), *Passion and Cunning, Essays on Nationalism, Terrorism and Revolution* (London, 1990) and *The Great Melody: a Thematic Biography and Commenting Anthology of Edmund Burke* (London, 1992).

Christopher Ricks is Professor of English at Boston University. His many publications include *Milton's Grand Style* (Oxford, 1963), *Keats and Embarrassment* (Oxford, 1974), *The Force of Poetry* (Oxford, 1984), *T.S. Eliot and Prejudice* (London and Boston, 1988) and *Essays in Appreciation* (Oxford, 1996) as well as editions of Tennyson (Harlow, 1969; London, 1987) and Housman (London, 1988).

Stan Smith is Professor and Head of English at Dundee University and co-director of the Auden Concordance Project there. His publications include *Inviolable Voice: History and Twentieth Century Poetry* (Dublin, 1982), *W.H. Auden* (Oxford, 1985), *Edward Thomas* (London, 1986), *W.B. Yeats: a Critical Introduction* (Basingstoke, 1990) and *The Origins of Modernism: Eliot, Pound, Yeats and the Rhetorics of Renewal* (Hemel Hempstead, 1994). He is General Editor of the Longman Critical Reader Series and of Longman Studies in Twentieth Century Literature.

Index